Czech–German Relations and the Politics of Central Europe

Czech–German Relations and the Politics of Central Europe

From Bohemia to the EU

Jürgen Tampke
Associate Professor
University of New South Wales
Australia

First published 2003 by
PALGRAVE MACMILLAN
Houndmills, Basingstoke, Hampshire RG21 6XS and
175 Fifth Avenue, New York, N.Y. 10010
Companies and representatives throughout the world

PALGRAVE MACMILLAN is the global academic imprint of the Palgrave Macmillan division of St. Martin's Press, LLC and of Palgrave Macmillan Ltd. Macmillan® is a registered trademark in the United States, United Kingdom and other countries. Palgrave is a registered trademark in the European Union and other countries.

ISBN 0–333–73449–1 hardback

This book is printed on paper suitable for recycling and made from fully managed and sustained forest sources.

A catalogue record for this book is available from the British Library.

Library of Congress Cataloging-in-Publication Data
Tampke, Jürgen.
Czech-German relations and the politics of Central Europe : from Bohemia to the EU/Jürgen Tampke.
    p. cm.
    Includes bibliographical reference and index.
    ISBN 0–333–73449–1
    1. Germans – Czech Republic – Sudetenland. 2. Sudetenland (Czech Republic) – Ethnic relations. 3. Czech Republic – Relations – Germany. 4. Germany – Relations – Czech Republic. I. Title.

DB2500.S94 T36 2002
943.71'00431—dc21   2002029401

10   9   8   7   6   5   4   3   2   1
12   11   10   09   08   07   06   05   04   03

Printed and bound in Great Britain by
Antony Rowe Ltd, Chippenham and Eastbourne

To Christine

Contents

Acknowledgements

This work would not have been possible without the generous financial assistance of the School of History and the Faculty of Arts of the University of New South Wales, Sydney, Australia.

The Collegium Carolinum and the Sudetendeutsche Archiv in Munich provided valuable and informative material.

Good advice and/or kind assistance came from Richard J. Evans, Heather Field, K. Erik Franzen, Dick Geary, Milan Hauner, Gerhard Hirschfeld, Bruce Kent, Bruce W. Memming, Bernd Martin, Hans Mommsen, John Perkins, Arnold Velden, Katharina Vadura and Stephen Wheatcroft. The author wishes to stress, however, that mistakes and all other shortcomings are solely his responsibility. Fritz Büchler assisted with translations from the German, and Monika Doláková, Anna Kozáková and Petra Kurtincová with translations from the Czech. A very special thanks to Gay Breyley for her assistance with the editing. Colin Doxford devoted many hours of his spare retiree time to discuss the more difficult parts of the manuscript and finally thanks to Christine for everything.

Glossary of Geographical Terms

Altvater-Gebirge	Rychlebské hory
Aussig	Ústí nad Labem
Böhmisch Leipa	Česká Lípa
Budweis	Budějovice
Brünn	Brno
Brüx	Most
Eger	Cheb
Gablonz	Jablonec
Iglau	Jihlava
Isergebirge	Jizerské hory
Königgrätz	Hradec Králové
Kremnitz	Kremnica
Krummau	Český Krumlov
Landskron	Lanškroun
Mährisch Schönberg	Šumperk
Marienbad	Mariánské Lázně
Moldau	Vlatava
Olmütz	Olomouc
Pilsen	Plzeň
Reichenberg	Liberec
Teplitz	Teplice
Trautenau	Trutnov

List of Abbreviations

ADG	Archiv der Gegenwart
BA	Benešův archiv
BdL	Bund der Landwirte
BdV	Bund der Vertriebenen/Vereinigte Landsmann-schaften und Landesverbände
BHE	Bund der Heimat Vertriebenen und Entrechteten
BHE/GB	Bund der Heimat Vertriebenen und Entrechteten/Gesamtdeutscher Block
BvD	Bund der vertriebenen Deutschen
CE	Common Era
CDU	Christlich Demokratische Union
CPSU	Communist Party of the Soviet Union
ČSR	Czechoslovak Republic
ČSSR	Czechoslovak Socialist Republic
CSU	Christlich Soziale Union
DGFP	Documents on German Foreign Policy
DNP	Deutsche Nationalpartei
DNSAP	Deutsche nationalsozialistische Arbeiterpartei
DSAP	Deutsche sozialdemokratische Arbeiterpartei in der Tschechoslowakei
FDP	Freie Demokratische Partei
FRG	Federal Republic of Germany
GDR	German Democratic Republic
KB	Kameradschaftsbund
LAG	Lastenausgleichsgesetz
NSDAP	Nationalsozialistische Deutsche Arbeiterpartei
ODS	Obcanska Demokraticka Strana
PDS	Partei des Demokratischen Sozialismus
SA	Sturmabteilung
SD	Sicherheitsdienst
SED	Sozialistische Einheitspartei Deutschlands
SOE	Special Operations Executive
SPD	Sozialdemokratische Partei Deutschlands
SdL	Sudetendeutsche Landsmannschaft
SdP	Sudetendeutsche Partei
SdR	Sudetendeutscher Rat

SS	Schutzstaffeln
USFR	United States Foreign Relations
VOL	Vereinigte Ostdeutsche Landsmannschaften
VdL	Verband der Landsmannschaften
ZdV	Zentralverband der Vertriebenen Deutschen
ZVU	Zentralverwaltung für deutsche Umsiedler

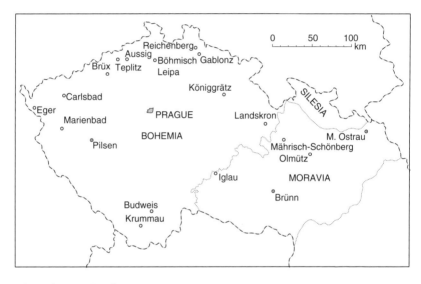

The Bohemian Lands

Introduction

On 7 May 1997, the American Secretary of State, Madeleine Albright, at a glamorous reception held in the Grand Ballroom of New York's Waldorf Astoria Hotel awarded the United State's European Statesman of the Year award jointly to the Czech President Vaclav Havel and the German President Roman Herzog for signing the Czech–German declaration on friendly relations and co-operative future developments. In her address Albright, herself of Czech origin, who had fled the country twice – in 1939 from the Nazi occupation and in 1948 after the establishment of the Communist dictatorship – praised the governments of the two countries for the successful completion of the negotiations and expressed her strong hope that after more than half a century of darkness, distrust would ease and give way again to the establishment of harmonious relations between the two peoples. The award, as had been the case with the treaty itself, was warmly received by governments worldwide and by the international media, and was welcomed by the great majority of Czechs and Germans. But there was not only praise. In the Czech Republic there were voices from both the left and the right of the political spectrum warning that clauses in the friendship declaration would jeopardize the post-Second World War political set-up by questioning the legality of the Potsdam Agreement of August 1945 which sanctioned the expulsion of approximately three million German-speaking people from their homes in Czechoslovakia on the conclusion of the Second World War. And indeed, the ink on the friendship declaration had scarcely dried, when the leaders of German expellee associations voiced their protests that there could be no friendship or co-operation until their grievances were settled. This new attempt on the part of the Sudeten German Homeland Association (*Sudetendeutsche Landsmannschaft*) to put their case before the international community was strongly supported by the *Bund der Vertriebenen*, the umbrella organization of the original eleven million German expellees (and their descendants) from eastern and south-eastern Europe. It brought to the forefront again an issue that had created a great deal of contention in inter-war Europe, had contributed to the renewed outbreak of hostilities in 1939 and, it had been believed, was finally settled by the post-Second World War settlements – the case of the Sudeten Germans.

Who were, and who are they? Although the name Sudeten originally refers to the mountain range to the north-east of what is today the Czech Republic, stretching across the Czech–Polish border from the *Isergebirge* in the west to the *Altvater-Gebirge* in the east, the term Sudeten German essentially is not a geographic but a political one.[1] Its origins go back to the peace-making process after the First World War, at the beginning of the 'Europe of the nation states' period when nationalism was at its height and when political thought, demands and ambitions had to be couched in nationalistic terms. It was then that the German-speaking people of the former Kingdom of Bohemia, the Duchy of Silesia and the Margravate of Moravia, who had all been part of the Cisleithanian part of the now defunct Austro-Hungarian Empire, were confronted by the fact that the First World War peace treaty had made them 'minority citizens' in the newly founded nation of Czechoslovakia. To counter the sudden creation of a Czechoslovak nationality, a new concept with little historical tradition behind it, these German-speaking people – or rather their leaders and spokesmen – created from their diverse regionalism their own artificial nationality: that of the 'Sudeten Germans'. Until then, in addition of course to being subjects of the Habsburg Monarchy, the dialects and customs of the *Nordböhmer* for example, or the *Egerländer*, or the *Südmährer*, or people from the tiny *Kuhländchen*, all related more closely to their Austrian and German neighbours than to one another.[2]

German settlement in this part of central Europe has been recorded throughout the second millennium of the Common Era and greatly contributed to the region's cultural, economic and political development. They lived together with their Czech neighbours in a bilingual community sometimes referred to as a *Zweivölkerland* – a two peoples' country – or a *Zweivölkerstaat* – a two peoples' state. The Bohemian and Moravian lands, of course, were not spared the great turbulence that characterized late medieval/early modern European history but – with the partial exception of the early fifteenth-century Hussite Rebellion – conflicts were not fought on ethnic grounds. The religious, political and socio-economic confrontations that marked the Reformation period in the sixteenth and seventeenth centuries saw Czechs and Germans in Bohemia fighting together for or against Catholicism. And ethnic rivalry played little part in the conflicts between the estates and centralized government, the nobility and the Crown, or the towns and the aristocratic landholders, which characterizes the beginnings of modernity.

Czechs and Germans contributed to Bohemia's cultural achievement that saw the province, and its capital Prague in particular at the apex of central-European culture. And the fact that Bohemia was among the richest parts of the Habsburg Empire, always a flourishing centre for trade and the key region for the Danube Monachy's early industrialization was based on the industrious efforts of both Czechs and Germans – even if at times one group may have contributed more than the other.

Ethnic rivalry did not arise in any significant way until the nineteenth century with the spread of modern nationalism that arose from the French Revolution of 1789 and that seems to have gripped many sections of the educated middle classes throughout Europe including the multi-ethnic Austro-Hungarian Empire. Attempts by the Habsburg rulers to stem the tide, motivated not only by power-political considerations but also by a concern for the well-being of the Empire's subjects, fell on deaf ears. And so did the many voices warning that the end of the transnational community might only too readily have fatal consequences. Nationalism triumphed in 1918/1919 but it soon became only too obvious that the new order was far more fragile and unstable than the system it replaced. For the German people in the Bohemian lands the collapse of the Habsburg Empire led to a loss of identity and they felt very apprehensive about their minority role in the newly formed Czechoslovak Republic. They had hoped to become part of Germany or Austria but these hopes had no chance of becoming reality. Having blamed the German Empire for causing the War, the last thing the western Allies would have agreed to was an enlarged German state. Moreover, loss of the German-settled parts of Bohemia and Moravia would have rendered the newly formed state economically non-viable. But the attempt to create nation states in the chequered multi-ethnic landscape of central, east-central and south-eastern Europe was bound to run into stumbling blocks. In Czechoslovakia the Czechs and Slovaks became the 'Staatsvolk' – they constituted the actual 'nationality', while the other ethnic groups – including approximately 3.3 million German-speaking people – became 'minority citizens'. These 'minority citizens' held 'minority rights' – a lopsided concept that found little appeal among the non-Czechoslovaks. Prague governments throughout the 1920s were coy to tackle this issue, i.e. to take effective steps that would bring the 'minority citizens' closer to the state.

Certainly after 1926 'activist' parties – parties that advocated a co-operative approach and who participated in the Czechoslovak Republic's political life – found the support of the majority of Sudeten Germans, as they were now starting to be called, but regrettably time was too short for this process to consolidate itself. When in the mid-1930s Czechoslovak governments did attempt to bring in legislation that addressed the grievances of the country's German population the tide had turned – domestically and at the international level. To the political instability of the inter-war years had been added the calamitous economic instability following the collapse on Wall Street. By May 1935 the irredentist Sudeten German Party (SdP) was the largest party in the Czechoslovak parliament. Four years later Czechoslovakia was no more; less than a decade after that most of the Sudeten Germans had joined eight million other Germans who, having barely escaped with their lives, were forced to leave their homes with a suitcase being their only possession. But whereas the *Volksdeutsche* in Yugoslavia, Romania or Hungary (who had no say in the Fatherland's policies) or the people of Pomerania, Silesia or East Prussia (none of which had been a major centre of National Socialism) justifiably asked themselves why it was they who had to pay the price for the Nazi catastrophe – the Sudetens did play a considerable part in their own downfall. The decision of so many of them (although not all) to back the SdP and their leader Konrad Henlein, coupled with the latter's decision to give full support to the Austrian lance corporal, led to the dismemberment of the first Czechoslovak Republic – the event that was to open the path to the Second World War. Like so many German-speaking people inside and outside the Reich who cheered so jubilantly after 1933 they did not know that the piper's tune was to lead to death and destruction.

The Czechs were the first outside the Third Reich – which since March 1938 included Austria – to experience the brutal reality of Nazi rule. Occupation by *Wehrmacht* soldiers of what was left of Czechoslovakia after the Munich Treaty of September 1938 on 15 March 1939 meant the beginning of six bitter years of oppression that was to reach its peak during the *Heydrichiáda* – the government of Nazi Security Chief Reinhardt Heydrich. The latter was send by Hitler into the Protectorate of Bohemia and Moravia (as the Czech lands were called under German occupation) in September 1941 to 'clean up' an increase in resistance activities here. His time as *Reichsprotektor* came to an end on 27 May 1942 when the troubleshooter himself was shot at and died a week later of his wounds. The assassination was carried out by the Czech resistance movement in cooperation with the British Special Operations Executive. The price for the death of one of Hitler's worst henchman was high: Nazi retaliation measures took the lives of 5000 people.

When the dreams of an Aryan 'Thousand Year Empire' had finally ended, a terrible punishment descended upon many German people including the Sudeten Germans. Intense, far-embracing Germanophobia, coupled to an equally staunch determination on the part of the victorious

Allies to once and for all eliminate the threat of future attempts to establish German hegemony in Europe, saw millions of people lose their homes, subjected to pitiless and often savage ejections from their *Heimat*, and forced to end up in a devastated country that initially was scarcely able to provide the basic necessities of human life. Yet accounts of these tragedies that fail to highlight the carnage inflicted upon Europe by Nazi Germany during the Second World War as the chief reason for the post-war catastrophe lack credence.

After their harsh expulsion from the land of their ancestors, the Germans of the former Bohemia and Moravia were the first to organize themselves politically and their associations were among the most active of the post-war expellees societies. Competent and dedicated leaders assisted their fellow refugees and expellees over the difficult post-war years when help and support from native-born citizens (and the latter's willingness to share the burden left by Nazism) was limited. A well-educated people with many qualities and skills, they contributed to the economic recovery of the Federal Republic and within less than a generation many of them did well in their new country – though their piece of the cake provided by the West German 'Economic Miracle' was much smaller than that of the locals.

When the international climate changed in the 1960s, and the heat temporarily went out of the Cold War, the Sudeten-German leaders were in the forefront in the fight against the new *Ostpolitik* of the Social-Democratic government of Willy Brandt (to acknowledge the post-Second World War boundaries in east-central and eastern Europe and to renounce all claims for revision). But their efforts were in vain and failure to stop the Federal Republic's recognition of these frontiers took the wind out of their sails.

By the late 1980s the 'Sudeten issue' had seemingly run its course. The slender hope on the part of the Association's officials and some of its members that the return of a centre-right government in 1982 would reverse the previous *Ostpolitik* proved illusory. The new government of Chancellor Helmut Kohl and his Liberal Foreign Minister Hans Dieter Genscher had no intention of disturbing the state of relatively peaceful co-existence between East and West that characterized the last Cold War years in Europe by digging up old corpses. There were still strongly worded articles in the Association's periodicals and equally strong speeches at their annual gatherings but few outsiders took any notice. They were speaking to the converted – a group that became ever smaller by the year.

Yet – one of the many unexpected surprises that followed the fall of the Wall – the end of the Cold War created a whole new ball game.

By the mid-1990s the Federal Republic of Germany had become the largest nation in Europe outside Russia, and economically by far the strongest. Czechoslovakia, on the other hand, had split up and the Czech Republic had joined the ranks of the struggling former Communist countries, keen to get into the European Union. This gave a new lease of life to the leaders of the expellee organizations who demanded that Czech entry into the EU should be made dependent on settling restitutions. The civil war in the former Yugoslavia also aided their cause. With television coverage showing day-by-day the tragic fate of people in Bosnia, Croatia or Serbia being forced to leave their homes, the *Vertriebenenverbände* could remind their fellow citizens that Germans were also dispossessed and expelled in the not too distant past. But it may well be that times cannot be switched back. With the imminent admission of former eastern bloc countries into the European Union, Poles, Hungarians, Slovenes, Czechs and others will again be part of a multinational political entity. Thus, less than a century after its demise, the traditional values of the Habsburg Empire – ethnic pluralism and transnationalism – may well be resurrected. Czechs and Germans too will live together in liaison. This books attempts to tell part of their history and hopes to make a small contribution to their harmonious future.

1
The Lands of the Weceslav Crown

The country around the Bohemian Basin and its adjacent mountain ranges to the south, west and north, which today constitutes the Czech Republic, is part of the diverse ethnic, cultural and religious landscape so characteristic of eastern-central, eastern and south-eastern Europe. Archaeological evidence has shown that Celtic tribes had lived here in the first two centuries before the Common Era – in fact the name Bohemia stems from the Celtic – to be followed by Germanic tribes who arrived in the third century CE and then moved eastward as part of the general European migration in the middle of the first millennium CE. Their place was taken by western Slavonic tribes in the sixth and seventh centuries. Bohemian princes are listed among those obliged to pay tribute to Charlemagne, the Carolingian founder of the Frankish Empire, for the first time in 805/806, and his successor in the eastern part of the Empire, Ludwig the German, laid claim to Moravia in 846. The ninth century also saw the region's conversions to western Christendom; in fact, one of the first Christian dukes, Wenceslas, the founder of the Přemislyden dynasty that was to rule Bohemia and Moravia until the beginning of the fourteenth century, was declared a martyr and a saint after his younger brother Boleslaw assassinated him in 935. The latter's rule lasted until 972 CE but his murdered brother became a Christian hero and the patron of the realm.

The Přemislyden were originally an influential Bohemian family who played a big part in uniting the small Slavonic tribes under the Czech banner and name. Their rule from the beginning was closely linked to the 'Holy Roman Empire of the German Nation', a monarchy that emerged from the eastern parts of Charlemagne's Frankish Empire in the tenth century and which covered most of central Europe from Cambrai to Marseille in the west, to central Italy in the south, Trieste and Bratislava in the east and the coasts of the North and Baltic Seas in the north. The term 'Roman' in this long-winded and complicated title was not a geographical expression (Rome, in fact, was not part of the Empire) but has to be seen as a legalistic term – the ancient Roman Empire was the only state-form that could claim legality in the eyes of contemporaries, in fact it was the only state-form known at the beginning of the Middle Ages. Only the German king, who at this time was the most powerful ruler in Europe, could join the ranks of the ancient emperors. The second most powerful ruler in the tenth century, the king of the West-Frankish Empire (today's France), had to justify his position with the second-best legitimization: that of being the successor of the Frankish kings. Hence the two most important empires in Europe at the time did not name themselves after their subjects but based their name on their source of legitimacy.[1] As this implies – it is equally important to stress – the reference to 'German nation' also has little to do with the modern meaning of the word. It was merely the legal confirmation that only the German king could wear the Emperor's robe. And from its inception there were always a large number of non-Germans living in the Holy Roman Empire as is shown, for example, in the medieval instruction of the papacy that their clergy in France had to differentiate between five languages and in Germany between three: upper-German, lower-German and Czech.[2] Language, until modern times, had little political significance.

Bohemia's status changed in 1002 from tributary to that of vassal of the German emperor.[3] This political, dynastic and religious link to the Empire was to serve rulers and country well. As the vassal duties declined – to eventually cease altogether – the Bohemian rulers reached great heights, obtaining some of the most prestigious positions at the Imperial Court. It was the Duke of Bohemia, for example, who was the cupbearer at the marriage of Kaiser Heinrich V to his English bride Mathilde. And their leading status among the German princes is shown by the fact that several Bohemian dukes were crowned as kings (the first one, Duke Wratislaw II, in 1085). Moreover in 1198 the Bohemian rulers were given the further privilege to have their monarchy based on hereditary succession.[4] If there were significant curbs on the power of the Přemislyden rulers then these did not come from the Holy Roman Emperor but the local Bohemian and Moravian nobility who carefully guarded their influential position and who firmly opposed any encroachment on their traditional rights and privileges.[5]

Attachment to the Empire was one factor that brought German influence to Bohemia and Moravia from the earliest days but it was not the only one. German monks came as missionaries from the ninth century onwards, establishing numerous cloisters and churches. Prague became a Bishopric in 973 and Olmütz (Moravia) in 1063. By the eleventh century German merchants were given special privileges in Prague, where the Přemislyden rulers had established their court. Prague, because of its favourable geographic location in the heart of Europe, soon became a rapidly growing centre for trade and commerce. In fact with the exception of ancient Rome, and together with Paris, Prague is ranked among the oldest capitals in Europe. And in the twelfth and thirteenth centuries German settlement in Bohemia and Moravia commenced in a major way.

The need to clear land of its dense native forest for cultivation and hence increase the country's potential to feed a growing population, coupled with the intention to utilize the region's rich mineral resources – all part of an overall tendency to stimulate economic activity – encouraged the Přemislyden rulers to attract settlers and experts from the agriculturally and technically more advanced regions of Europe. This meant that from around the middle of the twelfth century peasants arrived in large numbers from the west, particularly from the German-speaking parts of the Empire. They participated in the cultivation of the soil and they were soon joined by tradesmen, and later merchants, who helped to lay the foundation of urban settlements.

It should be emphasized, however, that these settlers did not come as 'colonizers' – let alone 'subjugators of the Slavonic indigenous people' but were there on the invitation of the rulers of the land and were often encouraged by tax concessions and other incentives. On the other hand it would be equally inaccurate to over-emphasize the German contribution by implying that Czech culture was merely the by-product of German civilization. The term 'immigrants' would not be correct either because in many parts of northern Bohemia, the country around the river Eger, the Böhmerwald, southern Moravia or Silesia, German-speaking people were the first to settle and these regions were in part settled by Germans only. Elsewhere in the lands of the Weceslav Crown they lived with their Czech neighbours in relatively peaceful cohabitation, and although this marks the beginning of a state of bilingualism or a 'two peoples' community' that characterizes much of the history of Bohemia and Moravia until contemporary times, ethnicity played little or no importance in the Middle Ages. All told, by the fourteenth century CE about one-sixth of the population was of German origin. Hence German settlement in Bohemia and Moravia has to be seen as part of the 'west to east shift' that was characteristic for much of the history of Europe over the last two thousand years: an economic, political and social *'Kulturtransfer'* from the west to the east.

German influence in the Kingdom of Bohemia first peaked in the four-teenth century. When the last male of the Přemislyden line was assassi-nated in 1306 their rule ended. It is evidence of the high esteem in which the lands of the Weceslav Crown were held – and of their strategically vital position in central Europe – that the leading dynastic houses at the time, the Habsburg, the Wittelsbacher and the Luxemburg – were keen to gain control of the Bohemian Crown. The last – the Luxemburg dynasty – succeeded, and for a century the Empire's political centre shifted to Prague. It was above all during the reign of Charles IV, crowned King of Germany in 1349 and Emperor of the Holy Roman Empire in 1355 that the Luxemburg dynasty reached its largest extent. Under him the Bohemian Kingdom included the province of Brandenburg in the north, stretched far into Silesia and the march of Lausitz, and in the south the frontiers were pushed almost to the gates of Nuremberg by the annexa-tion of the lands of the Palatinate along the Bohemian borders.[6] Charles IV also provided the Bohemian administration with modern centralized gov-ernment, orderly finances and an effective legal system based on the introduction of Roman law – ideas very much modelled on the policies of Philip the Fair of France.[7] Moreover, he established the first university north of the Alps, which had brought two thousand students and teach-ers to Prague by the end of the fourteenth century. Last but not least it was under him that Prague became the 'Golden City': a centre of Gothic art and architecture. The cathedral, numerous churches, the famous Moldau bridge with its two towers, the fine buildings of the 'Neustadt' – above all the castle, the *Hradschin*, were built during his lifetime. It is estimated that between 30–40 000 people were living in Prague at the end of his reign, the largest city north of the Alps. When Charles died in 1378 Archbishop Adalbert of Prague, who gave the funeral oration summed up his reign neatly and precisely: ' . . . so held his power in Bohemia and the empire that neither the empire lacked order nor Bohemia lacked care, and the men of the empire were content and the men of Bohemia found no cause of complaint'.[8]

His successors, his sons Weceslav (1378–1400) and Sigismund (1410–37) did not match their father's skill and ability – not an unusual fact in his-tory.[9] This would not have mattered a great deal in times of peace and sta-bility but neither the late fourteenth nor the fifteenth century was such a time. The Bohemian nobility, who had their powerful position curbed during Charles' rule, tried to recover their former predominance and attempted to take measures to prevent a further strengthening of the monarchy. This probably would not have presented such a difficult chal-lenge to the Bohemian Crown, had not the forerunners of the Reformation added religious to political animosity. And it was in Bohemia where the emerging split of western Christendom drew first blood.

Disagreement about doctrinal and structural matters, dissent, opposition and 'heresy' are as old as the history of the Christian Church. There were the Arian and Pelagian heresies from the fourth to the seventh centuries. The relationship between the Byzantine and Roman Church was marred by confrontation and bitter feuding from the eight century onwards until they finally split in 1054, and there is evidence of millenarian, chiliastic and other zealot movements throughout the Middle Ages.[10] However, criticism of the practices of the Catholic Church and papacy, and rejection of doctrine that was not based on scripture, did increase greatly towards the end of the Middle Ages, aggravated by the papal schism (1378–1415) when there were two – and eventually three – popes all claiming to be the supreme head of the church. Religious conflict became intertwined with traditional political rivalry and the continuing process of urbanization added a further dimension to the overall dilemma. The whole social strata – Crown, church, upper aristocracy, lower nobility, prosperous town-dwellers and not so prosperous urban craftsmen and artisans, and an increasingly exploited peasantry – was in a state of apprehension and uncertainty about its future.

John Wyclif is often credited with setting the process in motion. His biting attacks on the power and wealth of the late medieval church, the luxury and venality of the popes, on the monastic orders and the sacramental system by means of which the clergy could bestow or withhold God's grace, and above all his denial of the doctrine of transubstantiation, all had a powerful impact in England. Whether he was connected with the Lollards is doubtful but with its anti-clericalism and its opposition to the Catholic Mass the movement bears his stamp. Their followers came from the full range of society: peasants, urban craftsmen and artisans, the landed gentry, Oxford scholars and members of parliament. The Lollard heresy was suppressed before it was able to gather major momentum. The Hussite rebellion a generation later was a different story.

Like Wyclif, John Hus (1369–1415), a popular preacher in the Bethlehem Chapel in Prague and later rector of the University, criticized – though in different ways – the uselessness of the clergy, the sins of the papacy and the subsequent decline of morality. He, too, stressed the primacy of scripture over the corruption of the Church but he did not accept Wyclif's denial of the doctrine of transubstantiation. He was finally banned from Prague in 1413 because of his relentless opposition to the practice of selling indulgences. He challenged the Church hierarchy's decision in two trials, both of which he lost and which left him with only one option: to appeal to the next Ecclesiastical Council. When such a Council met an year later in Constance (1414–18) to end the schism, he was obliged to attend. Whether he was given a letter of safe conduct by King Sigismund is still a subject of debate.[11] However, and contrary to popular legend for-mulated centuries later – that saw the upright reformer being betrayed and unjustly sentenced to death by German jurors – Hus' accusers were Czech and his judges were Italian and French. It was the international organization of the Catholic Church that had put him on trial. As he was obviously losing his case he could have followed the example of Wyclif who decided that giving in to the establishment served his cause better than martyrdom. John Hus chose the latter option. He was burned at the stake on 6 July 1415.

If the King of Germany, Sigismund, who had been the protector of the Council of Constance, and who in 1419, following the death of his half-brother, was scheduled to take possession of the Bohemian Crown, had thought that the end of John Hus would mean a return of calm to his realm he was mistaken. As it turned out he was not able to take up his residence in Prague because Bohemia and Moravia had become involved in a civil war that ravaged the country for seventeen years. At the core of the conflict was the issue of lay communion. The demand for lay com-munion had played no particular part in the teaching of Wyclif or Hus, but was propagated by the more radical wing of the Prague reformers under the leadership of Magister Jacobellus von Mies. In fact the latter managed to introduce lay communion at a number of parishes in Prague whilst Hus was still on trial in Constance. This in turn split the country into two hostile camps: *Kelchler*, the supporters of lay communion and *Altkirchlicher* who upheld the Catholic tradition of the Eucharist as con-firmed by the fourth Lateran Council in 1215.[12]

Of course the social and political implications of the lay communion (*Laienkelch*) were far reaching. It eliminated the prerogative of the clergy to conduct one of the Church's most important sacraments. And if simple people could perform such a vital function, and, moreover, if lay people could conduct sermons in the vernacular, much of the Church's organi-zation and structure was superfluous. This meant above all that the immense wealth of the Church was at anyone's disposal. For a short time this combination of religious fervour and the prospect of material gain for many, coupled with the prevailing general uncertainty of the age and a crisis of the traditional governmental system, managed to achieve a rare phenomenon for the Middle Ages: it united diverse sections of the social strata under a common banner for which contemporaries coined the derogatory term the Hussites.

Not that the dissidents had all that much in common. Insistence on the supremacy of scripture was the one key-principle they all shared but this aside their ideas and thoughts covered the full political and religious spectrum from left to right. The moderate followers were known as *Utraquists* or *Calixtenes*, who believed in the communion of both kinds, *sub utraque Specie*. They centred on Prague and advocated a more balanced political structure consisting of an alliance of the wealthy and influential bourgeoisie in the capital with the nobility, and a monarchy that accepted the participation of the estates in government. They also stood for a more restrained approach as far as religion was concerned: there was to be a general reform of the Catholic Church, the function of priests was to be reduced but not to be eliminated altogether, and although the Church was to be stripped of its massive assets, the moderates were opposed to the abolition of all formal institutions and organizations. On the left were the 'Taborites' whose stronghold was the newly found town Tabor, named after the biblical mountain – a rural-based chiliastic movement that attempted to establish a communist theocracy based on early Christian communal church forms. They rejected such doctrines as those of purgatory and the mediation of saints, nor – to them – could priests in mortal sin validly administer sacraments. They also disapproved of penance, images, relics and the fact that mass was held in a foreign tongue. To them the pious laity, including women, had the right to preach, and church services could be held in any building suitable for divine worship.

Hostilities between 'Hussites' and the establishment started on a major scale in 1420. Initially, leadership of the revolutionaries was with the moderates in Prague but they were soon challenged by the extremists. The latter, who were among the first in Europe to make effective use of gunpowder, emerged victorious from this internal conflict – and for the next decade they also won their battles with all papal and imperial armies sent out to quell the uprising. Their armies invaded large parts of eastern and northern Germany as far as the Baltic Sea, leaving behind them a path of terror and destruction. By the mid-1430s war-weariness had set in on both sides and when the moderate Hussites managed to gain the upper hand again, after defeating the 'Taborites' and their supporters in a last battle at Lipany on 25 May 1434, negotiations with the Council of Basle[13] commenced and a peace treaty was signed in 1436. The council had made minor concessions on the question of the Laienkelch[14] but the towns and the nobility could keep the rich booty that the dispossession of the church had given them. The same year Emperor Sigismund II returned to his hereditary kingdom; there was no more challenge to his right to wear the Bohemian Crown.

The 'Hussite wars' had been fought by all sides with utmost brutality. Records list that scores of people were burned alive, drowned or pushed into disused mineshafts. Marauding armies added their share to the violence. The destruction of buildings, art treasures and books was massive. Many of Bohemia's magnificent churches and cloisters were razed to the ground and the damage done to towns involved in the conflict was substantial. As one leading historian of Czech–German relations aptly remarks 'one cannot praise the Hussite rebellion as a first sign of Europe's move towards the democratic ideal without mentioning the great suffering and pain that went in its wake'.[15]

Prague's time as the 'Golden City' had temporarily come to an end, and the long, steady rise of the Bohemian lands under the Přemislyden and Luxemburg houses to a position of prestige and prominence in Europe ended also. There does not seem to be unanimity among experts on the question of whether the Hussite movement was predominantly a Czech phenomenon – a sign of early Czech proto-nationalism – or whether such an interpretation would overemphasize the ethnic element in late medieval history.[16] And although the nobility in Bohemia – and to a lesser extent the towns – managed to temporarily strengthen their position *vis-à-vis* the monarchy, it is more convincing to view the Hussite era as a precursor of the sixteenth-century Reformation than a first step towards parliamentarianism or republican democracy.

The fact that the Church's power was greatly reduced after 1436 provides part of the explanation why Bohemia and Moravia escaped most of the violent confrontation that shook western Europe when the Reformation proper arrived, and why it also became an island of religious tolerance throughout the sixteenth century. Catholics, Utraquists, Lutherans, Calvinists, Bohemian Brothers, Baptists and Anabaptists lived here in relative tranquility. In 1526 the Bohemian estates offered the crown to the Habsburg ruler Ferdinand I, brother of Emperor Charles V. The decision of the estates, who had a long-standing policy of resisting monarchical encroachment, to choose a member of Europe's most powerful dynasty as their king was brought about by the arrival of the Ottoman Turks in central Europe. Hungary and the lands of the Stephens Crown also offered their crown to Frederick – and united they managed to repel the Turkish aggressors who had reached the gates of Vienna in 1529. But Habsburg rule also meant that in 1547 the fifteenth century's religious wars briefly reached Bohemia, after the country's estates refused to provide military support for the king's war against the Lutherans' Schmalcaldic League:[17] and were promptly charged with disobedience. The emperor won the war and the conflicts with the Bohemian estates.

Imperial troops occupied Prague and ten leading citizens were sentenced to death of whom six were executed – these included Czechs and Germans. And many Czech and German noblemen were punished by having part of their properties confiscated.

This setback notwithstanding, religious diversity continued in the kingdom and the estates soon set out to recover their former independence. Their greatest achievement came in 1609 when the Habsburg Emperor, Rudolf II, who resided in Prague for 30 years (from 1581 to 1611) issued a *Majestätsbrief* (an Imperial decree) that guaranteed religious freedom to all confessions and all inhabitants, including the peasants, and that gave the Bohemian parliament (*Landtag*) the right to legislate. But this success was short-lived. Little more than a decade later the Bohemians had lost all independence and had been placed firmly under Catholic Habsburg rule.

In 1617 the Bohemian estates elected the Archduke of Styria, and successor designate to the Emperor Maximilian II, Ferdinand, as their king. Educated by the Jesuits, Ferdinand was as determined to consolidate the position of the emperor in his crown lands and in the empire as he was bent on ending the Protestant heresy. The opportunity to do so arose earlier than expected. Disagreement about the execution of the Majestätsbrief[18] led to a vicious confrontation at the *Hradschin* between the Protestant members of estates and the Habsburg representatives of whom three in the end were thrown out of the window. They landed on the castle's dung-heap and escaped humiliated but with no serious injuries (one of them was later ennobled and given the title 'von Hohenfall' – having fallen from high). The Protestant majority of the estates, however, decided to sever their close attachment to the Habsburg dynasty and instead establish rule by independent patriarchal oligarchy not unlike the governmental system in Venice, the Swiss Federation or the Netherlands. The role of the kings was to be kept in the form of a constitutional monarchy: he was to be appointed by the estates and would be obliged to reside in the realm. And, most important, both the executive and legislative were also to be the prerogative of the estates.

The defenestration of Prague marked the beginning of the Thirty Years War, the most devastating conflagration in European history before the twentieth century. Although religion played its part, the war from the beginning was largely a political power struggle. On its international level it saw the main states of Europe in shifting alliances attempting to curb Habsburg hegemony; and, domestically, it was the decisive showdown between the new theories and practices of royal absolutist government and the traditional state-form that sanctified the rights of the estates.

The war, which was mainly carried out on the soil of the Holy Roman Empire, lay large parts of central Europe barren, including the lands of the Weceslav Crown. On average Germany lost one-third of its population, with losses in the most affected parts amounting to up to half of the pre-war levels. Politically it greatly altered the map of east-central Europe.

Shortly after the incident at *Hradschin* the rebels faced the final decision. In 1619 Matthias II had died and they now could either reaffirm their allegiance to Ferdinand, or finally separate from Habsburg. Encouraged by the support of both the Moravian and Silesian estates the Bohemian noblemen and their patrician allies chose the latter option. In August 1619 they decided to offer the crown to the head of the Union of German Protestant Princes, the Elector Frederick of the Palatinate – son-in-law of King James I of England – who was duly crowned King of Bohemia the following November. The hope of the estates that their choice would secure substantial military support from Europe's Protestant camp proved illusory. Only the Netherlands made a meaningful contribution by sending six thousand soldiers and by providing the insurgents' war fund with half a million Goulden – no small sum at the time. Ferdinand – now Emperor Ferdinand II – on the other hand, managed to assemble a formidable army led by the head of the German Catholic League, Duke Maximilian of Bavaria. The decisive battle was fought at the White Mountain near Prague on 8 November 1620. The Bohemians and their allies were absolutely routed.

Habsburg punishment was severe. Twenty-seven Bohemian leaders of the rebellion were executed. Two-thirds of the nobility had part or all of their property confiscated; in Moravia half of the manors changed ownership, the Habsburgs and the Catholic Church being the biggest winners. Town people and peasantry faced the option to either return to Catholicism or leave the country. The Lutheran and Calvinist clergy were expelled without exception. All told, about thirty thousand families left their homes and went abroad. The upper nobility doubled their number over the next generation but it was a new ruling class. The traditional estates – who had hoped to establish government based on an oligarchic system in which they would hold the key positions – were replaced by aristocrats loyal to the House of Habsburg. However, none of the reprisals were conducted along ethnic lines. Accounts claiming that the battle of the White Mountain was the beginning of 300 years of Czech oppression by their Habsburg – and hence German – overlords are incorrect.[19] Of the twenty-seven executed delinquents ten were Germans. The three officials who were thrown out of the window were Czechs. The expulsion of Protestants was not in any way conducted along ethnic – let alone 'national' lines. The new nobility, made up of Czechs, Germans, Spaniards, Italians, Flemish or Croatians, was not selected on national lines but because they had been reliable servants of the Habsburgs. The newcomers to towns and countryside who replaced expellees also came from many parts of Europe. Craftsmen, merchants and peasants were allowed to settle in the Bohemian lands not because of their place of origin but because they promised to be loyal Catholics and faithful subjects of the emperor. The conflict decided at the battle of the White Mountain was not whether Czechs or Germans were to be in charge of Bohemia and Moravia but whether the estates or an absolute monarchy would rule. And in the seventeenth century throughout most of continental Europe it was the latter that possessed the stronger power and controlled superior resources.

The damage done in Bohemia and Moravia was massive. Of the close to three million people who were estimated to have lived there before the war more than a third perished. This was brought about by the Thirty Years War, not by machinations on the part of the House of Habsburg. And claims that the latter's rule pushed the country into a period of darkness ('Temno') rest on a decisively subjective premise, and is not supported by the subsequent course of events.[20] In reality the Bohemian lands became a centre of European Catholic baroque, of a flourishing literature and the arts, of enlightened political thought. The losers of the White Mountain battle comprised not only Czech Lutherans and Calvinists but all Protestants in the lands of the Weceslav Crown; in 1620 not only Czech aristocrats but also the Bohemian and Moravian Protestant aristocracy lost their power and possessions. Finally, the political model envisaged by the estates in 1618/19 had no substantial support among the bulk of the population, neither in towns nor among the peasants, whose conditions in any case had further deteriorated under estate rule. The Catholic nobility also was weary about the course the uprising was taking; and, last but not least, the election of – and policies pursued by – Frederick as King of Bohemia, an ardent Calvinist, had undermined the Protestant alliance as well.

The outcome of the Thirty Years War, which finalized Habsburg possession of Bohemia, Moravia and Silesia, meant that the cultural, social and political tradition that had seen the lands of the Weceslav Crown affiliated with Protestant central Europe since the days of the Hussites was abruptly ended. In its place came the new alignment with Catholic southern Germany and southern Europe under the firm guidance of Habsburg Absolutism. It was a story of losses and gains for the Bohemian lands (as the Kingdom of Bohemia, the Margravate of Moravia and that part of the Duchy of Silesia that still remained with Austria after the 'rape of Silesia' by Frederick II of Prussia in 1742, were now commonly referred to). Gone was the religious tolerance of the Reformation era, the vigorous attempts to achieve a pluralist political model, and the lands' outstanding role as a pivot of central European Renaissance. Gains were to be the magnificent architectural masterpieces of the Catholic Baroque, and the picturesque rural landscapes – and rural lifestyles – characteristic of Catholic southern Europe; to this was later added enlightened religious reformism and, finally, enlightened political reformism.[21] Both peoples of the *Zweivölkerstaat* participated in this process. Their deeds have been well chronicled.[22] Suffice it to say there was no suppression of the Czech language with the implicit threat of its becoming extinct or being relegated to the level of local dialects, spoken only by the lower uneducated sector of society. The opposite was the case: Czech literary output flourished[23] and there was never any threat that government, administration and public services would stop communicating in Czech. Composers and musicians of both communities contributed to Bohemia's flourishing musical life, which, at the time of Mozart, ranked as the pinnacle in Europe. In fact, as his frequent visits show, Prague was a favourite city of the great composer.

Jansenism, a Catholic reform movement that had originated in the Austrian Netherlands and which emphasized predestination and a rigorous concept of morality, had influential followers in Bohemia. It was named after Cornelius Jansen (1585–1638), Bishop of Ypres, who restated traditional Augustinian doctrines on the question of grace, free will and predestination in a remarkably rigorous form. His assertion that everyone was irreversibly predestined to heaven or hell minimized the importance of virtue or good works for reaching salvation. The Jansenites attack on the papacy and on powerful religious orders, in particular the Jesuits, ensured that in eighteenth-century France, where the movement had considerable following, they became involved in the pre-Revolutionary political power struggle.[24] Outside France and the Netherlands Jansenism made its impact in Italy and in the Habsburg Empire. In fact two of the Empress Maria-Theresa's confessors, Anton Ruschitzka and Anton Günther, both of Bohemian background, were Jansenites. They belonged to a group of like-minded people at the imperial court in Vienna who managed to persuade the Empress to outlaw the Jesuits in 1773.

The nobility in the Bohemian lands, having submitted to the rule of the House of Habsburg after the battle of the White Mountain, still held for a century at least the most prominent and privileged positions in the state. They remained in charge of regional government and jurisdiction and continued to exercise considerable control over their subjects. This was curbed by the introduction of far-reaching reforms that commenced with reign of the Empress Maria-Theresa (1740–80) and peaked under her son Joseph II (1765–90) who is widely regarded as the leading example of 'Enlightened Absolutism' in Europe. Maria-Theresa, on conclusion of the Seven Years War (1756–63), relieved the burden on the peasantry by easing some of the feudal hardship. She also began to improve the realm's education system and to reform ecclesiastical abuses.

Her son, on becoming sole ruler after the death of his mother in 1780, started his government in impressive fashion. Within the first twelve months of his sole rule he substituted various punishment for the capital penalty, issued new legal codes based on the principle that all citizens are equal before the law, introduced far-reaching administrative reforms that further curbed the power of the nobility, in particular the Hungarian nobility, granted a limited degree of freedom to journalism and removed the control of censorship from the clergy to laymen of liberal principles. Joseph furthermore instituted public libraries and observatories, founded a medical college in Vienna, a new university at Lemberg, increased the number of public schools for the middle classes and encouraged the arts by offering various prizes. In 1781 he issued the *Unterthanspatent*, which abolished personal serfdom, and the *Strafpatent*, which abolished the *corvee* and limited the lord's right to punish peasants. As Matthew Anderson points out this won him peasant gratitude of a kind no other eighteenth-century ruler received or deserved.[25] In this year, too, he issued the Edict of Toleration which granted freedom of worship to Protestants and the Orthodox Church and throughout his reign the power of the Catholic Church was severely curbed. By 1790 seven hundred monasteries had been closed and the members of religious orders declined from 63 000 to 27 000. German was made the official administrative language for the empire; however, this was not an attempt to 'germanize' his subjects but to achieve greater administrative efficiency. Joseph also abolished numerous monopolies to foster trade.

This was doing too much in too short a time. At the end of Joseph's life the established interests in his dominion – Church, nobility, estates, privileged towns – all were in open or covert opposition to the monarchy. The fragile unity of the Habsburg Empire was threatened. Only by repealing many of his radical policies could his brother, Emperor Leopold II from 1790, restore stability to the disturbed lands.

The abandonment of Joseph's more radical reforms did not prevent him from being recorded by history as the 'Revolutionary Emperor'.

And there is a great deal of truth in this concluding sentence of an historian who was greatly impressed by his efforts:

> When Joseph died, the French Revolution had begun to destroy the old order. In France, the old order and the Crown which supported it had to go, because it stood in the way of a centralization of government and a unification of a hitherto stratified society, demanded by the spirit of enlightenment as well as by the economic needs of the time. In Austria Joseph had carried that process very far before the Revolution broke out in France. He had virtually abolished aristocratic privilege; he had destroyed all forms of the old feudal-type self-government, not only in the provinces but also in the corporations of the cities. He had, in fact, carried the centralizing and unifying measures begun by his mother to a point which made revolution redundant. The revolutionary on the throne had thus saved his countries from the bloodbath of revolution.[26]

The shock of the French Revolution halted all movements for reform. Staunch conservatism ruled most of continental Europe for many decades.

Half a century later there were new demands for reform – but this time they came not from above but below. The 1848 Revolution saw an attempt by sections of the educated European middle classes to establish their form of government: a nation state run under a system of parliamentary democracy. Democracy they did not achieve, but the concept of nationalism was to greatly influence the course of European history for the next century and a half.

In the slow and difficult progress of European – or, indeed, western civilization – towards what is called today 'civil society', the concept of nationalism and the idea of 'the nation state' contributed little. Rather, it has hindered humanity in its search for a better and fairer society by channelling massive resources into petty and mediocre political ideologies that at best glorified the trivial and, at worst, led many of Europe's people into xenophobia, racial hatred and, finally, genocide or, euphemistically 'ethnic cleansing'. The challenge to dynasticism had a devastating impact on Europe almost from its inception. Originally designed to help replace absolutist inefficiency with liberal concepts such individual freedom, representative government, careers open to talent and a stable and equitable civil and international order, nationalism soon deteriorated into a doctrine that promulgated little more than crude populism.

Although ideas of reconstructing the state along liberal and rational lines had been floating around among enlightened thinkers, literati, intellectuals and philosophers throughout the eighteenth century – without much impact beyond a small group of educated citizens – the chief reason for the creation of a nation state lay in the fact that the French revolutionaries, having cut their king's head off, faced a crisis of legitimacy. If government was no longer to be by divine or hereditary right new forms of authority were needed. In the French case it was the slogan of liberté, egalité and fraternité that aroused the loyalty of erstwhile subjects – now citizens. The newly formed French Republic demanded that the French now give their loyalty to the nation state instead of the dynasty – to *patrie* not to Louis Capet.

By 1815 the optimism of the eighteenth-century nationalists and of the French revolutionaries had largely disappeared. Large parts of Europe had experienced brutal warfare and red and white terror. Ideas of change and progress were viewed with suspicion, but the general European reaction could not alter the fact that revolution had occurred, and that certain of its achievements could not be undone, even though they could be twisted or perverted from their original aim. And to the educated middle classes of central Europe nationalism had lost little of its appeal; indeed, initially many of the educated middle classes thought that a liberal state could only function in the form of a nation state.

Anti-French feeling added to the growth of nationalism in central Europe: if the French were a nation then the German lands with their equally proud tradition in all fields had the same – if not more – right to become a nation. The last vestige of former German glory, The Holy Roman Empire of the German Nation had suffered an ignominious end at the hand of Napoleon Bonaparte in 1806. Furthermore, nationalist sentiments and convictions were strengthened by the fact that the ruling monarchical order after 1814, deadly frightened by the French Revolution, instead of trying to continue where Joseph II and other enlightened rulers had stopped, attempted in vain to turn back the clock.

Of the major figures behind the early rise of German nationalism such as Friedrich Schlegel, Adam Müller, Johann Gottlieb Fichte, Ernst Moritz Arndt or Friedrich Ludwig Jahn, none came from the German-speaking parts of Bohemia.[27] Czech nationalism is attributed in particular to Frantisek Palacký, whose nine-volume *Geschichte von Böhmen* presented the Czech peoples' contribution to European civilization and culture. To Palacký the history of the Bohemian lands was marked by constant contact and conflict between the Slavs on the one hand, and Rome and the Germans on the other. As expected, all positive values were with the former. And one of the leading British admirers of the Czech people put it, Palacký presented the true nature of Czech nationalism, a nationalism 'enriched and hallowed by the ideas of humanity, justice and rectitude'.[28] Like most nationalist works of the nineteenth century Palacký's *Geschichte von Böhmen* was little influenced by his contemporary, Leopold von Ranke's, noble aim to account 'wie es eigentlich gewesen war' but is marked by a great deal of pathos. And the fact that Palacký presented the case of a small European ethnic community trying to assert itself in a world of powerful neighbours makes his writing more sympathetic than the similarly subjective works of Heinrich von Treitschke, Thomas Babington Macaulay or Ernest Levisse. Nor was Palacký opposed to the Habsburg Empire. Indeed his comment during the 1848 Revolution that so essential was 'Austria to the importance of Europe that if such an empire had not existed it would have been necessary to create one' has often been cited. But his idea was that of a multinational autonomous association of free people with equal rights.

The 1848 Revolutions in central Europe did illustrate for the first time that the idea of nation state and liberal principles were not necessarily compatible; although as far as the Habsburg Empire was concerned the Revolution of 1848 also showed that ways could be found for the many ethnic groups of the Empire to live together harmoniously. The question of whether the new liberal German state should be *kleindeutsch*, i.e. without the Habsburg Empire, or *großdeutsch*, i.e. to include the latter with all its non-German ethnic groups, was one of the key questions of the Frankfurt Constituent Assembly. Most delegates preferred the *großdeutsch* solution but in the end, albeit reluctantly, accepted the alternative. Still, the final constitution passed by the assembly granted non-German ethnic groups equal language rights for their education, administration and in court, but this was on the provision that they would accept without condition their incorporation into the German state.[29] This was unacceptable to the representatives of the Czech national movement for which Palacký had become the chief spokesman. His position is shown in his rejection of the invitation to take up a position as minister in the 1848 Vienna parliament, when he argued that the liberal principles that should guide the relations of citizens within a society should also rule the relations of nationalities. To him the ideal order should not only remove the privileges of the upper class and abolish the last remnants of feudalism but should also give as much autonomy to the nationalities' new political units (*Länderkomplexe*) as was possible within the confines of the Habsburg hereditary monarchy.[30]

The freely elected *Reichstag* in Vienna, however, did find a solution that probably would have eliminated – or at least thwarted – the problems that were to curse the empire until its demise in 1918. Known as the 'Kremsier constitution' Czech, German, Italian, Polish and Slovene liberal and enlightened conservative politicians managed to reach a compromise between centralism, as was favoured by the German delegates, and federalism, either along ethnic or historic traditional lines, as was favoured by most Slavonic representatives. The final draft of the constitution allowed for a bicameral legislation to be elected by a liberal – though not full – manhood suffrage. The upper chamber, which was in charge of legislative matters, was to present the traditional crown lands, with the proviso that nationally mixed crown lands should be subdivided into homogenous districts whose representatives were added to the crown lands' delegation in the upper chamber. This would ensure that traditional political entities would be preserved, but also that there was a national organization on the lower administrative level to serve the interests of national minorities in the multinational crown lands. Important, too, was the granting of far-reaching autonomy to the communities on the lowest administrative level. The Crown was to have only a suspensive veto.

The victory of the counter-revolution put a quick end to the Kremsier constitution. Still, the realization that a basic reform at the communal or municipality level might take the wind out of the sails of the rapidly developing division along national or ethnic lines within the empire is also found in the constitution introduced after the collapse of the 1848 Revolution, by the Minister of the Interior, Count Franz von Stadion, in March 1849. The property census in his constitution was more rigid, the tenure of legislation longer and the imperial veto absolute. The national district organization was left intact but the crown land autonomy was reduced, and so was the federal element in the organization of the upper chamber. On the communal level there was to be autonomy close to that envisaged by the Kremsier lawmakers. Yet Stadion's constitution, too, was put on ice for a decade by the spirit of neo-absolutism that marked the years after the 1848 Revolution, and, when it finally became enacted in a watered-down version in 1860, its impact was limited.

The cause of European nationalism gathered further momentum in 1860 with the unification of Italy. The fact that only 2.5 per cent of the population did in fact speak correct Italian for everyday purposes illustrates again the brittleness of the concept to create states on the basis of a common language.[31] As one of the founding fathers of the Italian nation, the prime Minister of Piedmont, Mazzimo D'Azeglio, aptly commented 'We have made Italy, now we must make Italians.'

The year 1867 was a milestone for the development of Czech nationalism and the history of the Bohemian lands. The disastrous defeat of the empire at the hands of Prussia had led to a compromise with the

Magyar gentry resulting in the establishment of an Austro-Hungarian 'dual monarchy'. The emperor remained common ruler as emperor in Austria and as king in Hungary. Ministers of Foreign Affairs and Defence were also to be common to both parts of the monarchy, as would be the financing of those two items. All other matters were left to the governments in Vienna for the Austrian parts of the empire (i.e. the lands to the west of the river Leitha or 'Cisleithania') and in Budapest for the eastern parts ('Transleithania'). Although the constitution for the Austrian parts established the principle of full equality for all ethnic communities with an inviolable right to maintain their customs and language, there were soon demands from Czech politicians that a compromise like the one reached with the Magyars should be made with the Bohemian lands as well. This almost succeeded in 1871 when the Vienna government attempted to introduce political reforms that would have established a kind of 'trialist' solution for the empire: to replace the Austro-Hungarian dual monarchy with an Austrian–Bohemian–Hungarian 'trialism'. The 1871 reforms also attempted to introduce measures that would have greatly diffused the nationality problem. There were to be representatives chambers (*Landtagskurien*) along national lines, administrative districts based on common lingual background (*'sprachlich einheitliche Verwaltungsbezirke'*), acceptance of both Czech and German as official government language in those districts where one of the two ethnic groups accounted for a minority of at least 20 per cent, and separate budgets for the cultural needs of the two national communities. These reforms failed, in part because the German-speaking population in Bohemia and Moravia felt that the 'trialist' solution would greatly disadvantage them – although the 1871 reforms would have granted them that degree of national autonomy in the purely German-speaking parts of Bohemia, Moravia and Silesia that they were to fight for so hard – and, in the end, unsuccessfully – over the next decades. However, a further important reason why Emperor Francis Joseph refused to sanction the reforms lay in the opposition of the Hungarian parliament.

The German unification, pronounced amidst much pomp and splendour in 1871 at the Versailles Hall of Mirrors added fuel to the increasingly problematical situation brought about by rapidly rising nationalist and patriotic sentiments among the middle classes. In the short run it prepared the way for German nationalism to spill over to the German-speaking parts of the Bohemian lands, in the long run it laid the foundation for the close political and military alliance with the Second German Empire that was to prove so fatal for the dual monarchy. At the same time it created anxiety on the part of the Czech *Bildungsbürgertum* that they could be overwhelmed by aggressive German chauvinism. Palacký's enthusiasm for the Habsburg Monarchy, too, took a steep dive.[32]

Nevertheless, less than a decade later the Czechs managed to achieve considerable concessions when the government of Count Eduard von Taaffe agreed to the establishment of a Czech university, a major reform of the franchise that secured Czech majority in the Diets of Bohemia and Moravia and to the introduction of the principle of 'bilingual equality' in the courts and in the administration. This last law envisaged that all public servants and judges in the realm had to have command of both languages. Whereas this would have caused little difficulty in Moravia where the two nationalities greatly intermingled, it further poisoned the air in Bohemia with its large homogenous German regions. Demands for 'bilingual equality' added a further unsolved problem for the monarchy.

Throughout the 1880s German parliamentarians attempted again to achieve a separate administrative and judicial set-up for districts which contained only one of the nationalities. And a government-sponsored conference of Czech and German delegates held in Vienna in 1890 almost reached a compromise for Bohemia, but in the end again national obstinacy prevailed.[33] Czech politicians argued that such a division would result in the dismemberment (*Landeszerreissung*) of Bohemia. And, indeed, the more radical section of the German nationalists, in particular the followers of Georg von Schönerer, did show irredentist tendencies or advocated a *Zweiteilung* – a division of Bohemia into two separate entities.[34]

By now nationalism was in full swing. Whereas originally nationalist ideas found particular popularity among the *Bildungsbürgertum*, by the 1880s it had spread throughout the whole middle strata of society, down to the petty bourgeoisie. This resulted in the formation of countless patriotic associations in cities and towns: fiercely nationalistic athletic, school, and youth clubs, women's organizations and student fraternities. As one scholar of Czech–German relations aptly comments 'the process of nationalism turned the one [Bohemian] nation into two peoples'.[35]

By the turn of the century nationalism had spread beyond the middle classes to the labour movements and other sections of society, although patriotic enthusiasm was not the chief motive behind this process. Of all the lands of the Habsburg Empire the two motors of nineteenth-century Europe, population growth and industrialization, had its strongest impact in Bohemia and Moravia – which contained the most advanced industrial region of east-central Europe. There was large-scale migration from the countryside to the urban centres which began to tip the balance in favour of the Czechs in sensitive, strategically placed industrial districts.[36] The large-scale social and economic insecurity that affected most of the workforce before the outbreak of the First World War, the constant concern with daily 'bread and butter issues' such as job security, adequate wages or working conditions always led to tensions. This was a favourable ground for clichés, stereotyping or the need for a scapegoat. The threat of 'cheap Czech labour' or the 'greedy German (or, worse, German-Jewish) factory owner' were some of the clichés that widely made the rounds. In times of crises this could have fatal consequences. The main labour movement, the Austrian Social Democratic Party, attempted to dam the explosive potential of such sentiments.

Because of the multi-ethnic nature of the Danube monarchy labour and union representatives here were the first among the international socialists who had to face the problem of nationalism. The founding father of the Second International, particularly Karl Marx and Friederich Engels, had taken a somewhat blasé attitude on this issue. As a typical product of bourgeois society, nationalist sentiments in their estimates would wane more or less automatically once the bourgeois period of history had passed and socialist internationalism had been established.[37] Numerous resolutions passed by the Second International confirmed the bourgeois character of modern nationalism against which the proletariat was believed to have been immune. The tragic course of events in August 1914, when workers everywhere rushed to the defence of their country, showed how wrong they were.[38]

With the steeply rising workers' population in the Cisleithanian parts of the dual monarchy the nationality problem could not be pushed aside so simply. Initially, communications in the labour organizations were in German as most of the early labour leaders spoke both Czech and German, but as the rank and file was rapidly growing (and as only few workers were bilingual) publications and communications soon had to be published in both languages. In 1889 the nationality problem came to the official foundation of Austrian Social Democratic Party. Initially this party united all ethnic groups of the Austrian parts of the dual monarchy. Under its German leadership little attention was given to nationality issues for the first years. In 1893, however, the Czechs formed an autonomous faction, which in 1896 established itself as an independent Social-Democratic party. Nevertheless, the Social Democrats in Cisleithania were still united in the form of an umbrella organization, the *Sozialdemokratische Gesamtpartei Oesterreichs*. This *Gesamtpartei* at the 1899 Party Congress in Brünn adopted a concept that would change the Habsburg monarchy into a democratic federation of nationalities. Instead of the traditional crown lands there were to be autonomous territories that all had freedom of association and full autonomy in cultural and national matters.

The concept of federalism based upon a programme of cultural autonomy for the nations in Austria was further developed by three of the
most prominent leaders of the Austrian Social Democrats: Victor Adler,
Otto Bauer and Karl Renner.[39] Their fine thoughts on the issue, which –
had they become reality – may well have saved the empire, became
known as 'Austro-Marxism'.

The establishment of an independent Czech Social Democratic Party in
1897 did not prevent a reasonably amicable co-operation between Czech
and German labour over subsequent years. Only in 1913 did it come
to the final breach, but the Czech Social Democrats passed resolutions
in favour of a democratic multi-ethnic reconstruction of the empire
right until the eve of war.[40] All told, the largest parts of the industrial
working populations in the Bohemian lands remained immune to overt
nationalist sentiments.

An over-riding concern with 'bread and butter' issues was not confined
to the proletariat. The economic and social instability of nineteenth/
early twentieth century Europe ensured that basic matters of survival
were also of great concern to the middle strata of society, in particular
small shopkeepers and the 'petty bourgeoisie'.[41] Whether this left all that
much room to devote major energy to the fostering of patriotic, nationalist sentiments – so vital for the *Bildungsbürgertum*'s opinion makers in
the media, education system and parts of the political system – one may
doubt. In fact the result of the 1901 *Reichsrat* election showed that voters
had become tired of the bickering nationalist politicians after a particularly hectic period of confrontation that followed the Badeni crisis
of 1897.[42]

This leads to the question of how crucial or insoluble the problem of
nationalism really had become, before the Great War, to the Danube
monarchy. Or did the resounding victory of nationalism after 1918 and
the later catastrophes introduce an element of inevitability to the historical process that was not there at the time? Were the differences really so
irreconcilable as historians and politicians later made out?

In addition to the working class the Catholic Church in Bohemia and
Moravia also retained much of its transnational character. Again it was
above all material concerns that stood behind the establishment of separate Czech and German Catholic clergy associations at the beginning
of the twentieth century.[43] And capital, investment and big business fol-
lows its own rules and is not likely to be straight-jacketed in a major way
by narrow nationalist considerations.[44] Nor does there seem to have been
much evidence that the farming community, or the rural population at
large, was overtly impressed by calls for patriotic fervour.[45] And the same

goes for the Bohemian and Moravian nobility, which – although numerically small in numbers – had a disproportionate political influence in their diets because of the weighted franchise system.[46] It has also been pointed out that maximalist positions advocated in passionate speeches in parliament did not prevent members from pragmatically working behind the scene in boards or committees on everyday matters.[47] And all confrontations and divisions notwithstanding, until the turn of the century there were periods of lengthy co-operation in the *Reichsrat* and the diets.

There was certainly no lack of initiative on the part of the government in Vienna to find solutions. In 1897 the prime minister at the time, Count Kasimir von Badeni, again attempted to introduce language laws to enable the conduct of all official business throughout the Bohemian lands to be conducted in both the Czech and German languages. This meant that all German-speaking public servants would have had to learn the Czech language. Such a prospect led to a six-months campaign of obstruction in the *Reichsrat* on the part of the German delegates, culminating in an all-out donnybrook that could only be settled by calling in the police. The ordinances were then withdrawn. Further attempts on the part of the Vienna government – none of which lacked credence – followed but they failed to find a solution for the Bohemian stalemate: obstructionism by both Czech and German parliamentarians playing an important part. The laws constantly brought in front of the *Reichsrat* do not really support the common claim that the Imperial government tried to solve the empire's constitutional problems by playing the nationalities out against each other – at least not as far the Czechs and Germans were concerned.[48] In 1905 the Moravian *Landtag* did in fact find a compromise (*Mährischer Ausgleich*) but this model would not have provided a solution for Bohemia.[49] By 1913 parliamentary obstructionism had reached such proportion that both the *Reichsrat* and the Bohemian *Landtag* were incapable of providing effective government and Emperor Francis Joseph II had to call on emergency decrees to run the affairs of state.

The failure of the *Reichsrat* and the Bohemian *Landtag* to provide effective parliamentary government is listed among the chief reasons for the disintegration of the Habsburg Empire. The fate of the empire – so the argument runs – was sealed in 1914: the war only provided the final nail in the coffin.[50] There are good reasons to treat such interpretations with great caution. The fact that the Austro-Hungarian government had not solved all its problems by 1914 scarcely provides a compelling reason to believe that the empire was doomed. None of the European governments had solved the socio-economic and political problems that followed in the wake of population growth, industrialization and urbanization. And few European governments can claim to have tried as untiringly as did the Habsburg rulers. It certainly was regrettable that no solution had been found to make parliamentarianism work in Cisleithania but such problems do not inevitably cause the disintegration of empires. There is a tendency in works on central or east-central European history to emphasize the fact that *Mitteleuropa*'s parliamentary systems had not matured to the level of the more developed democracies of western Europe, in particular those of England and France. And that this in turn explains the fatal course that history took in *Mitteleuropa*. The absence of effective parliamentary government in Imperial Germany, for example, was at the core of the *Sonderweg* discussion that aroused much interest in the 1970s and early 1980s. The argument then advanced by German historians of liberal or social-democratic leaning was that a conservative alliance of rural aristocracy and heavy-industry leaders was bent on maintaining the non-democratic, semi-absolutist monarchical government at all costs, resulting in the militarist and expansionist policies of the Second German Empire.

The fact that the United Kingdom with its entrenched social and political divisions was the model European nations aimed at surprised historians across the channel. Among other things, they argued that the *Sonderweg* theory overemphasized the importance of parliament or parliamentary power as a measuring stick for constitutional progress. Regardless of whether the bourgeoisie dominated the actual governmental structures, they played a key role in any industrialized European society because of their dominance in virtually all other aspects of a country's life, i.e. in such areas as ownership of capital and investment, administration, the press, and the education and judicial systems.[51] And here the differences between England and Germany (or, for that matter the Habsburg Empire) were marginal.

There is even more reason to be sceptical of the claim that the French constitutional developments since 1789 were the guiding light for allegedly less advanced states of central and eastern Europe. The French Revolution had left the nation bitterly divided between Republicans and the supporters of the old order,[52] as is seen by the frequency with which further bloody revolutions occurred, or by the tragic fratricide that followed the Paris Commune. The conflict was aggravated by further divisions among the French caused by anti-clericalism, the Dreyfus affair and the rise of socialism. And the explanation for the Third Republic's survival until 1914 and beyond, is certainly not found in either the strength or the popularity of its constitution.[53]

All told, the sound nature of a pre-1914 government's policies – or the absence thereof – did not depend necessarily, or entirely, on the establishment of a properly functioning parliamentarianism. Applied to the Habsburg Empire, the fact that the dual monarchy finally collapsed after four years of twentieth-century total warfare does not mean that it was already doomed in 1914. Dynasties regarded as much more powerful collapsed under the strain of the Great War. The Habsburg Empire still made a lot of sense. It was a compact economic region with a healthy industrial growth rate and still had the unifying influence of the monarchy and the army.[54] Above all, there was no concrete or workable suggestion on what to replace it with. Nor did there seem to be any serious desire to draw up plans for a fundamentally different state system. Demands were for reforms from within – not for destruction. Parties advocating the dissolution of the empire were a small minority in both Cis- and Transleithania.[55] As far as Bohemia was concerned the chief political party of the pre-war decade, the 'Young Czechs', pursued 'positivist policies', i.e. attempting to achieve autonomy within the existing state structure;[56] the progressives – political parties openly hostile to Habsburg – had only two seats in the Vienna parliament.[57] Although Germans still held a disproportionately high share in industry, commerce and administration, the Czechs were catching up and the gap was steadily closing.[58] At the outbreak of war they had gained a great deal of autonomy, if not *de jure* so at least *de facto*.[59]

The gravest mistake on the part of the Habsburg rulers was their close political and military alliance with Imperial Germany. It meant that the empire became involved in the erratic course of Wilhelmine politics with their aggressive and expansionist quest for world power (*'Griff nach der Weltmacht'*). This in turn meant that in the summer of 1914 instead of conducting a small-scale war against the Kingdom of Serbia, a war that would have had the support of the big European powers who saw in the latter the chief troublemaker in the unstable Balkan region, the Danube monarchy found itself involved in a global conflagration.

This proved too much.

2
Czechoslovakia

The lack of success of 'positive policies' in the years preceding the outbreak of war in 1914 found the Czech population, as a Czech historian put it, in a state of declining enthusiasm or 'increasing reluctance [*Unlust*] towards Austria'.[1] Although all important political parties and political opinions at large were still 'positivist' in essence, there were signs of a growing feeling of disquiet and lack of fervour for the empire's cause. While the bulk of the Czech population was loyal at the outbreak of war (and remained so for most of the war), the massive enthusiasm found in much of the German parts was lacking. General mobilization was carried out without serious disruption throughout the empire, including the Bohemian lands. Karel Kramář, one of the political leaders of the Young Czechs and an ardent anti-German Russophile, criticized government policies, but his stance was isolated, even in his own party. The press in Bohemia and Moravia, from the left to the right of the political spectrum, mostly swung its support firmly behind the Crown. All Catholic newspapers published a declaration signed by the leaders of the two clerical parties, Mořic Hruban and Jan Šrámek, that 'At this great moment in which our Empire, and with it our nation and our country, finds itself, we and all of our people remain unswervingly faithful and devoted to the state and to its exalted monarch.'[2] At the other end of the political spectrum, the Social Democrat *Právo Lidu* was equally supportive, stating that the 'Czech nation, because of its international position, has to rely on Austria in the future, and it must work for a reform of the state according to its need'.[3] The diplomatic manoeuvering of the Central Powers to place Tsarist Russia in the role of aggressor, having already secured the labour movements' support in Germany and

Austria, worked for the Czech Social Democratic Party as well:

> the sympathies of the Czech people are not with those who represent
> official Russia nowadays, but who are in fact the biggest enemies and
> the cruelest oppressors of the Russian nation. Our sympathies are
> with those whom the Tsarist government shoot and kill in the streets
> of the Russian cities, whom they torture in their prisons, whom they
> deport to the icy plains of Siberia.[4]

A year later, the first massive battles on the eastern front at Galicia and
in Serbia having extracted their heavy toll, this support began to dwin-
dle. Disillusionment was compounded by the growing influence of Pan-
Germanism among the Central Powers – indeed, even left-liberal
opinions jumped on the expansionist bandwagon[5] – and opposition to
the empire's war effort began to emerge among the Young Czechs, the
Progressives and the National Socialists.[6] The arrest of Kramář and other
outspoken opponents of the empire's war policies at the end of 1915
gave further impetus to the cause of the anti-Habsburg front, which
largely consisted of a group of radicals in the Bohemian capital, gathered
around a loosely knit secret society that became known as the *Maffie*.

Most important, however, for the subsequent course of events in
the Danube monarchy, in particular for the foundation of the First
Czechoslovak Republic, was the conversion of Thomas G. Masaryk from
the position of reformist to that of enemy of the empire. Professor of
Philosophy at Prague University, Masaryk had headed the Czech People's
Party, usually referred to as the 'Realist Party' – a small political fringe
group that had broken away from the Young Czechs in 1900.[7] Masaryk
had a history of strong links with the West and it was he who, with modest credentials and the limited support of the Prague anti-Habsburg front,
had decided that the cause of ending the empire and achieving Czech
independence was best served by gaining the cooperation of the western
Allies. In the autumn of 1914 he undertook three trips to neutral countries
to test 'western opinion'[8] on the issue. He did not return from his last
trip to Switzerland, largely because he was tipped off that his arrest on
return to Prague was imminent. Instead he went to Rome, and from there
to a belligerent Paris and London. In Paris he was joined during the course
of 1915 by Edvard Beneš, a young professor of sociology at the time and
a student of Masaryk, and by Josef Dürich, a member of the Russophile
wing of the Czech *Maffie*. The three, together with Milanese Rastislav
Štefanik, a French citizen of Slovak origin, and by all accounts a colourful
personality, founded the 'National Council of the Czech Lands'.[9]

Despite this impressive name, the council's early achievements were modest. The activities of Masaryk and his aides in their work towards an independent Czech state were denounced by both the 'National Committee' and the 'Czech Union'. These two bodies, which had formed in the autumn of 1916, when it was announced that the Austrian Parliament would be recalled in May 1917, spanned the political spectrum. The Czech Union refuted the Entente's reply to President Woodrow Wilson's enquiry to the belligerents of 18 December 1916,[10] which among other things had demanded the 'liberation of the Czechs from foreign rule'.[11] At the parliamentary meeting itself, the union put forward a resolution for the transformation of the Habsburg monarchy from the dualist form into a federal state. Even at this late stage of the war, the two progressive deputies, with their demands for a new Czechoslovak state, were largely isolated and their party's programme was read in front of a half-empty assembly.[12]

With the food situation drastically declining throughout 1917 and, with living conditions at large deteriorating by the month, war weariness was gathering momentum. Strikes and food riots became more frequent, further fuelled by the news from Russia. However, although the empire's military fortunes continued to deteriorate, desertion among Czech soldiers remained low. Masaryk's attempt to form a Czech military force was blessed only with limited success. The largest army of recruits, Czech and Slovak POWs enlisted in Russia after the March Revolution, amounted to 39000 men, or 12 per cent of all prisoners.[13] By the time they were ready for military action, Russia was in the midst of civil war, which the Czech army in Russia soon entered, on the side of the anti-Bolshevik White Russian alliance.

Meanwhile, the attempts of the 'Czecho-slovak National Council' (which had succeeded the 'National Council of Czech Lands' in November 1916) to win the western Allies over to its cause had also failed to make progress between late 1916 and early 1918. Early in 1915 Masaryk had managed to have meetings arranged with the prime ministers of France and Britain, who had listened courteously to his ideas, but otherwise accorded his visits little significance. The situation had improved by the end of 1916, though, when the Entente's reply to Wilson's December note acknowledged for the first time the concept 'Czecho-Slovak'.

The Czech emissaries' decision to broaden the scope of their agitation from the original demand for Czech independence from the Austro-Hungarian Empire to the creation of a Czecho-slovak state is commonly explained by the fact that the addition of 2 million Slovaks to their ranks would strengthen the Czechs' position *vis-à-vis* the German populations of Bohemia and Moravia. Instead of 6.5 million Czechs facing 3 million Germans, in the future Czechoslovakia, 8.5 million 'Czecho-slovaks' would decisively outnumber the Germans, who were not expected to welcome the planned new political set-up. There are strong grounds to believe, however, that this was not all there was to the concept of Czechoslovakia. Given the political astuteness of Masaryk and Beneš, both men must have been aware that the inclusion of the Slovak parts of Hungary would mean that whatever they were likely to gain on the swings they would lose on the roundabouts. The increased strength of their position in relation to the large German minority would be countered by the inclusion of the Slovaks, whose cultural, economic and political background differed significantly from that of the Czechs – and among whom the Czechophile wing was in a minority.

Strategic considerations were also important. The western powers were not interested in the dismantling of the Habsburg Empire. As the Danube monarchy was seen as a stabilizing factor in one of Europe's most unstable regions, a further fragmentation of eastern and south-eastern Europe into small 'nation states' would have been envisaged as an aggravation of the situation. Hence, attempts to change the attitudes of western statesmen on this issue could only show promise of success if the new political entities that were to replace Habsburg were not only economically and militarily viable, but also sizeable states in terms of territory and population.

Throughout 1917 there was no indication that the West would change its stance on the future of the Habsburg Empire, although the United States' declaration of war against Austria-Hungary on 7 December 1917[14] was to add a new dimension to the peace-making process. On 5 January 1918, the British Prime Minister Lloyd George told the British Trade Union conference in London that:

> though we agree with President Wilson that a break-up of Austria-Hungary is no part of our war aims, we feel that unless genuine self-government on true democratic principles is granted to these Austro-Hungarian nationalities who have long desired it, it is impossible to hope for the removal of those causes of unrest in that part of Europe which have so long threatened the general peace.[15]

Three days later, Woodrow Wilson announced his famous Fourteen Points. These have played an important role in the evaluation of the post-First World War peace treaties. Ever since the signing of the peace treaties, accusations have been made that international guarantees allegedly made in the Fourteen Points were not followed and that the losers of the war were thus deceived and treated in a dishonest manner. Particularly in post-war German political and historical accounts, failure to follow 'Wilsonian principles' is listed as the chief injustice imposed on the German nation in 1918–19. Over the years, this interpretation has gained considerable popularity, not only on the losers' side, and has made its way into a legion of history textbooks worldwide. As far as the German-speaking population of the Habsburg Empire was concerned, it was above all Point Ten, which demanded autonomous development for the nationalities of Austria-Hungary, that stirred the emotions. It was alleged that this point guaranteed the unqualified right of each citizen to live in the country of his or her nationality and that a large number of German-speaking people were denied this right after the war. Even today this remains a key argument in the literature of Sudeten German associations and their supporters, who claim that the violation of international guarantees – brought about by Wilson's volte-face – victimized the German-speaking populations of Bohemia and Moravia. Surprisingly, the view that Wilson's tenth point was not adhered to during the negotiations at Versailles, St Germain and Trianon is also presented in scholarly works. The immense importance of this issue for the subsequent discussion in this book demands a short review of the true situation.

To begin with, the American president made his proposals in January 1918. At that time, United States troops were yet to arrive in significant numbers. Designed by an honest and much respected statesman, the Fourteen Points were intended as a basis, a starting point from which to commence negotiations to stop the terrible slaughter, an initial stepping-stone towards peace. No doubt Wilson also hoped that the success of his initiative would spare the Americans actual combat and loss of life. The fact that some of his points later became part of the peace treaties, or were incorporated into the Charter of the League of Nations, did not turn them *post facto* into a binding legal document or a set of immutable laws for the peacemaking process. They did not and could not constitute more than a first step towards finding a way to end the war; nor were they meant to. Any serious peace negotiations could only commence in collaboration with the USA's chief allies, the Entente powers, France, the UK and Italy, who had been carrying the full brunt of the war on the western and southern fronts for three and a-half years.

Summarizing briefly, the first five of Wilson's points deal with general issues: open covenants of peace and abandonment of secret diplomacy (one), freedom of the seas in times of war and peace (two), promotion of freedom of trade (three), reduction of armaments (four) and a fair settlement of colonial problems (five). Articles six to thirteen state specific demands for a number of countries involved in the war. There was to be withdrawal of foreign troops from Russia (point six), from Belgium (seven), from France, which included Alsace-Lorraine (eight), and from Romania, Serbia and Montenegro (eleven). The peoples of the multinational empires of Austria-Hungary and Turkey were to be given freest opportunity for autonomous development (points ten and twelve) and the frontiers of Italy were to be readjusted along recognizable lines of nationality (nine). There was to be an independent Polish state, with free and secure access to the sea (thirteen) and, last but not least, the formation of an association of nations to secure international stability and order (fourteen).

The meaning of Point Ten was clear from the outset. To establish the autonomous development of the numerous nationalities within the Habsburg Empire did not necessarily imply the breakup of the empire. Regardless of what has been claimed since 1918, Point Ten certainly did not constitute a legal basis for the establishment of an independent 'Sudeten German' state, nor a mandate for the German-speaking parts of Bohemia and Moravia to become part of Austria or Germany.

As it turned out, the Central Powers did not respond to Wilson's effort; hence, the president's attempt to set the peace process in motion failed, and for all practical purposes this was the end of the Fourteen Points, at least in their original form. The German government, along with the war leaders in Vienna, having won the war in Russia, was evidently still confident that Berlin and Vienna would determine the peace settlement. In particular, Imperial Germany's military leaders remained firmly committed to the fight for realization of their maximalist war aims. Germany's political parties, with the exception of the left-wing Independent Social Democrats, also rejected Wilson's proposals more or less outright, although acceptance of the Fourteen Points at that time would have left the governments of the two states in a far more favourable position to participate in the peacemaking process than was the case at the end of the year.

Ten months later and staring certain defeat in the face, newly formed governments in both empires contacted the American administration, attempting to negotiate from where Wilson had left off in January. However, the tables had now drastically turned. With the United States having also suffered severe casualties since then, the president had become far less conciliatory.[16] As far as Austria-Hungary was concerned, the American administration, in agreement with its Allies, rejected the offer, because the political reality in the now virtually defunct Habsburg

Empire had invalidated the tenth point of the president's January address. On 19 October, Secretary of State Robert Lansing informed the Vienna government that the president 'is no longer at liberty to accept the mere "autonomy" of these peoples as a basis of peace'.[17]

As far as Germany was concerned, President Wilson's Fourteen Points had caused concern among the Entente powers from the moment they were presented. Officially the British, French and Italian governments had backed his proposals. After all, they included some of the Allies' key demands – the withdrawal of German troops from France, Belgium and Russia, the guarantee of free access to the sea for Poland and readjustment of Italian frontiers – and, of course, the last thing they could afford to do at the beginning of 1918 was to put off their valuable new ally.

Behind the scenes, however, grave fears were held that 'holier-than-thou president'[18] Wilson, with his Presbyterian idealism and his belief that it was his God-given task to secure world peace and democracy, would monopolize the peacemaking process. There were strong suspicions that, in his zeal to 'create a liberal, capitalist world order, safe both from traditional imperialism and revolutionary socialism, within whose stable liberal confines a missionary America could find moral and economic pre-eminence',[19] he would give away at the peace table what the soldiers had fought for so bitterly – a settlement that would put an end to future German aggression. Their fears seemed well justified when French intelligence, on 5 October 1918, detected that the newly formed German government of Prinz Max von Baden had secretly approached the president for an armistice.

The realization that Wilson was considering a response to the German request without even consulting his European partners stung the Entente leaders, who, in a most angry manner, informed the president that they would not negotiate an armistice agreement on the basis of the Fourteen Points.[20] Wilson's harsh 15 October note to the German government, which stressed that there would be no headlong rush towards armistice and that armistice conditions could only be worked out in full consultation and cooperation with his Allies, did little to pacify the Entente's political and military leaders. After three weeks of further acrimonious confrontation – at one point the British Prime Minister Lloyd George angrily announced that if the Americans wanted to make peace with the Germans, they should do so, but that the British nation would then continue the war itself – the victorious powers finally drafted the armistice conditions which were handed to a German delegation on 8 November at Rhetondes in the Forest of Compiègne. With important qualifications, the Fourteen Points were to form the basis for peace negotiations.

In addition to the fact that Point Ten had already been declared null and void, the British prime minister also rejected Point Two, as it would have denied his country's power of self-protection. On British and French insistence, Wilson also added the following vital point:

> Further, in the conditions of peace laid down in his address to Congress of the 8th January, 1918, the President declared that the invaded territories must be restored as well as evacuated and freed, and the Allied Governments felt that no doubt ought to be allowed to exist as to what this provision implies. By it they understand that compensation will be made by Germany for all damage done to the civilian population of the Allies by the aggression of Germany by land, by sea and from the air.[21]

Equally importantly, a set of further armistice conditions made by the British and French governments followed Wilson's points. These were German withdrawal behind the Rhine and the establishment of Allied bridgeheads on the east bank of the river, the surrender of great volumes of military material and transport equipment, the immediate release of the prisoners of war without reciprocity and the internment of the bulk of German naval forces.

With Germany's war effort having completely collapsed and the country now also being in the throes of revolution, there was no alternative to acceptance of the armistice conditions. However, Germany's political leaders and the media initially failed to make the public aware of the full content of the armistice conditions. With the subsequent realization that it is not the losers who determine war settlements, there were loud cries of foul play. Although the final outcome of the peace process did not substantially deviate from Wilson's proposals, the claim that Germany was deceived (*'verschaukelt'*) at Versailles was to be an equally fateful myth for the history of the Weimar Republic as was the 'stab in the back' legend (*'Dolchstoßlegende'*) that was peddled by the political Right.

The failure of the January peace initiative did not mean that either President Wilson or the French and British governments had already consented to the breakup of the Danube monarchy at that point in time. Several months were yet to pass before they crossed the Rubicon. As late as May 1918, Wilson and Lloyd George were still attempting, separately, to make a peace with the Austro-Hungarian government that would have preserved the empire, although in a reduced form. They suggested a post-war Austrian state composed of the 'older units' – Bohemia, Hungary and Austria proper.[22]

The decisive change as far as the fate of the Habsburg Empire was concerned, Zbyněk Zeman argues persuasively, came with the last German onslaught and attempt to win the war, the '*Kaiserschlacht*' that began on 21 March 1918. The peace treaty of Brest-Litovsk meant that the military balance on the western front was tipped in favour of Germany, who had been able to transfer forty divisions from Russia. American troops, on the other hand, were yet to arrive in significant numbers. The battle lasted for four months and at times the British and French defence was stretched to breaking point. Now everything had to be thrown onto the scales to undermine the Central Powers' war effort.[23]

In addition to this, the Bolshevik seizure of power had created a new problem for the western statesmen – the spectre of communist revolutions spreading throughout Europe. And the successes of the Czech Legion in Russia against the Bolsheviks did not fail to make an impression. They added weight to the decision to hurt the Central Powers Alliance at its weak link – the Austro-Hungarian Empire. From 8 to 10 April, Beneš attended a meeting of the 'oppressed nationalities' in Rome, where representatives of the Habsburg Slavs, of Serbia and Romania, together with Italian and French politicians, had gathered to strike a first major blow at the ailing empire. The exiles demanded that the 'Allied states admit as combatants all those expressing their desire to be liberated from the German–Magyar yoke and made independent states'.[24] Although the Allies as yet did not accept these claims for independence, the meeting of the 'oppressed nationalities' did ensure that Allied military authorities recognized the value of the exiles' subversive propaganda against the Habsburg monarchy.

In May 1918 Masaryk went to the United States, where for several weeks he toured towns with large numbers of Czechs and Slovaks, advocating the coming of a Czecho-Slovak state. On 30 June a large gathering of the two peoples at Pittsburgh officially sanctioned the 'Pittsburgh Convention', which promised the Slovaks their own Diet and autonomous administration. During his visit he also met the US president, who had become much more amenable to the idea of breaking up the Habsburg Empire.

Meanwhile, the situation within the empire had drastically changed by the middle of 1918. The death of Emperor Franz Joseph in November 1916 removed the last linchpin holding the monarchy together; as hereditary ruler, he had been much loved and respected by the majority of his subjects during his reign of 68 years. The continuing war and ensuing ever-increasing hardship suffered by the bulk of the civilian population had greatly eroded the support base among the empire's non-German ethnic groups. Thus the inability of Franz Joseph's successor, Charles, to pull Austria-Hungary out of the war in the spring of 1918 virtually removed the last chance of the Danube monarchy's survival.

Following the French government's recognition of the right to Czechoslovak independence on 30 June, and of the National Council in Paris as the 'first basis of the future government',[25] Czech political leaders in Prague set up a 'Czechoslovak National Committee' on 13 July under the chairmanship of Kramář. On 14 August the British government acknowledged the Czechs as an 'allied and belligerent army waging regular warfare against Austria-Hungary and Germany'.[26] On 3 September the United States followed suit and on 14 October Beneš announced the formation of a provisional government with its seat in Paris. By this time the Habsburg Empire was in its final stage of rapid disintegration, swept away by nationalist or socialist revolutions. As far as the Czech lands were concerned, a mass demonstration in Prague on 28 October led the National Committee to take over the city's administration from the imperial authorities. Two weeks later, on 14 November, a provisional National Assembly, consisting of 214 Czech and 42 Slovak delegates, elected Masaryk (who was still in Washington) president, Kramář prime minister and Beneš foreign minister. On 22 December Masaryk returned to Prague, to a tumultuous welcome.

Less than two months later, on 6 February 1919, the Czechoslovak foreign minister presented his country's case to the Council of Five in Paris for international approval. Beneš gave an impressive performance. In contrast to the Polish delegate, who spoke before him, and who demanded boundaries for the newly formed Polish state that went back to those of the Polish–Lithuanian Kingdom of late medieval/early modern times, Beneš asked the council to respect and maintain the borders of the historic Czech lands as they had existed under Habsburg rule. To justify the breakaway of Slovakia from Hungary, he referred to the related ethnic and linguistic backgrounds of the Czechs and Slovaks among the western Slavonic peoples and to the principle of self-determination. Although his proposal for a Czechoslovak national identity did not survive the test of history, the period in which the two communities lived together and formed one state was marked by far less violence and bloodshed than was the case in Yugoslavia, the third of the nations newly created at the Peace Conference. As the late twentieth century was to show, the argument of the Serbian delegation, that Catholic Croatians and Slovenes, Orthodox Serbs and Muslim Bosnians – who shared little trace of common history – would somehow mysteriously form 'southern Slavonic' identity within a Yugoslav state, was to cost the Balkan people dearly.

Nevertheless, Beneš' optimistic assessment at Paris was one side of the story, the reality of the situation in the fledgling new state the other. Despite their ethnic and linguistic affinities, the two peoples had been following separate paths for most of the preceding millennium. Slovakia had become part of the Kingdom of Hungary – the lands of the St Stephen's crown – in the eleventh century; Hungarian dominance was evident in the fact that the region was referred to as 'Upper Hungary'. Economically and politically, this part of the Habsburg Empire was less advanced than the lands of the Weceslav Crown. The Hungarian ruling élites had also imposed fairly rigid Magyarization policies, especially during the fifty years before the outbreak of war in 1914, and these had thwarted Slovak social and cultural developments. The idea that Czechs and Slovaks constituted a single nation did not originate in any meaningful way until the 1890s, when groups of Slovak nationalists began to advance such a concept.[27] The guiding hand of Thomas Masaryk was present here, too, as the most prominent advocates of the Czecho-Slovak idea had been his students. These became known as the *Hlasists*, after their journal *Hlas* ('*The Voice*'). By the end of the war *Hlasist* ideas had gained acceptance among sections of the Slovak intelligentsia and the educated élite, who founded the 'National Council of the Czecho-Slovak Nation in Hungary' in October 1918. This group demanded autonomy for the Slovak people and the right to become part of the Bohemian lands (which were now referred to as the 'historical lands'). Czechophile ideas, however, had not gained wider acceptance among the bulk of the Slovak urban and rural populations, who, partly out of admiration for the Hungarian lifestyle and partly in the interests of professional advancement, had needed no coercion to accept the Hungarian government's Magyarization policies.[28]

Difficulties arose from the moment that both the Czech National Committee and the Slovak National Council announced the creation of an independent Czechoslovakia. There were contingencies of Hungarian troops in Slovakia and the administration, including the police force, was still under the command of the Hungarian authorities. Moreover, the new Hungarian government of Mihály Count Károly, which had taken over from the imperial authorities at the end of October, was determined that the 'Upper Hungarian province' was to remain with the 'motherland'. Six thousand Czech soldiers were moved into Slovakia to support the incorporation, but Allied pressure was needed before the Károly government would order the withdrawal of the Hungarian militias on 1 January 1919 and Czechoslovak authorities could take over.

Five months later, Hungary was under a Soviet dictatorship. Red troops renewed the attack on Czech forces in Slovakia and within a few weeks were in control of the south and east of the country. Again it was only the threat of French and Romanian forces attacking Hungary that led to their withdrawal. The peace treaties with Austria at St Germain on 10 September 1919 and with Hungary at Trianon on 4 June 1920 sanctioned international recognition of the Czechoslovak Republic. Internally, however, Slovak unhappiness with the limited degree of autonomy within the new nation led to an uneasy relationship that remained not unproblematic throughout the interwar years.[29]

Predicably, unease with the new political set-up was even stronger among the German political parties. The collapse of the Central Powers' war effort had caught most German-speaking people by surprise, as newspaper coverage had presented a positive picture of the military situation at the fronts until late into the year. Initially, all political parties, from left to right, rejected integration into the new Czechoslovak state; misinformation and misunderstanding of the peace-making process added to the overall confusion. In late October/early November, provincial governments in the major German-speaking parts of the former Bohemian lands were formed; German Bohemia (*Deutschböhmen*), Sudetenland, German Southern Bohemia (*Deutsch Südböhmen* or *Bohmerwaldgau*) and German Southern Moravia (*Deutsch Südmähren*) were constituted as part of Austria. Czech troops soon put an end to this by occupying all German border regions, which led to frequent clashes between Czechs and Germans. The worst of these occurred on 4 March 1919, when 56 people were killed.[30] News from Paris soon left little doubt that there was to be no break up of the 'Historical Lands'.

Allegations have been made that Beneš manipulated the figures accounting for German speakers to support his stance against any secession from the Czech lands. On the other hand, it has been pointed out that the statistics used, based on the last census taken in the Habsburg Empire, were unclear on subjects' nationalities and that the Czech foreign minister did not wilfully mislead the peacemakers. However that may have been, the reality of the situation required no misrepresentation of the statistics. None of the victorious powers would have consented to a peace that saw a German or Austrian state with a larger German-speaking population than the pre-1914 one. The suggestions of the former Harvard Professor for East European Studies, Cary Coolidge, that the German-speaking parts of the former Bohemian lands should be added to either Austria or Germany, were isolated; they were rejected outright by the British and French negotiators and also failed to gain acceptance from the American delegation.

With Europe's new post-war political order gradually establishing itself, opposition to the Czechoslovak state began to mellow. In fact, it is doubtful that the bulk of the German-speaking population, facing a 'catastrophic food situation' in the aftermath of war,[31] was overtly concerned with the nationalist aspirations espoused by their political leaders.[32] The German Social Democratic Party accepted the new state by officially constituting itself as the German Social Democratic Party in Czechoslovakia (*Deutsche sozialdemokratische Arbeiterpartei in der Tschechoslowakei* [DSAP]) in August 1919, although the party programme did emphasize the need for far-reaching autonomy for the state's minorities from the beginning.[33] Other parties were less compliant and remained uncooperative in the initial post-war years, as far as participation in government was concerned, but hardline irredentist policies were advocated only by the German National Party (*Deutsche Nationalpartei* [DNP]) and the German National Socialist Party (*Deutsche Nationalsozialistische Arbeiterpartei* [DNSAP]). These 'Negativist' parties, however, received only a small share of German votes during the 1920s.[34]

The constitution of the Czechoslovak Republic was drafted by the National Assembly that had formed in November 1918 and was passed by this very assembly, consisting only of Czechs and Slovaks, in February 1920. Initial commitments to validation of the constitution by a freely elected democratic constituent assembly were thus not honoured. Although the liberal character of the constitution has received acknowledgment and praise, the exclusion of the Germans and other minorities from participation in its creation has been justifiably criticized.[35] On the other hand, the reasons for the Czech decision to 'go it alone' as far as the constitution was concerned are readily discernable; the region's grave instability in the immediate post-war period, the insecurity of the domestic situation and the urgent need to place the new state on a legal footing were factors that created a climate not particularly conducive to the pursuit of faultless policies. With the German political parties' attitudes towards the republic ranging at best from modest, qualified acceptance through a noncommittal wait and see attitude to downright hostility, chances for a productive co-operation were slim. Claims that the absence of German representatives in the constitution-making process was the first fatal step towards the Munich disaster lack persuasion. The course of events in 1919 and 1920 did not set an irreversible process in motion; constitutions are not static documents, but are amenable to change and/or additions.

The privileged position enjoyed by many members of the German-speaking communities in the lands of the Weceslav Crown was reduced, but this did not mean that there was a complete role reversal after 1918, as is sometimes claimed. Germans are often represented as having ruled in the Habsburg Empire and then having to take the position of oppressed minority under the Czechs.[36] Such a view misinterprets the situation in both the empire and in the Czechoslovak Republic. Major land reforms were carried out, not always with adequate compensation, at the expense of large estate owners, most of whom were German. However, claims that the redistribution favoured Czech small landholders and disadvantaged German tenants are not supported by the statistical evidence.[37] Neither is the claim that the Czechoslovak government was deliberately pursuing economic policies detrimental to the German business community.[38] Difficulties that did arise in the 1920s, particularly for the textile industries, the largest industrial branch in the hands of German entrepreneurs, date from the final quarter of the nineteenth century, when German firms – in contrast with their Czech competitors – failed to modernize their production methods, a handicap that was characteristic for most light and consumer industries in the German-speaking parts.[39]

Of course, the tendency in times of hardship is to seek a scapegoat rather than the sources of a problem.

Criticism of Czechoslovak policies towards German public servants is more easily justified. The latter had been grossly over-represented in the Cisleithanian bureaucracy and the Prague government decided to correct this by dismissing, in one way or another, almost 50 per cent of German public servants. This brought their numbers roughly in line with the German proportion of the population (about one-quarter), but caused considerable hardship for tens of thousands of former employees and their families, as new employment opportunities were few and far between.[40] Further complaints include career discrimination and the absence of a significant number of Germans in the upper echelons of the public service, although it has been queried whether this was solely the fault of the Czech administrators.[41] Reservations have also been expressed about the alleged injustices of the Czechoslovak government's education policies, which were among the chief grievances listed by the Sudeten German Party in its attacks on the republic in the mid-1930s. The proportion of German primary and secondary schools corresponded statistically to the size of the community and the teacher–student ratio in German schools was lower than in Czech schools. (Both compared favourably with the situation in the German Reich.[42])

Improvements in Europe's economic and political climate that had become apparent by the mid-1920s assisted the easing of national tension in Czechoslovakia. Until then, Czechoslovak parties across the political spectrum had monopolized the government, but in 1926 two

German parties, the German Agrarian Party (*Bund der Landwirte*, BdL) and the Catholic German Christian Social Party, agreed to enter into coalition with Czechoslovak middle-class and conservative parties. This was brought about by the intention of the Czech and German Agrarians to introduce a levy on the import of grain. Such a policy, for obvious reasons, was firmly opposed by the Czech and German Social Democratic Parties. Nationalist solidarity was beginning to give way to more rational alliances, based on common socio-economic interests that crossed ethnic divisions. The term coined for the German parties that declared themselves willing to co-operate with the Czechoslovaks in the running of the country was 'Activists', as opposed to the 'Negativists' who continued to reject the republic. In September 1926 two German politicians took up ministries; the Christian Social Robert Mayr-Harting became Minister for Justice and the Agrarian Franz Spina Minister for Public Works. Three years later, after an election that saw numbers of seats increase for both the Czechoslovak and the German Social Democratic Parties, the leader of the DSAP, Ludwig Czech, was given the Ministry for Social Welfare in a centre–left coalition; with the depression imminent, this soon turned out to be a very important position. Although Activist ministers remained in government until the end of the First Republic, the devastating impact of Black Friday, October 1929, particularly on the German-speaking parts of Bohemia and Moravia, soon led voters to desert Activist parties in large numbers.

Historians have been careful not to over-emphasize the positive aspects of the Activist period.[43] Collaboration in the second half of the 1920s did not lead to concessions on the part of the Czechs on the vital nationality question, nor did it entice German Activist politicians to make firm commitments of loyalty to the Czechoslovak state. Still, the policies pursued in those years illustrate the republic's liberal democratic character; they must be ranked as signs of a positive trend, providing a potential that could have been built on, had stable times persisted. This was not to be and consequently Czechoslovakia's chief problem, that of nationality, was not solved.

Having already cursed the last decades of the Habsburg monarchy, the nationality issue lost none of its divisive potential after the Great War. The 'minority treaties' imposed on the new states in eastern and central Europe by the Allied peacemakers added their share to the dilemma. As an expert on Czech–German relations neatly puts it, 'The foundation of the Czechoslovak state in 1918 mirrored the belief of the age that the multinational state was outdated and not capable of adapting to democratic principles, [hence] the modern state form could only be realized in a democratic nation state.'[44] Having campaigned for the liberation of oppressed peoples from the Austrian *Völkerkerker*, the Czechoslovak Republic could hardly constitute itself as a Federation of autonomous nationalities, as this would have been an admission that the ČSR was, after all, also a multinational state. Instead, the Czechoslovaks now became the *Staatsvolk*, the people of the state or 'actual' nationality, while the remainder, the Germans, Hungarians, Ruthenes, Ukrainians and Poles, were classified as 'minorities' with 'minority rights'. Initially designed by the Allies to provide protection for the large Jewish population in Poland, minority treaties aimed to guarantee ethnic or national minorities equal rights with the majority *Staatsvolk*. Citizens were not to be discriminated against on the grounds of their mother tongue; thus the state was obliged to provide schools for minorities, who also had the right to use their first languages in business and administration, in court, the media and in religious observance. However, these rights were granted to individual citizens within minority groups, not to whole communities as collective bodies. This was to safeguard the state against attempts by minority groups to secede or to join the countries of their mother tongues.[45] As with so many of the plans made in Paris, the good intentions of the peacemakers withered away in central and eastern Europe's turbulent post-war political life.

As far as the German-speaking community in Czechoslovakia was concerned, the term 'minority' was scarcely applicable. Consisting of over three million people, the community still exerted immense economic, political and cultural power. The more farsighted of the Czechoslovak leaders recognized the need to 'win the Germans over', to quote President Masaryk,[46] to ensure the future of the new state. Masaryk's famous comment, made on his return to Prague in the turmoil of the revolutionary days, that the Germans originally came as 'immigrants and colonists', has often been cited as early evidence of ill will on the part of the new rulers towards the German minority. However, apart from being taken out of context, the remark is inconsistent with Masaryk's evident stance on German–Czechoslovak relations.[47]

The second prime minister of the republic, Vlastimil Tusar, who had replaced Kramář in July 1919, stressed that it was essential to 'have other bonds than the peace of St Germain and Versailles to tie the Germans to the state'.[48] Beneš too recognized the need for all the nationalities to live together harmoniously. The new system, he wrote early in 1919, would be similar to the Swiss one; this did not mean that the new state would adopt the Swiss political model, but was a reference to the spirit of Switzerland, a country where several nationalities coexisted peacefully.

The fact that the fateful decrees of 1945, which sanctioned the expulsion of most of the German-speaking population from Czechoslovakia, bear Beneš' name and signature, does not constitute evidence of a persistent Germanophobia throughout his political life. The influence of these two statesmen on the state's domestic policies, however, was limited,[49] as is apparent in the history of the central aspect of the new *raison d'état*, the language laws.

The Czechoslovak Minority Treaty of 10 September 1919 stipulated that 'All Czecho-Slovak nationals shall be equal before the law and enjoy the same civil and political rights without distinction as to race, language or religion.' Article 7 also stated that 'Notwithstanding any establishment by the Czecho-Slovak Government of any official language, adequate facilities shall be given to Czecho-Slovak nationals of non-Czech speech for the use of their language, either orally or in writing, before the courts.'[50] Article 9 added that 'Czecho-Slovakia will provide in the public educational system in towns and districts in which a considerable proportion of Czecho-Slovak nationals of other than Czech speech are residents adequate facilities for ensuring that instruction shall be given to the children of such Czecho-Slovak nationals through the medium of their own language.' Terms like 'adequate facilities' and 'considerable proportion' are of course rather vague and caused a great deal of debate, but initially the country's National Assembly took a relatively liberal position on the crucial language issue. The linguistic laws passed on 28 February 1920 declared Czecho-Slovak the 'state official language' (*staatlich offizielle Sprache*), but avoided terms such as *Hauptamtssprache* or *Staatssprache* (main official language or state language) with their connotations that the minorities' languages were *Nebensprachen* (secondary, subsidiary or peripheral languages) and of an inferior standing. Nor were minority public servants obliged by law to have a command of the 'state official language'.[51] However, these laws were not implemented, largely because the resignation of the Tusar government in September 1920 brought Czech nationalist politicians to the forefront. These were considerably less compromising on the position of the Czechoslovak *Staatsvolk* and its relation to the state's national minorities. It took a further five years before a new set of linguistic laws, far more rigid in content, was worked out and passed by parliament. The Czechoslovak language was now clearly specified as the *Staatssprache*; the importance and use of the minority languages in administration and the public services was substantially reduced. This led to a clear distinction between the *Staatsvolk*, the Czechoslovaks, and the 'others',[52] implying differing status and an unequal share in the state's affairs.

Access to all vital positions in the republic's upper hierarchy, in politics, industry or the intelligentsia, demanded mastery of the Czech language.

For the German communities, the language laws meant that 90 per cent of their citizens could use their mother tongue in dealings with the public sector. German was used in schools and there was no obligation to teach the *Staatssprache*. In fact, most 'average citizens' could lead their lives without ever being confronted with the Czechoslovak language. Except in the case of state public servants, the linguistic laws did not obstruct career advancement or professional development opportunities for Sudeten Germans, as the republic's German communities were increasingly referred to in late 1920s political circles. The imposition of *Minderheitsstatus* (minority status) and the associated consciousness of marginality, of belonging to a 'minority' rather than to the 'proper' *Staatsvolk*, overshadowed what was otherwise a more or less unmolested existence and did not serve to endear the Czechoslovak state to German ethnic groups. Long-term loyalty on the part of the latter could only be achieved with fundamental changes to the minority laws. There is no compelling reason, however, to believe that the obstacles to such changes were insurmountable; in fact, the idea of the republic's Germans becoming a *Zweite Staatsvolk* (a second 'national people') began to emerge in the late 1920s,[53] but time was needed for the post-First World War political set-up to establish itself more firmly before a trend towards increased autonomy could find majority support among the Czechs. And such time was not available.

Consolidation of the Czechoslovak state would necessarily be a lengthy process. Even had a solution to the nationality problem been found, the disaster of Munich 1938 would not have been averted. No policy of the Czechoslovak government could have altered the combined impact of Black Friday 1929 and January 1933. While the nature of Czech society and politics has to be regarded as an encouraging feature in the generally depressing political landscape of interwar Europe, there has been severe criticism of the Czechoslovak state, particularly from German historians. For example, the constitution's failure to grant collective legal and political rights to ethnic and national minorities, while granting full rights to individual citizens, ensured that German political parties were permanently barred from gaining office. Although in theory the constitution was acknowledged as most impressive (based on the model provided by the Third French Republic), real decision-making power is said to have rested with the Pětka, an unofficial commission made up of the leadership of the five major parties, which bypassed and effectively disempowered the parliament.[54] Czech society at large is said to have been distinguished by a pronounced state of 'pillarization' (*Versäulung*), that is, the establishment of party-based political empires that cosseted their followers virtually from the cradle to the grave. Shortcomings also included a dominance of professional politicians and a weak constitutional court. Hence, these arguments conclude that in reality the republic was a sham democracy, which, among other things, explains the smooth transition into the right-wing, semi-dictatorial form of government that led the short-lived second Czechoslovak Republic after the Munich sell-out.

Some of these arguments need refinement; others carry little conviction. Admittedly, the Czechoslovak minority and nationality laws were a retrograde step from the provisions provided by the Austrian constitution of 1867, but it should be spelt out more clearly how, for example, the absence of collective minority rights actually disadvantaged the German-speaking communities. Had the latter, constituting over three million citizens, managed to unite behind a single movement or party, the state's democratic set-up would have ensured that they could wield enormous political power. This is in fact what happened when the great majority of Czechoslovakia's Germans rallied behind Konrad Henlein's Sudeten German Party in the mid-1930s.[55] The uninterrupted presence of German parties in parliament (and of German-held ministries in the government) from 1926 to the end of the First Republic counters the claim that Germans were condemned to perpetual political impotence. It is also not altogether clear to the outsider precisely how 'pillarization' affected the country's individual citizens, or society at large, in a negative way – aside from the fact that such a state of affairs was in no way confined to Czechoslovakia.

No doubt there was room for improvement. Judged on some abstract, utopian ideal of a perfect democratic state, Czechoslovakia indeed fell short, but perfect democracy has shown itself to be either a spurious notion or a philosophical plaything. Compared with the uninspiring history of the Austrian Republic or the Weimar Republic, let alone the dictatorial or semi-dictatorial regimes that ran most of eastern, south-eastern and southern Europe, Czechoslovakia looked impressive, not only in comparison with non-democratic continental Europe. Post-war Britain had not overcome the deep social gulf that marked its pre-1914 history. Political power was still firmly in the hands of the Conservatives, with the trade unions routed in the 1926 strike. France was more deeply divided after the Great War than before. The Popular Front government pushed members of the French conservative establishment in droves into passively and actively sympathizing with fascism; nor should it be overlooked that the Third Republic, with its much longer history of democratic institutions, had no difficulty accepting a semi-fascist dictatorship after 1940. With the possible exception of the Scandinavian countries, there was no state in Europe where moderate Labour had such a strong say in the nation's affairs as was the case in Czechoslovakia. Switzerland, the oldest republic in Europe, was (and is) also not governed by the Westminster system of government and opposition at the federal level, but by an agreement of collaboration and rotation that involves the major parties.[56] As far as the much-cited absence of collective rights for minorities is concerned, the only collective 'right' held by the Welsh minority in the UK, for example, was the fact that the heir to the Kingdom's throne had been invested with the title Prince of Wales. And what collective right did the Bretons have in Third Republic France? Or the Basques in Spain?

The Czechoslovak Republic granted its citizens full civil rights – political and legal equality, liberty of expression, freedom of association, press and religion, access to education and basic health care, as well as a modest degree of social security. One of the factors accounting for the victory of liberal democracy over rival political ideologies in the twentieth century is that system's flexibility in tackling the difficulties and problems that invariably arise in human society. Of course, many of these problems are not solved speedily and some are never solved. No British government, for example, has yet solved the Irish question, but this does not detract from the admiration the United Kingdom receives for having played such a vital role in the development of parliamentarianism. The fact that the United States is still a long way from solving its ethnic problems does not detract from the country's actual achievements in the field of civil rights. That time was too short for Czechoslovakia to find a solution that would satisfy all its ethnic groups was not the chief reason for the country's ignominious end in 1938/39. External factors were far more important. To these our study will now turn.

3
The *Reichsgau Sudetenland* and the Protectorate of Bohemia and Moravia

The tendency to blame outsiders or outside forces for any ill fate that may have befallen a community is as old as human history. 'They [the troublemakers] came in from the outside,' the ancient Greeks used to say. In the twentieth century the most famous example of diversion from the reality of a situation by pushing the blame elsewhere is found in a comment made by the long-serving Prime Minister of Prussia, Otto Braun, after the Nazi seizure of power in 1933. Trying to explain the inglorious end of the republic, Braun claimed that the rise of Adolf Hitler could be summarized in two words: Versailles and Moscow – the harshness of the Versailles Peace Treaty and the Communist threat. In reality these two factors have to be ranked among the least important of the reasons for the Nazis' success. It was not the Versailles Peace Treaty that crippled Weimar Germany's economy[1] and the Communists – though a noisy and uncomfortable minority – were in no position to effectively challenge the German military and political establishment. The Czechoslovak Republic, on the other hand, can mount a respectable case for the claim that it fell victim to external forces.

The western Allies, having played a major role in the creation of the new political set-up in central-eastern and southeastern Europe, took limited interest in the region's stability after the peacemaking process was completed. The power vacuum left by the collapse of the Austro-Hungarian Empire was in no way filled. With the departure of Woodrow Wilson from the presidency in the autumn of 1920, the United States withdrew from active engagement in European affairs. The United Kingdom also showed little interest in committing itself to any security agreement on the continent. Only France entered into alliance treaties with the governments in Warsaw and Prague as part of its attempt to keep Germany at bay, but these agreements were very fragile.[2] Militarily the 'Little Entente', originally formed by Czechoslovakia, Yugoslavia and Romania in 1921 to counter threats of 'Habsburg revisionism', was a toothless tiger, and the League of Nations was to prove incapable of providing protection against aggression. Hungarian governments continued to resent the loss of 'Upper Hungary' and Czech–Polish relations were far from friendly. The precariousness of the ČSR's military and strategic situation did not become apparent during the relatively stable 1920s, but this soon changed with the Wall Street Crash.

The impact of the World Depression on the German-speaking areas of Bohemia and Moravia was devastating from the outset. Light and consumer industries, heavily dependent on the export of their products, lost as much as two-thirds of their market; in the glass and textile industries, unemployment skyrocketed. Job-seeking rates were far higher among the German population than among the Czechs: by 1932–33 German speakers accounted for two-thirds of the republic's unemployed.[3] As elsewhere in the industrialized world at the time, the ČSR's social security net failed to cope with such high unemployment, which in turn led to mass poverty. Contrary to claims made at the time – and later – there is little evidence to suggest that the Czechoslovak government pursued economic policies that deliberately disadvantaged the German citizens.[4] On the other hand, the prevailing spirit of economic rationalism ensured that Keynesian ideas also failed to find much of a following in the ČSR, which meant that the resulting longevity of the economic crisis was bound to have political consequences. Ominous messages soon appeared in the public sphere, such as this one written on a chimney: 'Auch du wirst wieder rauchen, wenn dich wird Hitler brauchen' (you too will smoke again when Hitler needs you).[5] By advocating a party programme that stressed the *völkisch*[6] identity of the Sudeten-German community, distancing itself from Hitler's form of National Socialism and by proclaiming loyalty to the Czechoslovak state – though on the basis of large-scale regional autonomy – Konrad Henlein's *Sudetendeutsche Partei* (SdP) scored 63 per cent of the German vote at the parliamentary election of 26 May 1935. The avalanche had begun.

By the mid-1930s the nationalist right in the German-speaking parts of the Bohemian lands was looking back at a long and illustrious history. Two Austrian nationalists who had a huge influence on the young Adolf Hitler came from here: Georg von Schönerer and Karl Hermann Wolf. The first was the parliamentary member for the Egerland for most of his political life. Described as the 'strongest and most thoroughly consistent anti-Semite that Austria produced'[7] – before Hitler, von Schönerer detested big business and liberal *laissez-faire* economics. Instead he advocated a classless ethnic community (*Volksgemeinschaft*) based on an 'early brand of "national socialism" – above all else radical German nationalism (meaning the primacy and superiority of all things German), social reform, anti-liberal popular democracy, and racial anti-semitism'.[8] The ideas of *Volksgemeinschaft* and *Volkstumspolitik*[9] were further developed by Wolf, who was born in Eger in 1862. After studying philosophy in Prague, Wolf turned to journalism and politics. Initially an ardent supporter of von Schönerer, he held the northern Bohemian seat of Trautenau in the Austrian parliament. Wolf made a name for himself during the Badeni crisis, when his obnoxious behaviour in the *Reichsrat* earned him the reputation of being the wildest political ruffian of the Danube monarchy.[10] Unlike von Schönerer, Wolf was not so much an anti-Semite as viciously anti-Czech. He left the Schönerer movement in 1902 to found the German Radical Party, which managed to win 22 seats in the 1911 *Reichsrat* election. Wolf was the idol of the Austro-German corps-fraternity students (*Burschenschaftstudenten*) – an undistinguished bunch of hoodlums, who in the last years of peace physically assaulted and terrorized students of other nationalities at all universities in the Cisleithanian parts of the monarchy.

A further strongly nationalist, anti-Czech political party, the *Deutsche Arbeiterpartei* (German Workers Party), founded in 1904 in Trautenau, combined *völkisch* nationalism with anti-Marxist, anti-capitalist socialism. Their pan-German aspirations having been shattered by the loss of the war, the party changed its name to the German National Socialist Workers Party (*Deutsche national-sozialistische Arbeiterpartei* (DNSAP)). The other Negativist party was the German Nationalist Party (DNP). Having been elected to the House of Deputies in the first parliamentary election held in April 1920, the party leader, Rudolf Lodgman von Auen, left little doubt about his thoughts on Czechoslovakia:

> We, the representatives of the German people in the Czechoslovak State, declare that the ideas and principles that guided the Allied Powers in drawing up the peace treaties were fallacious, that this state has developed at the expense of historical truth ... The Germans of Bohemia, Moravia and Silesia, and the Germans of Slovakia never wished to unite with the Czechs ... On the contrary, the Deputies of the Austrian Reich's Council elected in the Sudeten German districts in 1911 ... expressly declared their desire to join German Austria. ... We ... shall never recognize our Czech masters. We proclaim

with solemnity that we shall never cease our demands for the self-determination of our people. We do not regard ourselves to be bound by the laws of the Revolutionary National Assembly.[11]

Two years later, at a meeting of German members, he proclaimed to the National Assembly that 'Anyone who thinks that high treason is not the supreme duty of the deputies is committing a grave error.'[12]

As stated, neither DNP nor DSNAP did well in the elections of the 1920s. Lack of success at the ballot boxes, however, was compensated by the fact that these 'Negativists' and their vision of a Sudeten German *Volkstumsgemeinschaft* (community united by its shared ethnic and folkloric traditions) had a firm base in *Volkstums* organizations. Some of these organizations were large, for example, the *Deutsche Studentenbewegung*, the *Deutsche Kulturverband* and the *Bund der Deutschen*, but most German social and cultural activity took place within a legion of small clubs: *Heimatvereine*, *Turnvereine* (gymnastics clubs), numerous *Jugendvereine* (youth organizations), *Gesangvereine* (choral societies), *Schützenvereine* (rifle clubs), to mention only the best-known associations. These *Volkstumsorganisationen* proved more resilient and stable than the political party system in the face of the rapidly developing political crises of the 1930s.[13] Aided by the worsening economic crisis, club representation in the membership of both the DSNAP and the DNP began to rise, with the former drawing steadily closer to the National Socialists in the Reich. When the leaders of the DSNAP stepped up their campaign for cessation of the Sudetenland, a worried Czechoslovak government countered by issuing a decree on 29 February 1932 that outlawed the *Volkssport*, the paramilitary wing of the party, on the grounds of hostility to the state. Seven members were jailed. To escape a similar fate, the two Negativist parties dissolved themselves towards the end of 1932. On the advice of party leadership, most members joined the *Sudetendeutsche Heimatfront*, which had been founded by Konrad Henlein, a gymnastics teacher from the Egerland town of Asch, who also led the Sudeten-German Gymnastics Association. The *Heimatfront*, which soon changed its name to *Sudetendeutsche Partei*, aimed to rally the German-speaking population, across the political spectrum, behind the nationalist banner. United, they were to fight for social and economic improvements and for a better deal from the Czechoslovak government. The fact that from 1933 national and social issues went hand-in-hand for Sudeten Germans must be strongly emphasized.[14]

Because of Henlein's close collaboration with Hitler in the destruction of the First Czechoslovak Republic, the SdP has often been viewed as a mere front organization for the Nazi Party. Such an interpretation, though, is superficial. No doubt there were links to the NSDAP from the beginning, and after the 1935 election victory, the pro-Nazi wing of the party, largely consisting of former DNSAP members, started to gain the upper hand. Originally, however, Sudeten-German fascism was a homegrown phenomenon, having its roots in the *Kameradschaftsbund* (KB). Ideologically the KB was strongly influenced by the ideas of Othmar Spann, a Viennese Professor of Sociology, who advocated a political model based on the *Ständestaat* – a corporate state. In Spann's view, an educated élite should rule over a society made up of estates existing within a hierarchical order. Strongly Catholic, distinctly anti-democratic and anti-socialist, Spann's *Ständestaat* resembled the corporate state of Mussolini's Italy.[15] Structured along strict hierarchical principles, authoritarian and nationalistic, the KB's goal was a *'ständische'* Sudeten-German society, closely linked to, though not necessarily incorporated into, the Reich. All this had little to do with the racialist Social Darwinism of the Nazi Party, which led to a sharp confrontation within the SdP between followers of the KB and advocates of a strictly irredentist Sudeten-German policy in alliance with the NSDAP. The latter group was bound to win the conflict. After the May 1935 election there was considerable financial assistance from Berlin; the Führer's spectacular domestic and international successes, and the fact that most rank and file members preferred more radical policies, placed the SdP leadership's KB wing in a decidedly weaker position.[16] By 1937 former DSNAP members held most of the vital offices in the party. Henlein, however, managed to put his past affiliation with the *Kameradschaftsbund* aside and retained the leadership position.

Before 1933 the relationship between Czechoslovakia and the Weimar Republic is judged to have been 'correct but always fragile'.[17] Few problems marred the first half of the 1920s. The Weimar government had no interest in adding to its host of domestic and international problems by challenging the borders with Czechoslovakia – to the dismay of Sudeten-German nationalists. Meanwhile, the government in Prague could not lose sight of the fact that, with one-third of the nation's exports going to Germany, this country was the ČSR's main trading partner.[18] An arbitration treaty between the two states, as part of the 1925 Locarno agreements, marks the high point of interwar Czech–German diplomatic relations. The treaty stipulated the settlement of 'disputes of all kinds' – with the exception of those already covered by international agreements (which excluded disagreements about the Czechoslovak minority treaties) – through a 'permanent arbitration commission'.[19] Ironically, after Locarno, the situation deteriorated. Although official communications still referred to relations between the two countries as 'correct and friendly', the re-establishment of Germany's position among the leading European powers reawakened ambitions in ruling circles to renew the drive for hegemony in *Mitteleuropa*. Attitudes towards Czechoslovakia developed a tone of condescension, while trade rivalry contributed to the steadily worsening situation. In the late 1920s, concern about its declining export trade to the Balkan countries led the Czechoslovak Republic to mount a fierce international campaign against a planned Austro-German customs union; the campaign eventually succeeded in stopping the project. However, the Weimar government also managed to thwart plans to form a Danube federation, which was to consist of the Little Entente members, Austria and Hungary. The ČSR, being economically the strongest member, would have greatly benefited from such a federation, which would also have curbed the growing German influence in southeastern Europe.[20] Obviously the time of 'correct and official relations' had come to an end by 1933, but still there was no sign that a renewal of Imperial Germany's expansionist policies would aim to eliminate the Czechoslovak state.

This did not immediately change with the Nazi seizure of power. That Hitler intensely disliked the Czechs in his younger days is well recorded. He had hated the sight of Czechs in Vienna, 'arriving penniless and dragging their worn-out shoes over the streets of the city', only to 'install themselves in key positions soon afterwards'.[21] In fact, due to Wolf's influence, Hitler's disdain for the Czechs preceded even his antagonism towards the Jews.[22] Decades later, with his *Machtübernahme*, his achievement of political power, finally in sight, he is claimed to have proclaimed that 'the Bohemian–Moravian basin will be colonized with German peasants … The Czechs and Bohemians we shall transplant to Siberia or the Volhynian region … [because] … the Czechs must get out of Central Europe. As long as they remain, they will always be a seat of Hussite–Bolshevik subversion.' These comments are fictitious,[23] but their content, especially the use of the unusual term 'Czechs and Bohemians', otherwise found only in pre-1914 Austria, and the crude reference to the threat of 'Hussite–Bolshevik subversion' are thoroughly Hitlerian. However, '*Lebensraum*' matters in the early years of Nazi rule had to wait until the first hurdles were jumped. With rearmament well on its way, conscription reintroduced and, above all, with the triumphant occupation of the Rhineland by German troops in 1936, the way was cleared for the long-term goals of National Socialism.

The government in Prague, including the German Activist political parties, was well aware of the danger that was brewing. The success of the SdP had caused alarm bells to ring and there was still hope that the tide might be stemmed. Impressive as Henlein's victory was, after five years of social hardship and much suffering, a third of the German-speaking population still did not heed the call of the *Volkstumskampf* advocates. Unfortunately, progress towards an effective common policy that would revitalize democratic forces was slow. It was not until 18 February 1937 that Prime Minister Milan Hodža presented a memorandum to the German Activist parties suggesting a series of measures aimed at defusing tension between the two peoples. Particular attention was given to the language question, public investments, welfare and state employment. The commitment to consistently allocate funds and positions in the public sector – and to conduct state business in general – according to the principle of national proportioning meant that the republic's German population had in fact become the '*Zweite Staatsvolk*'. Government funding for the German-speaking parts was substantially increased; administrators were advised, when handing out contracts, not to routinely award projects to the lowest offer, but to also take the need for regional or local employment opportunities into consideration. This meant that the number of Sudeten-German firms receiving government orders increased significantly. In the subsequent twelve months, 7000 Germans entered the public service.[24] Coupled with the overall improvement in the world economy, these measures led to a marked decline in the unemployment rate.[25] By the middle of 1937, though, the Sudeten-German cause had long ceased to be merely a matter of socio-economic grievances.

The May 1935 election success also marked the turning point for the SdP. As stated, the party was split between the strictly irredentist wing, demanding incorporation of the Sudeten-German population into the Reich, and the KB wing, which also believed in German supremacy in central Europe, but in a less centralized, looser state form, somewhat similar to that of the medieval Holy Roman Empire. Such an autonomist model would allow for the incorporation of a Czechoslovak state in which Czechs would be ruled by German overlords. 'It is not our task to detach the Sudeten German regions,' Henlein's deputy and chief spokesman for the KB, Walter Brandt, explained, 'but to maintain the current set-up – not by way of forceful occupation, but through political and economic dominance, because what else can we do with the Czechs? They will have to be more or less incorporated into the German sphere of influence.'[26] With the SdP receiving major attention from Berlin, however, the KB's days were doomed. In addition to the solid financial support that had begun to flow into the party's coffers and the inevitable consequential strengthening of the former DNSAP members' position, news from the Reich painted a glorious picture. A booming economy, full employment, 'strength through joy', the construction of *Autobahnen* – it is no surprise that the assertion 'everything is better in the Reich' was heard more and more often. Nazi Germany's striking international successes, above all the remilitarization of the Rhineland, helped to convince party members and supporters that secession was preferable to autonomy. During 1936 Brandt and other KB members lost their leading positions, one after the other.[27] Karl Hermann Frank, a publisher and bookseller from Carlsbad, who had strong connections to the SS and SD, was Brandt's successor as party deputy, which further strengthened the pro-Nazi elements within the SdP. Under internal and external pressure, Henlein finally joined the Hitlerites. On 19 November Hitler was handed a lengthy memorandum, stating that conciliation between Czechs and Germans was 'practically impossible' and that only the Reich could solve the Sudeten-German problem. Henlein also reported to the Führer that he had been reliably informed that 'Beneš was determined to solve the [Sudeten-German] question for the Czech people and state by way of complete destruction of *Sudetendeutschtum*'. Although he was obliged to give an official impression of SdP loyalty to the Czechoslovak Republic, in reality nothing was dearer to him than the thought of incorporating all of Bohemia and Moravia into the Reich.[28]

The memorandum was well timed. A fortnight earlier, unknown to Henlein, the Führer had summoned Germany's military leaders, Defence Minister Werner von Blomberg, Army Commander-in-chief Colonel-General Werner Freiherr von Fritsch, Navy Commander-in-chief Admiral Raeder, Air Force Chief Hermann Göring and Foreign Minister Konstantin Freiherr von Neurath, to a meeting at the Reich Chancellery. Here, in a speech that took more than two hours, Hitler emphasized the urgency of settling the *Lebensraum* question. No minutes were kept, but several days later Hitler's military adjutant Colonel Hossbach wrote an account of the Führer's main points (this document entered the historical records as the Hossbach Memorandum). Having dealt with Germany's precarious international situation, Hitler concluded the first part of his address by stressing that only force could solve the problem and that only the questions of when and how remained. He then outlined three possible case scenarios. His first case pointed out that time was not on Germany's side and that the nation had to be ready to strike between 1943 and 1945 at the latest. Case two envisaged civil war in France, and should this occur, immediate action to be taken against Czechoslovakia. Case three dealt with the possibility of France's involvement in conflict with another power – Hitler particularly had Italy in mind – in which case Germany would have to attack Austria and Czechoslovakia without delay. Hitler suggested that the last two scenarios could eventuate as early as 1938.[29]

As it turned out, the Hossbach Memorandum was used as evidence against the major Nazi war criminals in the Nuremberg trials at the end of the Second World War. It led the United States attorney to argue that as early as 5 November 1937, German plans were becoming definite in regard to both timing and victims. In his well-known and controversial book *The Origins of the Second World War*, British historian A. J. P. Taylor rejects suggestions that the Hossbach Memorandum was a blueprint for German policy, as none of these case scenarios came to pass. Taylor interprets Hitler's exposition as 'in large part day dreaming, unrelated to what happened in real life'.[30] He describes the conference as a manoeuvre in domestic affairs, designed to isolate the highly successful Minister for Economics and President of the *Reichsbank*, Hjalmar Schacht, who had begun to criticize and oppose further expansion of the armament programme.[31] Taylor is correct in pointing out that the actual course of events did not follow any of Hitler's scenarios; indeed, most participants at the meeting were to be dismissed from their posts within three months – they were scarcely the people to whom Hitler would reveal his innermost thoughts. However, the ominous direction Hitler's thoughts and intentions were taking is evident in the content of his 'daydreaming'. The speech may not have been a timetable for aggression, but the course for the journey was certainly spelt out.

Two weeks later, Henlein was on his way to Berlin, where an audience had been arranged with Hitler for 28 March. It was then that the Führer gave his famous instruction to always present demands that could not be satisfied in negotiations with the Czechoslovak government. He also gave his assurance that the Czechoslovak problem would soon be solved. Having received the Führer's special blessing, Henlein lost no time in acting. At an SdP congress at Carlsbad on 23–4 April, already held in the style of a Nazi Party rally, he demanded full autonomy for the Sudeten Germans, including the right to embrace the National Socialist ideology, which would have effectively finished the Czechoslovak state. Needless to say, Prime Minister Hodža's set of suggestions, made on 28 March, for the harmonization and management of nationality and minority matters, received no mention in Henlein's speech. Subsequent offers on the part of the Czechoslovak government, to establish national diets (*Kurien*), made in early July, or to create three German districts (*Gaue*), made in August, were met by new demands – in line with Hitler's order.[32] From the evidence it seems that the concept of autonomy, which would have meant remaining part of the Czechoslovak state, was becoming increasingly unpopular among the Sudeten Germans.[33] Among other factors, they would still have been confronted with the republic's economic difficulties, in contrast to the reputed comfort of the Reich, where – so propaganda told them – the Nazis had virtually created a workers' paradise.

On 28 May, buoyed by the triumph of the *Anschluss* of Austria, Hitler announced to his generals and to leading figures from the Foreign Ministry that he was 'utterly determined that Czechoslovakia should disappear from the map'.[34] Two days later a revised 'Case Green' reiterated his 'unalterable decision to smash Czechoslovakia by military action in the foreseeable future';[35] the provisional deadline for completion of preparations was 1 October. By now the familiar Nazi thuggery had well and truly arrived in Bohemia and Moravia. The municipal elections of May and June 1938 were marred by intimidation and molestation of those still willing to oppose the fascists. Even so, 15 per cent remained brave enough to vote against the SdP.[36] Bullying and browbeating of suspected dissenters continued throughout the summer into early autumn. On 7 September, in a last desperate effort to save the nation, Beneš, since December 1935 President of Czechoslovakia, offered what amounted to a virtual acceptance of the Carlsbad Points – the creation of an autonomous German state within a Federal Republic. This was backed up by the government decision to make immediately available a further one billion Czech Crowns for investment in the trouble-stricken German parts of the country.[37] But this was all in vain.

The hectic course of events that marked the month of September 1938, ending with the Munich Agreement on 30 September, has been well covered elsewhere. Suffice here to recall that on 19 September Beneš was presented with the demand to agree to the secession of the German-speaking parts, with its associated threat of consequences. Deserted by its western Allies and presuming that Soviet assistance[38] could only be limited, the Czechoslovak government complied, preferring to save its people from a senseless bloodbath. There was still a week of frantic manoeuvring between Hitler, who was determined to have his war, and virtually everyone else – with the exception of the equally bellicose new Foreign Minister Joachim von Ribbentrop – desperately trying to pull the world back from the brink of disaster. Neither the obvious lack of enthusiasm for war among the German people nor a deeply sceptical army leadership managed to deter the Führer, who was, according to the British Ambassador Henderson, by now 'quite mad'.[39] 'Long live war', he exuberantly told Henlein at the height of the crisis, regardless 'if it lasts from two to eight years'.[40] Even Göring had cold feet at the thought of going to war with Britain over Czechoslovakia. Having weeks earlier scoffed at the 'little splinter down there', made up of 'ludicrous dwarfs' and agents of the 'eternal Jewish–Bolshevik grimace', who the Germans, proud to be 'shooters and not shitters' (*Schiesser keine Scheisser*),[41] would soon deal with, the Field Marshal now urged Hitler to change course.[42] However, it was not until Benito Mussolini had come to the assistance of the British Premier Neville Chamberlain and the French Premier Edouard Daladier, that the path for a negotiated settlement of the 'Sudeten German question' was finally cleared.

On 1 October 1938 the First Czechoslovak Republic ceased to exist. The same day the great majority of the Sudeten-German population celebrated its 'homecoming' to the Reich with utmost enthusiasm. And while most of the outside world was relieved that peace had been preserved, albeit at the expense of the Czech people, the more thorough observers knew that an unmitigated disaster had occurred. Their feelings are summed up in an embittered comment by the *Daily Telegraph*'s longstanding correspondent in Vienna, Eric Gedye, that the German minority, 'easily the most privileged in Europe', was at 'no time politically persecuted, always arrogantly conscious of the backing of Germany's sixty-six millions' and that 'its real grounds for complaint were limited to certain economic disabilities – which were in part politically necessary because of the Germans' disloyalty to the Republic – and to petty officiousness practiced by some of the local Czech officials. ... Their minor grievances had been continually exaggerated, inflated and trumpeted abroad by the German propaganda machine, because they were an instrument to forward the German plans for hegemony in Eastern Europe'.[43]

In the light of the subsequent course of events, the British and French governments' decision to refrain from challenging Hitler over his ambitions towards Czechoslovakia in 1938 has been severely criticized by historians in the English-speaking world. A. J. P. Taylor, for example, whose *Origins of the Second World War* constitutes a singular condemnation of Neville Chamberlain's appeasement policies,[44] reasons that with a statesman like Hitler there are only two options: full opposition from the very beginning or no opposition at all. Taylor deems Munich a sell-out. Likewise, Peter Calvocoressi argues that 'not going to war in 1938 was not only shameful but inexpedient and foolish'.[45] And according to Vojtech Mastny, 'apart from considerations of international morality, the principal folly of the appeasement policy consisted in the willingness to sacrifice Czechoslovakia without receiving in return any tangible security guarantees'.[46] More recent assessments of appeasement policies have been more cautious and less antagonistic. Attention is now directed back to the immense war weariness among the French and British populations, ensuing from lingering horrid memories of 1914–18. Reluctance to take up arms again over 'a quarrel in a far away country between people about whom we know nothing' was not confined to Chamberlain, who, as 'a former businessman', was worried that war would destroy the reviving British economy,[47] or to the pro-German wing of the Conservative Party, but was shared by the great bulk of the people. The ruthlessness of Hitler's foreign policy needed to be clearly exposed one more time before governments, armed forces and the public at large would have to accept that only force would stop the dictator.[48]

Still, the tragedy of it all remains. The Czechoslovak army was prepared to fight in September 1938, its soldiers highly motivated and its arsenal among the best in Europe. The border with Germany, though considerably lengthened after the *Anschluss* of Austria, was still made up of mountainous terrain that would have favoured defence over attack and that would not have been conducive to *Blitzkrieg* tactics. German war games were claimed to have established that it would take eleven days to overrun Czechoslovakia, but war games are notoriously unreliable. A French declaration of war would have required the transfer of a large number of German militia to the west. And with the *Westwall* far from being completed,[49] the psychological impact on the German population and army leadership of hundreds of thousands of French troops assembling in striking distance of the Rhine does not need major guessing. The same goes for the Soviet build-up of troops along the Polish border. Even if, as recent works suggest, the Soviet Union's massive partial mobilization north of the Pripiat Marshes was primarily designed for warfare against Poland, the possibility of the *Wehrmacht* facing a third front, or indeed of large numbers of Soviet troops soon coming to the assistance of Czechoslovakia, could well have seen the end of Adolf Hitler.[50] Hitler had not yet gained full control of the army leadership; even the *Reichswehr* Chief of Staff, General Franz Halder, in whom Hitler had great faith, had been involved in plans for a *coup d'état* in the event of war over Czechoslovakia. Leading figures in the civilian administration, too, would have supported moves to finish off the Führer.[51] Instead, five months later, the latter had collected a rich booty, including scores of engineering works and electrical and machine tool factories. In particular, the Skoda works, along with modern textile and chemical plants, were now at the Reich's disposal, as were large quantities of gold and foreign currencies and a huge supply of armaments.[52] Above all, Germany's military and strategic position had been immensely enhanced. The Nazi catastrophe was ready to reach new dimensions.

The euphoria of most Sudeten Germans at the sight of *Wehrmacht* soldiers marching into the Bohemian lands to the tune of the *Egerländer Marsch*[53] could not hide the fact that, for tens of thousands of people in the seceded regions, the Munich Treaty spelt doom and disaster. The developments leading up to Munich had already been accompanied by extensive bloodshed, instigated chiefly by the newly formed Sudeten-German volunteer corps.[54] To escape the violence of Henlein thugs, 25 000 people had already fled to the Czech parts of Bohemia and Moravia before the end of September. After the incorporation of the German-speaking parts into the Reich, the stream of refugees fleeing the clutches of the *Wehrmacht*, SS and fanatical SdP supporters quickly swelled to approximately 150 000 by the end of the year. Most of these Czechoslovak citizens were of Czech ethnicity, but over 12 000 Germans and almost 22 000 people who were either of Jewish faith or had been identified as Jews under the Nuremberg Laws were also among the refugees.[55] Initially about 30 000 German Social Democrats and Communists had fled the arrival of German troops or sought to escape the scorn of their compatriots. On the insistence of the Berlin authorities, the government of the Second Czechoslovak Republic ordered some 20 000 of them to return. Of these, between 7000 and 8000 spent several months in concentration camps; some received lengthy jail sentences. Other opponents of the '*Anschluss*', including members of the KB,[56] were also incarcerated. Fifty thousand Czech employees of the Czechoslovak State, including public servants, teachers, railway and postal workers and members of the armed forces, were made redundant by the Munich Treaty and its aftermath and consequently compelled to move to the territory of the Second Republic.[57] Thus, although the numbers directly expelled by order of the new authorities appeared small, fear for life and limb and the simple need to survive ensured that well over 200 000 people were forced to leave. The dividing line between expulsion and flight was rather thin.

For several weeks, opponents of SdP policies, Social Democrats, Communists, Jews and Czechs continued to suffer physical assault and maltreatment at the hands of other civilians,[58] but the main wave of terror in the two months following secession was the work of the *Sicherheitsdienst* (SD) and the Gestapo. Approximately 10 000 opponents of Nazism were arrested or sent to concentration camps. The campaign reached its climax on 9 November, *Reichskristallnacht*, when, as everywhere in Germany, Nazis burnt synagogues and assaulted and murdered Jewish people, ostensibly in response to Herschel Grynszpan's assassination of a German diplomat in Paris on 7 November. The majority of the population, however, disapproved of such pogroms.[59]

An outcome of the Munich agreement was the creation of the *Reichsgau* '*Sudetenland*', made up of the German-speaking parts of western and northern Bohemia, northern Moravia and southern Silesia, with the incorporation of southern Bohemia into Bavaria and southern Moravia into Austria. About 215 000 Germans continued to live in the territory of the Second Czechoslovak Republic. The *Reichsgau* was a new political concept, an attempt to combine and unify party, state and administration – a long-standing Nazi goal. Henlein was given the chief position of *Reichsstatthalter*, responsible for administration of the *Reichsgau* and accountable only to the Reich's ministry of the interior and, of course, to the Führer. Beneath the *Reichsstatthalter* was the *Gauselbstverwaltung* (a system of self-administration), particularly designed to strengthen the 'Sudeten German identity'. One step lower were the three government districts, each headed by a *Regierungspräsident* (government president); at the bottom of the pyramid came the traditional regional and local administrative offices and institutions. Most positions in this hierarchy were held by Sudeten Germans. A considerable number of public servants from the *Altreich* (the Germany of pre-1938 borders) had to be employed, as the full-scale dismissal of Czechs, Jews, Social Democrats and Communists from the administration had left a vacuum that could not be immediately filled by Sudeten Germans. However, only the police and security apparatus (Gestapo, SD and SS) came predominantly under the control of *Reichsdeutsche*, that is, Germans from the *Altreich*.[60] This invalidates later allegations that responsibility for events between 1938 and 1945 in the *Reichsgau Sudetenland* must be shouldered exclusively by the *Machthaber* (powers that be) in Berlin. And the soaring number of applications for NSDAP membership and entry into the SA following the 'homecoming' to the Reich[61] does not support the claim that the Sudeten Germans, too, should be ranked among the passive victims of the Nazi era.

As stated, the enthusiasm and jubilation that accompanied the *Anschluss* into the Reich was genuinely shared by the great majority of Sudeten Germans, which is not to say that most of them endorsed the xenophobic hardcore racialist – soon to become genocidal – and ultra-aggressive aspects of National Socialist ideology. Rather, the widely held belief that incorporation into the Nazis' *grossdeutsche* Reich would fulfil aspirations for national self-determination and would lead to substantial socio-economic improvement constitutes a more convincing reason for the general euphoria. This honeymoon period, however, was short-lived. The Nazi policy of *Gleichschaltung* (synchronization), implemented almost immediately after the *Anschluss*, involved the elimination of a large number of clubs and associations, thus riding roughshod over longstanding local traditions. Workplace friction also soon developed, as many Sudeten Germans regarded their *Reichsdeutsche* colleagues as arrogant and inconsiderate; this led to claims that Sudeten Germans were being disadvantaged in their professional development. The initial euphoria was gradually displaced by a prevailing sense of inequity – as newcomers to the Reich, Sudeten Germans felt they were not accepted as *Volksgenossen* on equal terms.[62] Moreover, economic recovery was not as solid as expected – and as had been promised. Unemployment did begin to decline substantially by the beginning of 1939, but this was off-set by a fall in real income for most employees. There was also no reso-lution of the serious housing shortage that had existed since before the *Anschluss*.[63] All these factors contributed to the erosion of the image of the glorious social conditions alleged to prevail in the Reich. Six months after Munich, the mood among the Sudeten Germans had grown posi-tively sombre; a few months later, they found themselves at war.

Incorporation into the Nazi state had also failed to bring any major gains for the business communities of the Bohemian and Moravian Germans. The textile and machine manufacturing industries were absorbed into the German war economy, which served to fill their order books, but the much-needed modernization of other branches of industry did not eventuate. The bulk of the loot expropriated from Jewish and Czech properties went to concerns within the Reich – the Hermann Göring plant did best, but the chemical giant IG Farben, the leading optical equipment producer Carl Zeiss Jena, all major banks and numerous insurance companies all helped themselves to generous chunks of the booty. This is not to say, however, that Sudeten-German firms, entrepre-neurs, party members and members of the public at large completely missed out on the benefits of the plunder.[64]

Czech people who remained in the seceded German parts of the former Czechoslovakia – estimated at 290 000 in the *Reichsgau* and 410 000 throughout the former German parts[65] – did not fare well. They were stripped of most civil rights and all Czech political and cultural associa-tions were outlawed, which meant, among other things, that there were no Czech libraries. The Czech language could only be spoken in the private sphere and with high schools and grammar schools forced to close down after Munich, Czech education was confined to elementary schools.[66] Despite these measures, the more radical Sudeten-German admin-istrators and race theoreticians remained dissatisfied and demanded the removal of all Czechs from the German regions. However, this plan to solve the 'Czech question' by way of *Umsiedlung* (transfer or resettlement) did not find favour with the Nazi leadership; Hitler and his chief authority on racial policy, Reinhard Heydrich, preferred the *Umvolkung* (ethnic trans-mutation or assimilation) solution. The concept of *Umvolkung* had been developed by the *Reichsprotektor* of Bohemia and Moravia, von Neurath, and his representative Karl Hermann Frank, Henlein's former deputy of SdP days, following the rape of Czechoslovakia. Von Neurath's policy for Czech people in the *Reichsgau* and Protectorate was to 'assimilate Czechdom, that is, Germanize about half the Czech population'.[67] The other half of the Czech people were to be deprived of power in various ways, eliminated or removed from the country. Those affected included 'in particular mongoloids and a large section of the [nation's] intellectu-als'. Frank understood Germanization as 'national mutation of racially suitable Czechs', but he added that those who could not be racially absorbed, as well as members of the intelligentsia who were hostile to the Reich and other destructive elements, should be dealt with by means of 'special treatment' – *Sonderbehandlung*.[68]

The magnitude of these morbid plans for the fate of their erstwhile fel-low citizens was not known to the general Sudeten-German populace, some of whom did show allegiance to former friends and neighbours. But benevolent attitudes towards the Czech people were confined to a minority. The majority had no qualms about the oppressive measures taken by the authorities. Indeed, the brutal 'punishment' meted out to the villages of Lidice and Ležáky after the assassination of Heydrich, for example, found broad support.[69] These times left their traces.

The Sudeten-Germans' future was to be determined by the war. As else-where in the Reich, the *Reichsgau* initially showed solid support, if not excitement, at the news of the Führer's brave decision to stop tolerating Polish provocation and aggression. And as long as the *Wehrmacht* scored one success after the other, the situation in the *Reichsgau* remained 'stable and quiet',[70] although food supplies and overall living conditions steadily deteriorated. The United States' entry into the war, followed by the defeat of the Sixth Army at Stalingrad, sapped the morale of most citizens; resig-nation at the thought of a prolonged war were reported throughout the region.[71] Yet, with the knowledge that a one-way street had been entered in September 1938, the secession decision was resiliently upheld; signs of remorse were scarce. There was no significant resistance movement in the *Reichsgau*. Of course, it would scarcely have been possible. With most of the political left having been wiped out after the *Anschluss*, Communists and Social Democrats could only mount token efforts and always remained an easy target for Gestapo and SD. Several hundred of them were executed for resistance activities and as many as 22 000 were allegedly arrested.[72]

Nazi attempts to monopolize religious beliefs and practices did lead to opposition from members and followers of the Catholic Church. According to Czech historian Jaroslav Macek, the Gestapo in the *Sudetenland* investigated 1143 Catholic priests, an impressive figure, as the total number of clergymen was around 1640. Among these, 318 were interrogated, 231 seriously cautioned, 118 barred from further teaching and 11 from conducting sermons. One hundred and ten were arrested and 85 sent to concentration camps, 23 of whom did not survive. A number of lay brothers and lay sisters also fell victim to Nazi religious oppression.[73]

Neither the fact that close to 200 000 of their men had died at the front, nor the first dropping of Allied bombs on Sudeten territory in December 1944, nor the appalling sight of refugees fleeing from the advancing Red Army, could entice the Sudeten Germans to change course. Added now to the traditional dislike of the Czechs, whether due to a belief in German superiority or to a conviction, however justifiable, that the German speakers had been victimized under Czech rule, was a new fear of Czech reprisals for events leading up to and since Munich. With news coming in from London of plans for large-scale expulsion, it is not surprising that the Sudeten Germans were among the last to leave the sinking ship. It was not until Russian and American troops had literally arrived at their doorsteps that the people realized their *Reichsgau Sudetenland* was little more than a bursting bubble.

For Czechs the collapse of the Third Reich and the *Reichsgau* would mean that the long period of humiliation and oppression that had begun with Munich was over. Back in 1938, news of the sell-out of Czechoslovakia had barely reached the outside world when the Polish Foreign Minister, Joseph Beck, shortly before midnight on 30 September, presented the government in Prague with a 12-hour ultimatum for secession of the industrial area of Teschen on the Czechoslovak–Polish border. This was accepted and little more than a month later, on 2 November, an arbitration meeting held in Vienna under the auspices of the German and Italian foreign ministers assigned to Hungary an extensive portion of southern and eastern Slovakia. It was then that the term 'hyenaism' gained wide circulation in western Europe.[74] Government in the short-lived Second Republic passed into the hands of an authoritarian, conservative cabinet under the presidency of Emil Hácha. With little room to move, the prime aim of the Hácha government's policies was to avoid any possible conflict with the Reich. The political Left was outlawed and an Enabling Act authorizing the executive to legislate by decree in case of emergency severely curbed the role of parliament. Slovakia received internal autonomy, with a separate government and a diet; the same arrangement was made with the Carpathian Ukraine, further east. Thus the Second Republic had become a federal state. Extensive privileges were granted to the German minority still living in Czecho-Slovakia,[75] as the country's name was now officially spelt. While these measures provided a degree of internal stability, they were not able to secure the republic's longevity.

Hitler soon recovered from the setback at Munich. Just three weeks after the settlement, new directives to the *Wehrmacht* included the 'liquidation of the remainder of the Czech state'[76] among its short-term options. This was not an expression of the Führer's longstanding antagonism towards the Czech people, or brought on by his disappointment at having been denied the war he had sought in September, but rather the outcome of economic, strategic and military considerations. By the end of 1938 the massive rearmament programme had begun to overheat the economy. Germany, in addition to a serious balance of payment crisis and a rise in inflation, faced a chronic shortage of foreign exchange, raw materials and labour. Continuing where he had left off on 5 November 1937, Hitler stressed in numerous speeches that the problem of securing 'living space' for the German people had become intertwined with the need to solve the nation's economic problems, thus making territorial expansion ever more urgent. With the successful *Anschluss* of both Austria and the *Sudetenland*, internal opposition to the Führer's aggressive foreign policies had dwindled; industrial, agricultural and military leaders now supported his ambitious plans. These plans had in their sights the bulk of Czecho-Slovakia's wealth and resources, which remained in the Czech heartlands of Bohemia and Moravia, to the east of the incorporated German-speaking regions; of particular interest were Czech arms and ammunition that could be of use to the German army. (It is estimated that the arsenal that fell into German hands after the occupation of Czecho-Slovakia was sufficient to equip twenty divisions.)[77] Strategically, full control of Czecho-Slovak territory would greatly strengthen the Reich's position against Poland.

The first documentary evidence of German plans for a full-scale invasion of Czecho-Slovakia dates from 17 December 1938, when the Chief of the Armed Forces High Command, General Wilhelm Keitel, on Hitler's instruction, issued an order to begin preparations to march into Bohemia and Moravia.[78] Throughout January and February directives concerning 'operational preparedness' for 'Y-day' (the day of the crossing of Czech borders) were issued to select military units.[79] At the same time Berlin encouraged Slovak nationalists to finally free themselves from the 'Czech yoke'. Supported by a virulent anti-Czech German propaganda campaign, the *Hlinka-Garde* and associated semi-fascists had stirred up enough trouble in Slovakia for the Prague government to intervene. On 9 March President Hácha dismissed the Slovak cabinet and declared a state of martial law. The Führer's hour had clearly come again, but it still took Hitler several days to sufficiently bully the Slovak Prime Minister, Father Joseph Tiso, to have the Slovak Assembly declare its independence on 14 March. And the request for German 'protection' (needed to justify the occupation of rump Czecho-Slovakia to the international community) did not come until a day later, after German warships on the River Danube had fired on Slovak government offices.[80] Also on 15 March, at 4:00 a.m., after having been hastily summoned to the Reich Chancellery the previous evening for a massive browbeating from Hitler before the assembled Nazi establishment, Hácha signed a declaration agreeing to the imposition of a protectorate over the remainder of Czecho-Slovakia. At the same time Hácha telephoned Prague, ordering Czech troops not to resist the invasion of German troops, which commenced at 6:00 a.m.

Hitler himself arrived in the Czech capital in the late afternoon, to a sullen reception and empty streets. He stayed less than 48 hours at the *Hradschin*, finalized the terms of the German protectorate and left, to show only occasional subsequent interest in the Czechs and the protectorate.

The protectorate decree was read out over Prague radio on the morning of 16 September by von Ribbentrop. Hitler allowed the Czechs to keep their own president and form of government, while at the same time ensuring that all power remained with the appointees of the Reich. To this end, Hácha was appointed to the position of *'Staatspräsident'* of the protectorate and his cabinet became the government of the day. A multi-layered legal and administrative structure was introduced, maintaining the Constitutional Court and the Supreme Administrative Court of the previous republic, while establishing a complicated system of regulations and laws, the application of which varied according to nationality. The laws fell into three categories: (i) those of the German Reich, which were extended to include the newly occupied territory, (ii) laws originating from the Protector himself in the form of decrees and (iii) original Czech laws covering anything not overridden by the former two sets of laws. Also, two levels of citizenship were created – Germans became citizens of the Reich and as such were subject only to the laws of the German Reich and its courts, while Czechs and other remaining nationalities became nationals of the protectorate and were subject to all three of the above forms of law, as well as to both Czech and German courts. Any remaining Czech institutions automatically became subordinate to those of the German Reich and protectorate; decisions made by Czech courts could therefore be overturned by the Protector and handed to a German court for arbitration.

The decree then proceeded to outline the structure of the protectorate, which was to be 'autonomous' and 'self-administered'. Czech figureheads in relation to the presidency and the government were to remain parallel with those of the German administration. To ensure the fulfillment of his desires in this area and to protect the interests of the Reich, Hitler created the position of *Reichsprotektor*. As the Führer's representative, the *Reichsprotektor* had the duty of ensuring that Hitler's policies were enforced. In effect, the Reich Protector had control over all aspects of life in the protectorate, from confirmation of government positions to the final say on laws and decrees. The Czecho-Slovak National Assembly was abolished and the last remaining political parties dissolved. In their place President Hácha appointed a fifty-member Committee of National Solidarity. General Alois Eliáš was given the position of prime minister. Finally, the Reich was to manage the protectorate's foreign affairs, communications systems and finances, as well as providing its military defence.[81]

Effective power was clearly in the hands of the *Reichsprotektor*, Freiherr Konstantin von Neurath, and his deputy, Karl Hermann Frank. Von Neurath had been dismissed from the position of German foreign minister in February 1939 as part of a major reshuffle in the diplomatic service. Although officially second in command, Frank was undoubtedly the more influential of the two men. He was also invested with the title of state secretary and – of particular significance – because of his close connection to the Chief of Reich Security, Reinhard Heydrich, Frank was put in charge of the SS and police apparatus in the protectorate.[82]

As far as President Hácha was concerned, protectorate status meant that his government still enjoyed an extremely modest degree of independence over the country's domestic policies; the decrees also enabled the National Solidarity politicians to preserve some dignity in the face of great adversity. Von Neurath's term as Protector was initially marked by relatively restrained German policies, although the emphasis here must rest on 'relatively'. A first wave of arrests saw all suspected Communists and refugees from the Reich imprisoned; most of the former were released after a brief interrogation by the Gestapo, while most of the latter were sent to concentration camps. The more oppressive policies that began to be implemented by the middle of the year bore Frank's handwriting. On 4 June the state secretary gave a menacing speech at Budweis, warning the Czechs that dire times were ahead should they cause trouble.

Four days later, when a German policeman was murdered in the mining town of Kladno, the Gestapo arrested the entire Kladno council and a number of other people, despite the lack of evidence of Czech complicity. Some of those arrested died as a consequence of mistreatment. Moreover, the Czech municipal councils of six cities were dismissed and replaced by German commissioners. A further series of stiff laws intended to intimidate the Czech population followed and, from June 1939, specification of Jewish identity was to be determined according to the notorious 'Nuremberg Laws'. This was the first step towards the eradication of approximately 78 000 protectorate citizens who were either of Jewish faith or were designated as Jews and a further 6000 Roma people.[83]

The outbreak of war on 1 September 1939 led to the arrests of at least 2000 people – left-wing politicians, intellectuals, members of former nationalist organizations, clergymen and others suspected of potential resistance – and to their internment in concentration camps.[84] On 28 October, Frank again provoked confrontation between German students, SS and SA men and Czech citizens commemorating the foundation day of the Czechoslovak Republic. On 15 November, the funeral of a student who had died of wounds inflicted by security forces in Prague turned into an anti-German demonstration. A furious Hitler not only ordered von Neurath and Frank to close all Czech universities for three years, but also ordered the detention of a large number of students. Frank complied by having nine 'ringleaders' shot and by deporting 1200 students to concentration camps. This sufficed to temporarily pacify the situation in the protectorate. As the war progressed, Czech industry began to play a major role in fulfilling the Reich's armaments requirements. Apparent reluctant acquiescence to Nazi rule, however, could not hide the intense hatred that was developing among the great majority of the Czech population – not only towards the occupiers, but towards anything 'German'.

This was of little concern to the theoreticians of the 'Master Race', who continued to draw up vicious plans for the 'solution' of the 'Czech problem'. Following on from schemes previously drawn up by the *Reichsprotektor* and his deputy,[85] the Nazi racial specialist Professor Konrad Meyer-Hetling developed a plan for Himmler, confirming the suitability of about half the Czech population for Germanization. As far as the remainder was concerned, Himmler and Heydrich agreed that 'racially poor' or ideologically unreliable Czechs should be used as slave labour and/or evacuated.[86] Bohemia and Moravia were to become purely German regions. 'In the end there is no room for the Czechs in this part of the world', Heydrich, who had arrived in the protectorate in late September 1941 to replace von Neurath, told a meeting of high German officials in his inaugural address on 2 October 1941. The chief of the security police saw no sense in further attempts at the old-fashioned method of making Germans out of 'Czech riff-raff' (*Tschechengesindel*). The population had to be analysed according to racial and *völkisch* (national or ethnic) principles, whereupon the 'racially and ideologically unsound' (*schlechtrassig und schlechtgesinnt*) were to be removed to the east. 'Racially unsound but ideologically sound' (*schlechtrassig gutgesinnte*) Czechs should be sterilized. The 'racially sound but ideologically unsound' (*gutrassig schlechtgesinnte*) were to be placed in a purely German environment and, if this still failed to make them good Germans, they were to be simply put against the wall.[87] When Czechs continued to stubbornly resist Germanization, Frank threatened to withdraw privileges even for the *gutrassig und gutgesinnten*:

> If the Czechs do not submit, then a day will come when it will be definitely too late for a change of heart. They will then no longer be in a position to disturb order and peace in the heart of the fighting Reich. … It is ridiculous to believe that it would then be a matter of some political haggling, autonomy or so-called Germanization.[88]

The urgent needs ensuing from total war, however, temporarily put paid to these schemes. In January 1943, with the military situation becoming ever more precarious for Germany, Hitler ordered the shelving of all Germanization plans until the end of the war.[89]

Heydrich's appointment as Deputy *Reichsprotektor* in the autumn of 1941 was brought about by an increase in the number of short-term strikes and acts of sabotage following the German invasion of the Soviet Union. There had also been threats of resignation from the Hácha government in response to attempts to further Germanize the Czech school system and to make German the only official language. Annoyed by news of instability in the protectorate, Hitler had decided to send Heydrich in as troubleshooter. With von Neurath out of the way (forced to resign because of 'failing health'),[90] the security chief quickly lived up to his reputation: within two months he had 404 people sentenced to death and a further 1300 – mainly members of the Czech resistance – arrested and sent to concentration camps. Few survived. In early October Heydrich also staged a show trial of Prime Minister Eliáš, who was charged with having connections to the Czech underground and the Czech Exile Government in London. Eliáš too was sentenced to death, but the execution was not carried out until June 1942. Apparently Hitler ordered the postponement of the execution to ensure the good behaviour of the Czechs by holding the prime minister hostage.[91]

'Cleaning up' the protectorate, however, was also to be Heydrich's last assignment. On 27 May 1942, on his way to work, he was ambushed and fatally wounded by two Czech exiles, Jozef Gabčik and Jan Kubiš, who had been flown in from London with the aid of the Special Operations Executive (SOE), the British subversive warfare agency, and parachuted to a location near Prague. The security chief died a week later in a Prague hospital. The two assassins and a third comrade, who had supported them as a lookout, managed to escape. It took the Gestapo three weeks to track down Gabčik and Kubiš, who had hidden in the St Cyril and Methodius Orthodox Church in Prague; apparently another SOE agent had betrayed them for a large monetary award.[92] The assassins and five other parachutists engaged the SS and police units in a gun battle for several hours, before finally preferring suicide to surrender.

On receiving the news of Heydrich's assassination, Hitler was outraged. In a first fit of frenzy he ordered the immediate shooting of 10 000 Czechs and the wholesale arrest of the Czech intelligentsia. Frank flew to Berlin, where he managed to calm the Führer down by pointing out the harm such action would cause to the protectorate's armament production and to the prospects of German victory. The order was rescinded. Still, the price for having gotten rid of one of the Nazis' most notorious henchmen, who had ranked closely behind Himmler as the chief architect of the 'final solution' to the 'Jewish question', was extremely high. Over the next weeks and months, a wave of terror descended upon the protectorate. On 10 June, the entire male population of the village Lidice, near Kladno, was rounded up and shot; the women were sent to the Ravensbrück concentration camp. Of the 98 children, 81 were deemed racially unsuitable and later killed; the others were placed for adoption by German families. The village, which had allegedly given shelter to SOE agents, was then burned down. The same fate befell the hamlet of Ležáky, where 24 men and women were shot, their children sent to Ravensbrück. In addition, 1357 people were killed by order of summary courts.[93]

Victims of the *Heydrichiáda*, as the wave of terror that marked the security chief's reign and its aftermath is referred to in Czech, also include the former Prime Minister Eliáš and the priests who sheltered Gabčik, Kubiš and their helpers. Vengeance taken for Heydrich's death included the dispatch of 1000 Jewish people from Prague to Majdanek; only one of these survived the war. And in October 1942, another 252 people, including whole families, were massacred in the Mauthausen concentration camp on suspicion of direct or indirect involvement in Heydrich's assassination. A group of Czech and German historians, recently commissioned by the governments of both countries to investigate the two nations' linked past, estimates that altogether 5000 people lost their lives in measures of revenge for the security chief's death.[94] Hácha and his group, who had already submitted to full collaboration with the Nazi regime, were not able to intervene in any way and consequently lost any remaining credibility and support among the Czech people.

The killing of Heydrich, prepared over several months with the vital assistance of the domestic *odboj*[95] organization *Jindra*, represented the high-water mark of Czech resistance. Against difficult odds Czech resistance activities achieved a credible contribution to the Allied war effort. The country had fallen into German hands under orderly and peaceful circumstances, which eroded the basis for illegal activities. Occupation continued for six years, longer than in any other European country, which placed additional strain on the capacity of resistance movements to replenish constant loss of leadership and rank and file members; the Gestapo could also rely on the assistance of Sudeten Germans in the protectorate's administration and police force, who were familiar with conditions in the Bohemian lands and who were well acquainted with the Czech mentality. All arms and ammunition had been handed over peacefully and new supplies could not be flown in until the frontiers drew closer to the protectorate. Last but certainly not least, the terms of Munich had deprived the country of most of its heavily forested, mountainous regions that would have been vital for partisan warfare. Thus, until the later stages of the war, resistance activities had to be confined to clandestine operations – sabotage of all kinds, intelligence gathering, providing relief for families of the imprisoned and shelter for resistance activists, distribution of anti-German leaflets, listening to foreign broadcasts (which was punishable by long jail sentences or death) and recruitment of new members. Resistance had already commenced during the Second Republic and greatly increased with the outbreak of war. Underground operations had reached formidable proportions by the summer of 1940, becoming a prime source of intelligence from the Reich[96] and peaking with the assassination of Heydrich a year later.

The *Heydrichiáda* decimated the Czech resistance movement, but failed to eliminate it altogether. Local and regional *odboj* organizations gradually recovered and finally established a Czech National Council. In August 1944 a broad-based popular front covering most of the political spectrum and part of the army staged a national uprising in neighbouring Slovakia, which initially managed to topple the Tiso regime. Inadequate preparation and lack of coordination led to the defeat of the uprising by German forces, but only after heavy fighting.[97] Several thousand partisans fled to Czech territory, where they were joined by resistance fighters flown in from London. All told, the number of partisans fighting the German war effort during the last months of the war is estimated at 8000.[98] They constituted the core of Czech and Slovak troops who took on the retreating German forces in the spring of 1945.

After the *Heydrichiáda* the bulk of the population continued to quietly endure its fate, receiving some comfort from the changing fortunes of war that saw the steady erosion of Nazi Germany's military situation. An uneasy truce between the Czechs and the German occupiers continued. The German administration was reluctant to pursue policies of massive oppression (as they had done in Poland), as this would have jeopardized the protectorate's war production. Faced with the Reich's overwhelming superiority, the Czechs refrained from entering into an unequal confrontation that would have cost a great deal of blood without delivering tangible results. Their level of collaboration was kept as low as possible – sufficient to prevent large-scale reprisals, while attempting to keep the German war machine's gains at a minimum.[99]

After Heydrich's death, effective power passed into the hands of Frank, on whom Hitler bestowed the official title of 'German State Minister for Bohemia and Moravia' in August 1943. This may have contributed to the apparent turn-around in Frank's behaviour towards the Czechs, who were temporarily treated in a more conciliatory manner than had previously been the case.[100] It was, however, too late to halt the escalating hatred among the great majority of the population towards Frank himself and towards anything German. Nor did it save his neck after the war.[101]

The seemingly passive policies of the government and the greater part of the Czech population towards the Nazi occupation and the allegation that they 'meekly submitted' to the will and policies of the *Reichsprotektor* lead the Czech-American historian Vojtech Mastny to comment on the 'collaboration by considerable segments of the population – the politicians, bureaucracy, business and labor went to lengths which were both unnecessary and dishonorable, short-sighted despite immediate material advantages, and ultimately damaging to the nation's self respect'.[102] Surely this criticism is too harsh. In no country occupied by Nazi Germany, including those that escaped the full-scale terror meted out to the people of Poland and the western Soviet Union, did the great majority of the populace risk bloody retaliation in return for the meagre advances to be won by resistance, which was in any case unlikely to con-tribute to the outcome of the war. Acquiescence, opportunism, moder-ate or 'tactical' collaboration and even outright collaboration were common throughout occupied western Europe.

As an historian of collaboration in France succinctly put it 'there seemed to have been almost as many collaborationisms as there were proponents and practitioners of collaboration'.[103] Mastny himself, a few paragraphs after his blunt condemnation of the Czechs, raises the suspicion that 'fur-ther research into the wartime history of Europe may prove that people in other advanced industrial countries, bred in the traditions of democ-racy, tolerance and humanism, were surprisingly susceptible to a regime based on the very antithesis of these traditions'.[104] Recent literature does indeed justify this suspicion and provide evidence of the prevalence of what Mastny presents as a surprising paradox.[105]

If anything, the Czech record ranks favourably in comparison with those of western countries as far as resistance and collaboration is con-cerned. Resentment of Nazi policies, which were much harsher here than in the West, ensured that, beneath what may have looked like a rel-atively calm surface, a volcano was waiting to erupt. Six years of occupa-tion took a heavy toll. The Czech education system was greatly curtailed at all levels.[106] Huge landholdings were taken over. By September 1940 the German Settlement Society in Prague acquired 53 000 hectares of land in southern Bohemia and Moravia. Compulsory German management was imposed on a number of large Czech farms, totalling 337 000 hectares. Military needs led to the confiscation of a further 80 000 hectares; for this purpose 245 parishes were evacuated, forcing 80 000 Czech rural dwellers to leave their homes. Large parts of industry and finance went into German hands, with Reich German and Austrian capital in the protec-torate increasing by 571 per cent.[107] And apparently Sudeten Germans filled positions in the private and public sectors, from Frank at the top to minor officials at the bottom.[108] Because Czech industry was fully converted into wartime production, other branches of the economy, in particular consumer industries, were neglected. Overuse and lack of maintenance caused deterioration of equipment, machine tools and plants. Heavy demands upon agriculture and forestry exhausted soils and forests; worn-out farming machinery was a further cost. Overall damage was estimated by the Czechoslovak government after the Second World War to have amounted to $US 11 500 million.[109] Working conditions deteriorated, with the working day extended and workers tied to their jobs. Virtually the whole Czech population of working age (men between 16 and 65, women between 17 and 65) was mobilized in support of Germany's war effort. Although written almost 40 years ago, Radomír Luža's summary is still valid:

> Forced labor, the prohibition of strikes, and close control by the National Labor Center served only to strengthen the bitterness of the taste put in the Czech mouth by the regime under which terror, coercion, and jail were regular practices. The Nazi policy of the stick for the intelligentsia and the carrot for the farmer and workman failed to lessen Czech labor's hatred for a system that had brought national catastrophe. The organizational efficiency of the Nazi economic machine was seriously impaired by Czech awareness that the only economic criterion was the welfare of Germany. Germanization, economic subjugation, and police terror with executions and arrests drove the Czechs to passive resistance.[110]

The number of human lives lost in the pre-Munich territory of Czechoslovakia is estimated in recent studies at between 337 000 and 343 000.[111] The fact that these numbers, statistically, are comparatively low in the scheme of Nazi barbarism in eastern Europe does not serve to reduce the level of ire felt by the population.

German troops retreating from the eastern front entered protectorate territory in the spring of 1945, leaving a trail of destruction. Officially designated by Hitler a *Vernichtungskrieg*, the war against the Soviet Union had, from the start, seen large-scale annihilation of the civilian population by the SS and *Wehrmacht*; these tactics did not change with the drastically declining military situation. Most units, unable or unwilling to see that the war had been lost, continued with customary savagery as they retreated from the Red Army. Whole village populations were killed, scores of public executions were held throughout the country and partisans and their helpers were burned alive.[112] State Minister Frank again excelled in ordering the harshest of measures. But the worst was yet to come. A Czech historian recalls:

> At the beginning of 1945, the German National Socialists had trains carrying prisoners from Auschwitz and other concentration camps driven through the territory of Bohemia and Moravia; the closing stages of the horrific Shoah were passing by before the eyes of the Czechs. On the open carriages of coal trains, a monstrous mobile theater was played out, in which the Third Reich demonstrated what it, in its final throes, remained capable of inflicting on the human being. The fate of the prisoners was even harsher in this 20-degree cold on

the carriages than in the actual concentration camps – for several days at a time there was nothing to eat or drink, no protection from the frost; people were dying continually – of hunger and thirst, freezing in the icy wind, but also by the bullet, by blows from clubs or truncheons; most died standing, as the rag-clad, half-naked 'detainees' were crammed together and not even able to fall to the floor.

In February 1945 the second act of this truly black theater was played out, as German guards drove tens of thousands of prisoners of war, mainly Soviet, like a herd of cattle, through northern Bohemia. From this the third act took its lead, as prisoners from more concentration camps, senselessly evacuated as the Russians advanced, were transported to Bohemia and Austria.

Before Czech eyes the SS guards and Wehrmacht (the latter somewhat less intensively) demonstrated here just how hard humanity can be kicked, how deeply it is possible to disregard any consideration of humanity. And it is impossible not to comprehend that those who saw these times – similar to the way the English spoke of the 'Huns' during the 'Blitz' – found here their judgment of the Germans, rightly or wrongly, unfortunately confirmed. The chronicler of the municipality of Dolní Sloupnice noted at the time: 'No propaganda against the Germans could be so effective as the sight of these miserable creatures and the brutal treatment dealt them.'[113]

In addition to the ruthless warfare came news of concentration and extermination camps even more horrifying than Theresienstadt near Leitmeritz, where of the almost 140 000 people of Jewish faith, or who were designated to have been Jews under the Nuremberg laws, brought there during the war little over 17 000 survived.[114]

It was this apocalyptic scenario that, by the end of the war, had led to an alliance of the people of the occupied countries, resistance movements, newly established provisional governments and military and political leaders of all countries affected by Nazi aggression, right up to the 'Big Three' peacemakers at the top, who united behind the one goal of removing all possible basis for future German aggression. This was why the German-speaking communities of central-eastern, eastern and southeastern Europe became 'Hitler's last victims',[115] as a recent study aptly puts it. Claims that single out the inadequacies of the United States' peacemaking policy or the evil of Marshal Stalin or the alleged deceitful behaviour of Edvard Beneš miss an important point.

4
Expulsion and Forced Resettlement*

The Munich tragedy marked the low point in the life of Edvard Beneš. He resigned from the presidency on 5 October and retired to his country residence, where, physically and emotionally exhausted, he spent several days in bed, whilst outside a vast press campaign blamed him for the disaster that had befallen the nation. Deserted by everyone but his family and closest friends, he left Czechoslovakia for London before the month was over.

* The terminology of the topic covered in this chapter is of major political and moral importance. Article XIII of the Potsdam Agreement uses the terms transfer for the expulsion of the great majority of the German-speaking population of Czechoslovakia, so do emigree Czech historians (note e.g. R. Luža, *The Transfer of the Sudeten-Germans*). German historians – with the exception of Marxist historians based in the earstwhile German Democratic Republic – rarely accept this term, even those who cannot be suspected of any anti-Czech bias put the word transfer in inverted commas. The Sudeten-German Association, or historians writing on the organization's behalf, reject *Odsun*, the Czech term for the transfer, which translates into German as *Abschub*. They insist that only the term *Vyhnání* (German *Vertreibung*) is the correct description. Czech historians repudiate this claim as it implies that the course of events in 1945 was solely the product of the Czech peoples' desire for punishment and revenge. Although they do not deny that excesses occurred in the immediate post-war period, they stress (correctly in the author's opinion) that the international factor, i.e. the determination of the Great Powers to prevent a repetition of the Nazi catastrophe, has to be taken into consideration. The joint Czech–German Historians' Commission agreed on the German terms '*Vertreibung und Aussiedlung*'. This causes difficulties with the translation into English. Expulsion in English could stand for *Vertreibung* or for *Ausweisung*, the latter term being not quite as severe as the former. The term *Aussiedlung* could be translated by resettlement, which in English has also the meaning of *Umsiedlung*. This term, the official designation used in East Germany after the war, is altogether unacceptable to German historians today. The author suggests that forced resettlement is the closest term; see also below pp. 148–50.

Here he began to recover slowly. In a first reply to his attackers, he insisted that he had taken the right path to prevent Czechoslovakia from becoming another Spain, where the civil war had wreaked havoc. He had bowed to overwhelming pressure, but he was resolved to fight another day:

> For Germany and for the world, I was the symbolization of the republic, of its policy up to date, and the person who held high the flag of the struggle for the borders, for democracy, of resistance against nazism, for the conception of either an all-European resistance, or of honorable compromise. Munich was a shameful capitulation and a betrayal of all that.[1]

Beneš's contempt for the policies of the western Allies led him to the gloomiest of prognostications. The West might have thought it had averted war, but in reality Munich made war inevitable:

> I don't know when it will break out, perhaps next year or perhaps in two or three years' time, but I myself think that it cannot be longer than a year. ... Poland will be the first to be hit: Beck has helped Hitler against us, but he is in fact helping him against Poland and the others. France will suffer terribly for having betrayed us, wait for that, I am watching the internal decay of France. ... And Chamberlain will live to see the consequences of his appeasement ... Hitler will attack them all, the West and Russia as well, and finally America will come in ... They did not want to understand, the war will force them to pursue the kind of policy we had been trying to follow for twenty years ... The war will be followed by tremendous political and social changes, changes of the generations ...[2]

Most of all, Beneš was disappointed with France, the country he had most admired. Towards the end of the year he was offered a professorship in sociology at Chicago University, which he accepted, but he was determined to return to Europe. No sooner had he taken up his chair in the division of social sciences than, on 15 March 1939, he received the news of Czechoslovakia's final destruction. To him this invalidated Munich once and for all. From now on he indefatigably worked towards one goal: the re-establishment of a Czechoslovakian state, free of the destructive forces that had brought about the end of the First Republic.

An early boost came when, on 28 May, the editor of the American magazine *Foreign Affairs*, Hamilton Fish Armstrong, arranged a meeting with the US President, Franklin D. Roosevelt, at the latter's Hyde Park residence north of New York. The visit lasted for three and a-half hours and, according to Beneš's accounts, Roosevelt was highly critical of the French and British policies. The president is said to have labelled Chamberlain's insistence on appeasement as a fundamental mistake. In his memoirs Beneš writes that he put three questions to Roosevelt: first, did the US government believe in the renewal of Czechoslovakia?, second, did Washington uphold its condemnation of Germany's destruction of the Czechoslovak state? and third, would the United States recognize a Czechoslovak government in exile and support Czechoslovak resistance? According to Beneš, the US president held back only in regard to question three, stating that America's support would depend on the circumstances when war broke out. In Roosevelt's opinion, however, this was only months away.[3] Beneš was equally pleased with his talks with Roosevelt's deputy, Sumner Wells, and with the Secretary of State, Cordell Hull.

On his return to London in mid July, Beneš received further encouragement when Sir Winston Churchill gave a lunch in his honour. Churchill, apparently with tears running down his cheeks, promised in his speech that the peace that would be made in the future would not be made without Czechoslovakia.[4] The widely expected outbreak of war on 1 September was, of course, the most important stimulus for Beneš's relentless drive to have his nation resurrected. By the end of the year he was able to announce, in a New Year's message, the creation of a National Council, recognized by France and Britain and granted the right to represent the Czechoslovaks abroad. The National Council was also in charge of the Czechoslovak army in exile, consisting of 4000 troops that had joined the Allied forces. On 10 May 1940, Churchill became prime minister. Beneš congratulated Churchill in the warmest manner and received the assurance that Churchill would do everything in his power to achieve the liberation of the oppressed peoples of Europe. After Dunkirk the British government agreed in principle to have the National Council transformed into a provisional government – although this did not include any commitment as far as Czechoslovakia's territorial boundaries were concerned. The next twelve months saw the president busy forming a government and consolidating his position among the Czechoslovak politicians in exile. The entry of the Soviet Union into the war on 22 June 1941 brought a further breakthrough for the 'Metternich of democracy', as A. J. P. Taylor once described Beneš;[5] on 4 July the Soviet Ambassador to London, Ivan Maisky, promised full recognition of Czechoslovakia and of the provisional government. This Beneš had in writing a fortnight later, on 18 July. The same day he was informed by the Foreign Office that the British government also gave definite status to his government, but, because of His Majesty's Government's agreement with the United States, no changes would be made during the war in regard to European frontiers. However, at a garden party held at Buckingham Palace, Churchill assured Beneš 'that everything was all-right now'.[6] Beneš, now back in the full swing of politics, had completed the first stage of the long and difficult journey towards the re-establishment of the nation of Czechs and Slovaks.

Understandably in the light of events, the new Czechoslovakia would not be the same as the one that was finished in September 1938. The avoidance of another Munich demanded above all the support of a loyal and reliable citizenship; this meant that a solution would have to be found that would curtail those who had opposed the notion – and existence – of a Czechoslovak state. And the chief oppositionists had come from the German-speaking communities. During the dying days of the First Republic, in a last desperate effort to find a less savage solution for his country than the one demanded by western statesmen, Beneš had presented a so-called 'fifth plan'[7] to the French government – he offered the secession to Germany of Moravian, northern Bohemian and western Bohemian borderlands, which lay before the chief Czechoslovak defence line, on the condition that the Reich would take in an additional one million Sudeten Germans. The republic could cope with the remaining 1 to 1.2 million Germans; half of them were democrats, socialists and Jews, who Beneš wished to grant protection from the massacres that had occurred in Austria and elsewhere.[8] Two years later, after the collapse of France and the recognition of the Czechoslovak government in exile by Britain and the Soviet Union, Beneš returned to the question of the German communities' position in a future Czechoslovakia. In a number of communiqués to the DNSAP members who had managed to escape to London, to British diplomats, to the resistance movements at home and to members of his government in exile, Beneš argued against the 'unrealistic hope, naively held by some, that it would be possible to get rid of or expel three million Germans' from the historical lands. But it would be possible, and indeed necessary, to oust several hundred thousand Nazis from the country and to arrange for an internal transfer of several hundred thousand Germans (he gave no precise figures) from the interior to the border regions and, at the same time, to move the Czechs from the border regions to the interior. This would create a nation of two distinct, internally homogeneous parts – a Czech centre and a German region consisting of three cantons situated adjacent to the border. There would be local government under a federal system. Because the three cantons lay outside the state's chief defence line, the Sudeten Germans could withdraw from the ČSR if they wished to do so in the future, without leaving the country defenceless, as the Munich agreements had done.[9] Had they been accepted as a starting point for attempts to overcome Czech–German antagonism, these suggestions might have sown the seeds for a less catastrophic end to the millennium-old history of Czech and German cohabitation in the Bohemian lands, but they never got off the ground.

The committee of the DSAP in exile (the *Treuegemeinschaft* or 'group of allegiance'), to whose leader, Wenzel Jaksch, Beneš had offered six seats in the planned National Council (*Staatsrat*) – which was to constitute the exile government's parliament – did not reject the proposals outright, but made cooperation conditional on an assurance of full and equal partnership in a new Czechoslovak state. The committee's policy was based on a DSAP resolution made at the Holmhurst estate in Loughton/ Essex on 10 March 1940, which proclaimed the need for a federal Czechoslovakia – as part of a European federation – in which the Sudeten Germans would have their own government and parliament.[10] As Jaksch, in the not too distant past, had advanced the concept of a large Central European federation, more or less under German economic dominance, Czech political opinion had become sceptical about his sincerity on the Sudeten-Germans' role in a post-war republic.[11] His demand, made in a memorandum dated June 1939, that the 'Sudeten Germans also should have the right to free decision on whether they wish to form an autonomous member in a federation with the Czechs, within the historical provinces of Bohemia and Moravia, or, as a German province, become part of the [Central European] federation',[12] did little to soften this scepticism. His further postulation that the DSAP members in exile should put their autonomy demands in the sharpest fashion, so that Czech refusal would again provide them with space for tactical manoeuvring,[13] bore the mark of Henlein tactics. There is disagreement among historians as to whether Jaksch had decisively changed his stance on these issues by the time of the Holmhurst meeting,[14] but, whatever the answer, the matter of Social Democratic participation in the Czechoslovak National Council was shelved for the time being.

More disconcerting for Beneš than the German exiles' response to his suggestion were reactions from the resistance movements in the protectorate, who made no secret of their thoughts on the issue. Their response stressed that the historical frontiers were not to be tampered with, even if some Germans remained in the ČSR; the idea of border cantons was rejected and the dispossession of Sudeten Germans promoted. As several ministers in his government expressed similar reservations, the president decided against further attempts at a federal solution to the problem of the Germans in Czechoslovakia.[15]

In the spring of 1941, the Czech underground at home came out with a particularly strong anti-Sudeten German programme,[16] which Beneš tried to dilute. He sought to maintain a German-speaking population of one million and to ensure that those who remained be allowed full participation in the political life of the post-war republic. As a first step towards this goal, he again advocated the entry of Sudeten Germans into the National Council,[17] but this renewed attempt to admit members of the former DSAP into the *Staatsrat* met with an even more vicious response from home. Beneš was reminded in no uncertain terms that the Czech people would not understand why, after all the injustices suffered, the historical borders could not be restored. Sudeten Germans were responsible for many of the ghastly atrocities committed against Czechs. It was Sudeten-German security men who had shot the students. Executions, arrests and confiscations were the work of Karl Hermann Frank. Any negotiations with Sudeten exiles, let alone their entry into the *Staatsrat*, would lead to the strongest dissatisfaction with the exile government among the populace.[18]

As German entry into the *Staatsrat* was again postponed, Jaksch and the majority of Social Democrats rejected the demand for such a substantial reduction in the number of Germans permitted to stay in a post-war ČSR.[19] The *Heydrichiáda* further eroded whatever chance there may have been for a mutually satisfactory settlement. The Social Democrats' Committee refused to distance itself from demands for severe punishment of those responsible for the terror meted out to the Czech people. This lowered the standing of Sudeten Germans, said to be among the culprits, in the international community, which was becoming ever more hostile, not just to Nazism, but to Germany and Germans generally. By the end of 1942 Beneš and Jaksch had reached untenable positions. The latter and his supporters would eventually return to the concept of the Sudeten Germans either becoming part of a large Central European federation or of a democratic greater Germany. Hopes that the West, when faced with the logistics of transferring large numbers of people, would support such schemes and abandon the envisaged expulsions, formed the basis of this optimism.[20] The president, on the other hand, continued to consolidate his push for the resurrection of a pre-Munich Czechoslovakia.

Quite independently of these activities, debate had developed around the idea that post-Second World War Europe would see major population transfers in attempts to stop the threat of national rivalries again leading to armed conflict. As early as the 1930s, think-tanks in Britain and France had looked into possible methods of solving ethnic conflict in eastern and southeastern Europe. These included the creation of stricter nation states, that is, of states without ethnic minorities. In particular, attention was drawn to the ostensibly successful population transfers between Greece and Turkey and between Greece and Bulgaria, carried out under the auspices of the League of Nations in the early 1920s. Although there was still the occasional reference to these transfers in political and diplomatic circles, the escalation of the war soon moved the emphasis away from broad and essentially vague discussions about the future of nations and nationalities in a post-war world to the specific problem of how to deal with one nation in particular – Germany, or, more precisely, to the question of how to stop future German aggression. The idea of removing Germans from their homes in eastern central Europe was raised for the first time at top political level by the British Foreign Minister, Sir Anthony Eden, and Josef Stalin, at their meeting in Moscow on 17 December 1941. Matters raised then, and the subsequent history of the expulsion and resettlement of the Sudeten Germans, must be seen not only as part of long-term trends in the development of European nationalism, but have to be viewed primarily as a consequence of a renewed attempt on the part of the German Reich to dominate Europe, undertaken this time by a regime of unparalleled viciousness. Against this background, and assisted by the ever growing hostility towards Germany that followed air raids on London and other locations in the UK, Beneš succeeded in having the Munich treaty of September 1938 annulled by the British War Cabinet on 6 July 1942. At the same meeting, Cabinet also agreed in principle to the transfer of the German-speaking populations from eastern central Europe. The Soviet Foreign Minister, Vyacheslav Molotov, had already assured Beneš, as early as 9 June 1942, that the Soviet government had never recognized the Munich treaty in any case and that Czechoslovakia should keep its pre-Munich borders.[21] Shortly before his departure to the United States on 6 May 1943, Beneš received a message that the Soviet government also agreed to the transfer of the German-speaking population. This was confirmed by the Soviet ambassador for governments in exile, Aleksandr Bogomolov, on 5 June 1943. Beneš also had no difficulties gaining the consent of the US President. Roosevelt, known for his pronounced Germanophobia, had already told Beneš, on his May 1939 visit, that for him 'there was no Munich'. In discussions held by the two men during Beneš's stay in the spring of 1943, Roosevelt agreed to the transfer proposal.[22] His view was widely shared by the State Department.

In November 1944 the Czech government submitted a memorandum to the European Advisory Commission that had been formed, with its seat in London, on the basis of an agreement reached at the Moscow conference of Foreign Ministers, in October 1943, to look into questions of post-war Europe's political order. The memorandum spelt out that the 800 000 Germans expected to remain in Czechoslovakia would constitute no threat to the state. It was estimated that 500 000 Henleinists and Nazis would escape before the conclusion of hostilities; war casualties were expected to amount to 250 000 and the remaining 1 600 000 were to be transferred to Germany, a process that was to take over two years. Those expelled would be allowed to take with them all movable property; compensation was to be paid for immovable properties, with revenue from reparation claims against the Reich. Germans who preferred to stay in the republic had to apply for Czechoslovak citizenship, which was automatically granted to active anti-Nazis. They were to enjoy full democratic and human rights, but minority rights were to be eliminated. To ensure that Germany would accept the expelled persons, the Czechoslovak government asked the European Advisory Commission to include the principle of transfer in the armistice conditions of the German capitulation.[23] Initial responses from the Great Powers suggested that all three preferred to discuss the matter among themselves before presenting any binding proposition. The British government replied in January 1945 that, although it had studied the Czechoslovak proposal 'with care and sympathy', no premature action should be taken, as the memorandum dealt with problems that could not be settled by the United Kingdom alone, but had to await the post-war peacemaking process. Initial Soviet reaction is also said to have been 'lukewarm'.[24] The United States gave a lengthy reply:

The American government fully appreciates the injuries suffered by Czechoslovakia at the hands of the Germans and of the German minority during the past decade or so and is prepared to examine the problem in an effort to seek a satisfactory solution for the future. This solution, of course, will also have to take into account the needs of Czechoslovakia referred to in your note, and also the broader aspects of the problems in its relations to general measures for the peace and security of Europe as a whole, as well as the particular problem which will face the Governments accepting the unconditional surrender of Germany ... There will also undoubtedly arise questions with regard to the transfer of Germans from other territories. Since this problem may therefore involve an aggregate of some millions of people, it would be a matter of major concern to the occupying powers in the maintenance of order in Germany during the absorption of such people from abroad simultaneously with the repatriation or resettlement of millions of displaced persons now within Germany. The American Government therefore feels that transfers of the kind contemplated in Your Excellency's note should only be carried out pursuant to international arrangements. ... Pending such international arrangements, the American Government feels that no unilateral action should be taken to transfer large groups, and understands ... that the Czechoslovak Government does not envisage any unilateral action to do so.[25]

Thus, with the three Great Power governments having agreed to the transfer in principle, but postponing firm commitment and advising the Beneš government not to act alone, no plan for the operation's scope and logistics was in place as the war drew to its close. The official Allied confirmation did not come until the declaration at Potsdam on 2 August that the 'three Governments, having considered the question in all its aspects, recognize that the transfer to Germany of German population, or elements thereof, remaining in Poland, Czechoslovakia and Hungary, will have to be undertaken. They agree that any transfer that shall take place should be effected in an orderly and humane manner.' The same day, Beneš signed the Constitution Decree, stripping all Czechoslovaks of German or Hungarian nationality of their Czechoslovak citizenship, with the exception of those who qualified as recognized antifascists. This ensured that, by the end of the decade, only 230 000 Germans remained in Czechoslovakia.

The fact that Beneš played such a consistent part in the shaping of the expulsion policies, from the formulation of the 'fifth plan' to the final transfer, has led to charges that the president's diplomatic manoeuvrings hid his real intention, which is said to have been, from the outset, the creation of a German-free Czechoslovakia. Hence, he was chiefly responsible for what eventually happened to the German-speaking communities in Bohemia and Moravia; after all, it was he who signed the decisive Beneš Decrees. It is difficult to see, however, how such a view could be substantiated by the evidence. Aside from the fact that, for a long time, Beneš took a comparatively moderate and conciliatory stance on the issue, a great deal had happened between late September 1938 (when in a last attempt to save a feasible Czechoslovak state, he had submitted plan five to the French Premier Leon Blum), and May 1945. In the interim the world had witnessed six years of total war – a war which saw the abandoning of every principle of human decency. A conflict had taken place in which tens of millions of human beings perished, which left large parts of Europe in ruins, and from which ensued a widespread desire to establish a peace that would, once and for all, prevent a repetition of such a catastrophe. This must not be lost sight of, but there are further reasons why responsibility for what eventually happened in eastern central Europe cannot be attributed primarily to one or a few individual politicians. Milan Hauner's comment in the continuing debate about 'Munich 1938', that the literature suffers 'a fundamental disproportion between excessive concentration on the diplomatic negotiations on the one hand and disparagement of the factors of military strategy on the other',[26] is valid in assessments of the outcomes of the Second World War. No doubt diplomacy played a part and legality has to be assigned to treaties and agreements, but as Hitler reminded the world so brutally during the 12-year history of the 'Thousand Year Reich', a treaty can be reduced to a scrap of paper without mechanisms to enforce it. So, although the outcome of the Second World War in part resembled what had been discussed among the Allied leaders, and some directions for post-war settlements resulted from wartime meetings of the 'Big Three' and other top-level gatherings – are the reasons for the post-war expulsion and transfer found exclusively, or even predominantly, in the diplomatic records of the time?

It is hard to answer this question in the affirmative. As far as '*Grosse Politik*' was concerned, the Atlantic Charter issued by Roosevelt and Churchill on 14 August 1941 was essentially designed for the US populace. The United States had not yet entered into the war and the nation's men and women had to be assured that, if they were forced to go to war again, their sacrifices would be in defence of liberty and freedom, America's proud traditional values. Article two of the Charter also stipulated that there should be no 'territorial changes that do not accord with the freely expressed wishes of the peoples concerned'. Roosevelt in particular wanted to avoid the First World War mistake of making far-reaching political concessions while war still continued. Because the Atlantic Charter has joined the long list of alleged betrayals or broken promises on the part of the Allies it is again recommendable to recall what was actually said on board USS cruiser *Augusta* on 12 August. Secretary of State Wells took the minutes:

> Mr. Churchill then said that he desired to bring up for discussion the proposed joint declaration by the President and himself. The President said that he believed the best solution of this problem was for an identic [*sic*] statement to be made in London and in the United

States, probably on Thursday, August 14, to the effect that the Prime Minister and the President had met at sea, accompanied by the various members of their respective staffs; that these members of the two Governments had discussed the question of aid under the terms of the Lease-Lend Act to nations' resisting aggression, and that these military and naval conversations had in no way involved any future commitments between the two Governments, except as authorized under the terms of the Lease-Lend Act; that the Prime Minister and the President had between them discussed certain principles relating to a better future for the world and had agreed upon a joint declaration which would then be quoted verbatim.

Mr. Churchill dissented very strongly from the form in which the President had desired to make it clear that no future commitments had been entered into. The President stated that that portion of the proposed statement was of extreme importance from his standpoint inasmuch as a statement of that character would make it impossible for extreme isolationist leaders in the United States to allege that every kind of secret agreement had been entered into during the course of these conversations.

Mr. Churchill said that he understood that side of the question, but that he believed that any categorical statement of that character would prove deeply discouraging to the populations of the occupied countries and would have a very serious effect upon their morale. He likewise made it clear that a similar effect would be created by British public opinion. He asked if the statement could not be worded in such a way as to make it positive rather than negative, namely, that the members of the staffs of the Prime Minister and of the President had solely discussed questions relative to the furnishing of aid to the countries resisting aggression under the terms of the land-Lease Act. The President replied that he believed that the statement could be drawn up in that way and that if he then were queried in the United States he need merely reply that nothing had been discussed or agreed upon other than that which had already been indicated in his public statement.

I then gave the President, Mr. Churchill and Sir Alexander Cadogan copies of a redraft which I had made this morning of the proposed joint declaration before Mr. Churchill had arrived and had had an opportunity of going over it with the President, and the latter had approved it. Mr. Churchill then commenced to read it. He suggested that there be inserted in the text of the third point before the word 'self-government' the words 'sovereign rights and'. This was agreed upon.[27]

Although qualified by point five of the Charter ('the destruction of Nazi Germany after which all nations could live safely within their boundaries'), point two did cause considerable concern among the Czechoslovak, Polish and Yugoslav governments in exile, which prompted Churchill to announce in the House of Commons that the Charter excluded Germany, a statement repeated subsequently on several occasions by the British government.[28] And as the most draconian schemes for a Carthaginian peace for Germany were to come from the Roosevelt administration,[29] there is little reason to believe that the US view was different. After all, it was Roosevelt who initiated the insistence on Germany's 'unconditional surrender' that was announced after his meeting with Churchill at Casablanca in January 1943.[30] 'Unconditional surrender' ruled out any possibility that the defeated Germany could apply to the Atlantic Charter to prevent territorial changes. Discussions at the meetings in Casablanca, Quebec, Moscow, Teheran, and Yalta dealt above all with strategic matters and with the question of how the Axis powers should be treated after their defeat. As far as national issues were concerned, only the post-war Polish boundaries received major attention (at Yalta) and the issue of population transfers was only once on the agenda – at Teheran, when the European Advisory Commission was instructed to solicit submissions from the allies concerned.

How much did the busy activities at lower diplomatic levels in actuality contribute to the post-war expulsion policies? A lot of ink, for example, has been spilt among academics and in diplomatic circles over the Greek–Turkish population transfer, constituting an unconvincing attempt to establish a legal precedent for the transfer of large populations, but how relevant are these predications to what happened in real life? More important for the development of a widespread 'transfer mentality' among Germany's enemies, which made the expulsion of so many people possible, was the fact that the appalling sight of mothers and children, of old people, of sick and injured dragging themselves along with the fewest of possessions – images now brought into the homes of German people through a number of television programmes – was in no way a new or unique phenomenon. Following the outbreak of war in September 1939, approximately nine million had been forced from their homes in one way or another as part of the implementation of Nazi racialist ideology.[31] This figure does not include the 'resettlement' of the six million people of Jewish faith or those designated as Jews under the Nuremberg laws. Those who castigate the Allied leaders for recklessly signing away the fate of millions of people should bear in mind that these policies were formed during a conflagration that virtually demanded the mustering of the globe's resources, to stop a political system that did not hesitate to dispose of millions of human lives deemed worthless and to enslave millions more in its adherence to racialist ideologies that can only be classified as insanity. Nor should sight be lost of the fact that one of the 'Big Three' powers had been the target of an unrestrained 'war of annihilation' (*Vernichtungskrieg*), directed against Slavonic 'subhumans' (*Untermenschen*), which is estimated to have taken the lives of at least seven million civilians alone.[32]

During the war London had become a centre for émigré politicians from occupied Europe and many negotiations about past, present and future took place there. The UK thus assumed an important position in the peacemaking process that did not correspond to the extent of its wartime contribution. Churchill, though very critical of his predecessor's appeasement policies, was reluctant to again commit huge infantry forces to a full-scale war on the European continent because of his own horrid memories of the First World War and the British people's sacrifices. After the fall of France, Britain alone would not have been able to muster sufficient infantry forces to defeat Nazi Germany (of course, defeating the *Luftwaffe* was an important achievement). In the summer of 1942, for example, Soviet troops were facing 269 German divisions (including troops of their allies) on the southern sector of the Russian front alone. Nine German divisions were all that was needed to guard the Atlantic Wall.[33] This did change with the long-awaited opening of the Second Front on 6 June 1944, but, because the British troops made up the northern wing in 'Operation Overlord', as the Normandy landing was code-named, and hence were advancing against northern Germany, they were a long way from Czechoslovakia. However, for His Majesty's government to have a dominant voice in the debates that would shape the political map of eastern central Europe, the presence of British troops was necessary. So, the busy diplomatic activities that went on in the British capital must be placed into context. High-ranking diplomatic officials such as William Barker, Arthur Brown, Frank Roberts, Oliver Harvey or Philip Nichols listened to and conferred with Beneš and many other émigré politicians. They advised, supported or cautioned and a committee was even appointed,[34] all of which makes for interesting records of a bustling diplomatic life in the British capital, but this wheeling and dealing could have only a limited impact on the actual course of events.

Last but not least in the assessment of diplomatic factors in the build-up to the post-war expulsions, it should be noted that population transfers formed only one of several schemes proposed by the Allies to put a stop to future German aggression. Not all schemes were compatible.

At the first meeting of the 'Big Three', in Teheran from 28 November to 1 December 1943, both Churchill and Roosevelt put forward plans that would have dismantled the German Reich. Sir Winston suggested the isolation of Prussia and the creation of a Danube federation that included Bavaria, whilst Roosevelt argued for a division of Germany into five autonomous states. Over subsequent months Churchill widened his concept: Germany should secede all territory east of the River Oder, there were to be several German states and Prussia was to lose its chief industrial regions. All this culminated in a plan worked out by the US Minister of Finance, Henry Morgenthau, and the Secretary of State, Summer Wells, and presented to Churchill and Roosevelt at their second meeting in Quebec in August 1944. This 'Morgenthau Plan' would have finished off Germany altogether. The Ruhr industrial region and the major German ports were to be internationalized. Germany, stripped of all war-making industries and divided into two larger and a number of smaller states, was to be turned primarily into an agricultural and pastoral country. Such a solution, resulting in a dismembered Germany, would have ruled out population transfers of the magnitude envisaged. As stated, diplomacy in itself does not provide the key to the tragic events that befell the Sudeten-German communities in 1945. To explain the development from the harsh demand that Czechoslovakia's German-speaking population be limited to 800 000 or at most 900 000[35] to an even more horrid reality, it is useful to return to the site of a war torn Europe – to the military factor and the situation 'on the ground'.

Actual warfare reached the protectorate at the end of March/early April. It was short but intensely savage. For the Czechs, after the betrayal of the Sudeten Germans at Munich, the humiliation of the German invasion in March 1939, six years of protectorate rule that had culminated in the *Heydrichiáda* now came full scale combat warfare – and all this stands for – against the German enemy – not the Nazi German enemy, or the Reichs-German enemy but the German enemy. This further eroded whatever little room there may have still been for the Czechs and Germans in the Bohemian lands to have their long period of cohabitation end in a more sanguine solution. Terror and bloodshed marked the retreat of the German forces up to the last day of the war. 'On April 19 SS Units burned down the village of Ploština, tied up its 23 inhabitants and threw them into the burning houses', 'the same day they abducted 19 patriots from the village of Újezd near Olmütz tortured them for two days before setting them alight', 'On May 5th 1945 after having plundered the village of Javorisko, in the district of Litivel, the SS burnt it down. During the execution the SS troops shot in the nape or killed all

38 male inhabitants from the age of 15–70 years.'[36] And on the records go. Clashes between SS units and Czechoslovak insurgents reached a gruesome climax in Prague. Initially there were attempts to limit the potential bloodshed involved in the hand-over of the capital to the Czech National Council but SS divisions 'Wallenstein', 'Reich' and 'Wiking', which were stationed around Prague,[37] saw it differently. Supported by low flying *Luftwaffe* aircraft dropping incendiary bombs SS troops attacked the city on 6 May. Again the police record should be cited:

> In Pankrác and Krč members of the S.S. began maltreating the Czech population as early as May 6th, when they succeeded in penetrating into this quarter of the city from the south, supported by armed German civilians. Their violence reached its height on May 8th at 6:30 P.M., when a mass advance was begun on Krč. The worst acts of violence were committed by young men between 17 and 20 years of age. The doors of houses and flats were burst in, houses and shops were plundered, dwellings were demolished, furniture shot to pieces and set fire to. The inhabitants were driven from their homes, forced to form a living wall with their bodies to protect the German patrols, and constantly threatened with automatic pistols. Many Czechs lay dead in the streets. …A great many dead bodies of Czech civilians were later found in a little church. They included men, women and even children from one to three years of age, all killed in a terrible way. Their heads and ears had been cut off, their eyes gouged out and their bodies run through and through with bayonets. There were some pregnant women among them whose bodies had been ripped open. Twenty-three men from an estate were shot in the courtyard after being tortured for a long time. The state of affairs in Krč is best shown by the fates of the inhabitants of two of the many houses broken into. In house No. 295 alone, 37 persons were murdered, ten of them being children between the ages of 6 and 15, 13 Women, two of them pregnant, and 14 men.[38]

This does in part explain why, after the departure of the last German troops, 'all hell broke loose over the Germans in Prague'. Here is a German chronicler's account:

> With few exceptions, even those only tenuously associated with the Sudeten German unity movement (*Einheitsbewegung*) before 1938, with the ideological and propaganda world of the National Socialists or with the administration of the German Protectorate, right down to

the smaller functionaries, very wisely fled. Those who stayed were mostly innocent, those whose doors in Prague were now smashed, whose windowpanes shattered, who were driven onto the streets, often half dressed, with blows and furious shouts. A circle was being closed – the memory of the victims of raging, uniformed and hated mobs in autumn 1938, of the persecution of the Jews, of the shootings of demonstrating students in November 1939, of the hundreds executed before the assassination of Heydrich in 1942 and the thousands thereafter. All these acts of violence should indeed be called to mind and reflected upon, not because like may be repaid with like, but because the same suffering was inflicted on Jews, Czechs and Germans, because of their origins, because of their language, also because they were men or because they were women, in different particular ways and yet in the same way, in the course of those ill-fated seven years. In those hellish seven years, the threatening voices outside the house, the shots on the street, the fear in the darkness, the screams of the persecuted, the sadistic irony and the wretched, trembling failure of one's own strength rumbled and pounded repeatedly through the heads of people in the Bohemian lands, like an infernal symphony. It was just that this pounding was not simultaneous, just that different fronts were formed at different times, and shaped so deeply, that still today, after fifty years, it remains difficult to recognize, or want to recognize, the common ground.

In any case, the Prague Germans, many of them women, were hounded onto cobblestone barricades, which had to be dismantled, surrounded by howling people, beaten and sometimes bashed and trampled to death. In a sport stadium on the left bank of the Moldau, frightful events took place. Terrible lynching murders in the lanes of the old city were also reported. Making living torches out of Germans was not the worst of it.[39]

Summary executions by armed bands or 'people's courts' (*Volkstribunale*), killings, lynch killings and other forms of violence were reported throughout Bohemia and Moravia.[40] The worst incidents outside Prague were the Brünn 'death march', in which up to one thousand people died,[41] and the massacre of close to a hundred Germans that followed an explosion at an ammunition factory at Aussig.[42] An Austrian historian gives this gloomy summary of the turbulent state of affairs:

The end of the war and the end to danger did not yet mean that order was restored and the considerable delay in restoring it was due to politically motivated revolutions and transformations at all levels of the power structures. That enabled people to rise to prominence within the social structure, such people as can be found in any society, but who, in normal circumstances, are kept within bounds by laws and by control mechanisms. But a *de facto* lawless period, a period when one third of the population is branded 'socially or politically unreliable' and thus beyond the law, favors social elements who believe they can now indulge their idiosyncrasies without let or hindrance, that they can take the law into their own hands and settle their personal or political scores autocratically and without fear of punishment... A green light flashed for human traits that normally reside in the remotest and most hidden corners of the human soul, aggression and sadistic tendencies. The 'people's fury' erupted.[43]

On 4 April 1945, the Czechoslovak government-to-be arrived in Košice (Kaschau) in eastern Slovakia, where a day later the Košice programme (*Kaschauer Programm*) was announced. Article VIII of this programme dealt with the republic's minorities. In accordance with the Great Powers' answers to the Czechs' European Advisory Commission memorandum, the Košice programme refrained from specific reference to the Sudeten Germans. It stated that those members of the German and Hungarian minorities who had actively fought against fascism and Nazism could retain full rights as Czechoslovak citizens. The others would have their citizenship cancelled. If they chose to 'opt again for Czechoslovakia, public authorities will retain the right of individual decision in the case of each application'. But those Germans and Hungarians who had committed 'a crime against the Republic and the Czech and Slovak people, will be declared to have forfeited their Czechoslovak citizenship and, unless they are under the sentence of death, will be expelled from the Republic forever'.[44] With the conclusion of the war, all Czechoslovakia's leading politicians, including Beneš, publicly demanded a final settlement with the nation's German population and thereby endorsed the expulsions that were being carried out.[45] This has led to claims that it was political manipulation from above that led the Czech people to turn so viciously against the Sudeten population, countering allegations that the politicians at the top in fact reacted to pressure from below. To the outside observer, it seems that the populace did not need pushing, nor did the government need pressure; rather, the Czechs and Slovaks were virtually unanimous in their desire and determination that the new state be free of the German[46] – and to a lesser extent the Hungarian – population. No doubt Beneš too had by then given up on anything less than the maximum solution he had so long opposed. Had he not, his voice would have been that of a loner swimming against the tide.

A semi-anarchic state of affairs in the immediate post-war period, which left effective power with regional and local councils, or in the border regions with administrative councils (*Verwaltungskommissionen*), saw countless 'national militias', 'citizens' militias', 'revolutionary guards', partisans, plain desperados and, last but not least, Red Army soldiers forcing Germans out of their houses and homes. The Soviets who occupied most of the country gave a free hand, while the Americans in their zone, which stretched from Carlsbad over Pilsen to Budweis, managed to stop the worst excesses and closed the borders to Austria and Bavaria until orderly transfer arrangements could be made. Calls from the Prague government to refrain from violence were not heeded.[47] In the various 'internment camps', 'political prison camps', 'labour camps', 'concentration camps', 'assembly camps' or 'German camps', where many expellees awaited their transfer, 'literally catastrophic conditions prevailed'. The death toll in these camps is judged to have possibly been as high as 5000.[48] Records of this phase of 'wild' or 'spontaneous' expulsion during the first weeks and months after the war list harrowing tales of murder, rape, humiliation and plunder. These tragic stories have been well chronicled; indeed, of the many issues involved in the complex history of Czech–German relations, the expulsion of the Sudeten Germans from Czechoslovakia has seen by far the most publications.[49] Understandably, as the great majority of these accounts have been written by victims, or on their behalf, these works deal almost solely with the suffering and hardship; such recollections could not be expected to engage in profound analysis of questions around the causes of the victims' ill fate. Not quite so understandable is the fact that subjectivity and one-dimensional interpretations are not confined to lay publications. As early as the mid-1950s, the British journalist and historian Elizabeth Wiskemann noted with some irritation that 'since the war broke out books pour from German academic institutions in condemnation of the expulsion of Germans by the Poles and Czechs between 1945 and 1947 as if no expulsions had occurred in the preceding years'. This, Wiskemann believes, is due to the fact that the academics concerned did not comprehend the extent to which 'the Germans were hated over the world by 1945, most German authors write with incredulity about this – to them – shocking fact and are therefore unable to gauge its influence'.[50]

Since then a number of Czech historians have also become very critical of the expulsion of the German population. They argue that post-war

Czechoslovakia would have been better served, economically, politically and socially, had their forefathers overcome their anger and rebuilt a new society with their German neighbours; this may also have prevented the Communist disaster.[51] Such decent sentiments are certainly to be welcomed, but after six years of Nazi carnage, there was scarcely a less realistic point in time to expect a people, Czech or any other, to tame 'their ego, their selfishness [*Selbstsucht*] and their pride',[52] in short, to immediately forgive the injustices dealt them and make a fresh start. Studies of this kind also seem to presume that most Sudeten Germans, dismayed by what the Nazis had tricked them into, would have become loyal Czechoslovak citizens, had they been offered the chance to stay in their *Heimat*. In the light of history before and after the expulsion, this has to remain speculative.[53]

Between 17 July and 2 August, the leaders of the three Great Powers met for the last time at Potsdam. As far as Czechoslovakia was concerned, the Allies, guided by preceding events, did not regard a future cohabitation of Czechs and Germans in a new Czechoslovak state as feasible, as is implied in paragraph XIII of the Potsdam Agreement.[54] As stated, on the last day of the Potsdam meeting, 2 August 1945, Beneš also signed the constitution decree, which removed Czechoslovak citizenship from all German or Hungarian nationals except those accepted as antifascists. A series of further decrees over subsequent months dispossessed all German landholders of their properties and confiscated all German assets as part of reparations for damage done to the Czechoslovak state under Nazi rule.[55] The decree of 25 October 1945 provided that 'no compensation will be granted for nationalized property which at the actual time of termination of the occupation belonged to (a) the German Reich, public persons as defined by German law, the Nazi party, or German formations, organizations, enterprises, undertakings, as well as other German legal persons, and (b) physical persons of German ethnic nationality, excepting those … who actively participated in the fight for the liberation of the country or suffered under Nazi and Fascist terror.'[56]

Officially, Potsdam marks the end of the 'spontaneous' expulsions. In reality, people were still being pushed across the borders to Austria and Germany, though in much reduced numbers[57] until the commencement of the 'orderly' or 'regular transfer' in January 1946, at which time it is estimated that 730 000 people had already been expelled. Ordinance 115/1946, passed by the Czechoslovak Provisional Assembly on 8 May 1946, virtually granted an amnesty to those responsible for grave crimes committed during the 'wild' expulsions. Addressing this fact, the Czech government has more recently stated, in point III of the joint Czech–German parliamentary declaration of 21 January 1997, that:

> The Czech side regrets the great hardship and injustice imposed upon the Sudeten Germans after the war by their expulsion from the former Czechoslovakia and forced resettlement, as well as the dispossession and expatriation of innocent people, carried out in the context of claims of collective guilt. The Czech side regrets in particular the excesses that occurred, contrary to elementary humanitarian principles and to existing legal norms at the time, and that ordinance 115 of 8 May 1946 made it possible for these excesses to be viewed as not contravening the law and hence to go unpunished.[58]

The second stage of expulsion is documented as having taken place under more organized conditions. 'The process of collective expulsion, as regards fairness and justice, can never be "normal" ', a German historian writes in a recent text, 'but the later resettlements ... followed a pattern that excluded brutal crimes. Despite all the inhumanity the forced loss of one's *Heimat* brought to the individual, the act of expulsion [at this later stage] did not often entail the endurance of unlimited horror.'[59] The Americans insisted that the expellees be allowed to carry with them up to 50 kilograms, initially (this was later raised to 70 kilograms), in personal belongings, a week's food supplies and 500 Marks (later raised to 1500 Marks). There were special conditions for recognized antifascists, employees deemed indispensable and spouses in mixed marriages. The Americans also insisted that only whole families were to be expatriated, but this was not always complied with. Often husbands were forced to remain at their workplaces, putting the burden of resettlement on their wives. Large-scale deportation to the Soviet Zone did not commence until June 1946. The Soviets did not allow for the increase of the original limits of 50 kilograms and 500 Marks – offences against the transfer regulations were reported more often from the Soviet zone than from the American one. At the peak of the operation, in the first half of July 1946, twelve trains carried 14 440 people each day into the two zones. As this stretched the zones' capacities to provide food and shelter beyond their limits, deportation levels were soon reduced. In November the period of 'regular transfer' came to an end. By this time, 1 440 000 Sudeten Germans had reached the United States zone of occupation and 790 000 the Soviet zone.[60]

The number of people who perished during or as a result of these expulsions is still a topic of heated and emotional debate. Figures calculated by various sources in the Federal Republic of Germany, from the 1950s to the 1980s, suggest that between 216 000 and 272 000 Sudeten Germans lost their lives in the expulsions.[61] However, these are based on shaky statistical evidence, as pointed out by the Czechoslovak émigré historian Radomir Luža in his 1964 monograph *The Transfer of the Sudeten Germans*.[62] More painstaking work has been done in recent years on this sad but important topic,[63] suggesting that the real number of people killed is but a fraction of the figures initially advanced. Current estimates put the number of transfer victims at around 30 000; while research is not yet complete, a significant correction of this assessment is unlikely.[64]

The post-war fate of the German-speaking communities of Czechoslovakia was extremely harsh. This has never been in doubt. Indeed, these events constitute the final chapter in the Nazi catastrophe. That the great majority of Sudeten Germans were still alive, it must be conceded, was a privilege in itself, after the slaughter that constituted the Second World War. While tens of millions of people had had their lives cut short in one brutal way or another, the expellees' stories did not end with their expulsion. But the immediate post-war burden fell much harder on the shoulders of the refugees and expellees than it did on those Germans not deprived of their *Heimat*. Those who were displaced had lost everything – home and homeland, all that was known and familiar to them, all that shaped and maintained their identities, the whole social and economic structure of a region, a community and an individual. In the long run, they were to be given another chance, but amidst the despair and deprivation of the early post-war years, that run must have seemed long and distant indeed. In the face of this, though, the question remains, how, after all the events of the preceding decade, a meaningful cohabitation between the two peoples, the Czechs and the Germans, could have been possible.

As far as the Czechs and Slovaks are concerned, could a less drastic step than mass expulsion have saved them from communism? This is the case argued by, among others, Czech revisionist historians. Perhaps, although no German who had actively participated in the destruction of Czechoslovakia or had behaved dishonourably during the Nazi years would have been permitted to stay under any circumstances. Whether the remainder would have immediately been granted full civil rights again, including the right to vote, is uncertain, given the emotion-charged atmosphere of that time. However, if one is to engage in counterfactual 'what if' history, it might be useful to raise the question of what would have come of the expulsion of ethnic Germans if Czechoslovakia had not become part of the Soviet Bloc. This is not quite as absurd as it may at first seem; after all, as victims, regime opponents and dissidents had to bitterly concede, the Czechoslovaks brought the communist disaster on themselves. There were no Soviet troops on Czechoslovak soil after December 1945; the Czechoslovak Communist Party emerged from the 1946 election as by far the strongest political party (and, according to Zbyněk Zeman, would have further strengthened its position had a parliamentary election been held[65]). It is true that the Soviets put firm pressure on the Gottwald government to follow their lead and walk out of the Paris Marshall Aid conference in June 1947, but if the Czechoslovak delegation had not been compliant and had refused to do so, the Stalin administration would have had to send in troops to enforce submission to orders from Moscow. With the Cold War already in full swing and with the United States still holding the atom bomb monopoly (and with the Pentagon devising plans that targeted 22 Soviet cities for nuclear attack in the event of full scale war[66]), military invasion of Czechoslovakia would have been an extremely dangerous step to take. On the whole, Czechoslovak–Soviet relations had been amicable, as is shown by the Czech–Soviet friendship treaty of December 1943. Besides, elsewhere in Europe, alternative solutions did emerge as possible, for example, the 'Finlandization' of Finland and the 'Austrian solution' for Austria. These two countries were allowed to be 'western' as far as their economic and political systems were concerned (that is, to adopt the practices of a capitalist free market economy and of democratic political pluralism), but both states had to agree to remain militarily neutral and not to join an anti-Soviet military alliance. Had such a solution been available for Czechoslovakia, the country would have become part of the 'West', which was rapidly moving towards a state of civil society by shaking off the chains of the past, such as dictatorial government, gross social injustices and restrictions on citizens' liberties. Under such a scenario, it would have been difficult for the Czechs and Slovaks to resist claims from the expelled German-speaking people that righting the wrongs of the past should include settlement of their grievances – that they should be granted the right to return to their traditional *Heimat*. In the 1950s and 1960s, with the powerful backing of 'Big Brother' in Moscow, the Czechoslovak government had little difficulty disregarding such demands. And when the Soviet Empire eventually collapsed, more than 40 years after the expulsion and transfer, most of the wind was taken out of the former Sudeten-Germans' sails; outside the professional expellee organizations, the number of people with a serious interest in turning back time had drastically declined.

5
Expellee Politics

Arrival in Germany did not end the refugees' and expellees' ordeal. For those who were pushed across the borders in the 'wild' expulsions of the immediate post-war months, the best that could be said was that the absolute worst was over, there being no further threat to life and limb. A German doctor who worked in a collection camp felt that the 'people had gone through too many terrible things, so they were happy to escape from the Czech hell ... They had nothing more to lose, but had already lost everything and could only gain. Regardless of what life might bring in the future, it could not be worse than what they had lived through here.'[1] However degrading the experience of being housed in hastily built and overcrowded camps was, 'at least instead of hunger and fear there was now hope and even the entitlement to food rations'.[2] The bulk of the expellees were able to wait in their homes until it was their turn to be 'transferred' in trains provided by the Czechoslovak rail system to the American or Soviet occupation zones. As their eviction took place under comparatively less traumatic conditions (they could use decent washing facilities on arrival, were given physical examinations, were deloused, received medical care if needed and were provided with food), the shock of 'forced assimilation' did not immediately follow 'forced resettlement'.[3] This came after the expellees' short stay in receiving camps, when they arrived at their allocated destinations.

Germany was in chaos. Six years of total war had resulted in the destruction or severe damage of millions of dwellings. Allied saturation bombings had laid cities in ruins; the transport, communication and administration systems were in shambles. Besides the expellees, millions of demobilized troops, homeless local civilians, non-German displaced persons and liberated prisoners of war were in need of food and shelter. Large Allied armies occupying the country were claiming available quarters and placing further strain on scarce resources. Against this unpromising, if not seem-ingly hopeless background, the governments of the victorious powers insisted on a policy aimed at integrating the expellees as speedily as pos-sible. They did so for external and internal reasons: to remove any basis for future ethnic strife in central Europe and to thwart the scope for large-scale social and/or political unrest within war-torn Germany. The execution of this monumental task in the American and Soviet zones, where the great majority of the Sudeten Germans had ended up,[4] was assigned to German administrators at state, regional and local levels, although the occupation authorities in the early post-war years remained in charge of the process and intervened if they thought it necessary. As early as September 1945, the American zone, which covered the states of Bavaria, Württemberg-Baden and Hesse, saw the appointment of a State Commissioner, with a set of emergency laws to deal with the refugee problem soon to follow.[5] Proceedings in the Soviet zone took a similar course, with the establishment of the Central Administration for German Resettlers (*Zentralverwaltung für deutsche Umsiedler* – ZVU), also in September 1945.[6]

The speed with which the Allies insisted on the whole forced resettle-ment programme being carried out led to severe social, economic and political dislocations. Because most of the housing losses had occurred in urban centres, large cities and the major industrial centres were closed to any intakes. This meant that vast numbers of expellees had to be crowded into rural areas – villages or smaller towns, where population density was low, damage not so pronounced and where most dwellings were still habitable. In the west of Germany, the states with the least urban concentration were Schleswig-Holstein and Lower Saxony in the British occupation zone, where most *Reichsdeutsche* from eastern Germany had been directed, and Bavaria, but all rural regions had to accept an influx of people that went well beyond their capacities. This was to have severe consequences. The existing local population was obliged to accept the newcomers into its houses and homes, which led to appalling condi-tions in terms of overcrowding, hygiene and privacy, with the expellees receiving by far the worst of this emergency set-up. The conservatism characteristic of most rural regions added its share to the difficulties; village communities, often inward-looking and suspicious of outsiders, were now forced to live in closest contact with large numbers of strangers from distant places, who had been accustomed to different lifestyles and who had sometimes adhered to different religions.

Consider the case of the small Hessian village of Gersdorf. In 1949 Gersdorf had a population of 176. The expulsion brought a further

128 individuals to the village, of whom 109 were expellees from the Sudetenland. While the original inhabitants of Gersdorf were accustomed to a Spartan lifestyle and avoided close contact even with their neighbours, let alone outsiders, the newly arrived Sudeten-German expellees from southern Moravia had different customs. In their *Heimat* work had been easier and people had enjoyed an easygoing, convivial way of life. Their social norms included bowing and hand kissing to express gratitude or greetings. An initial strengthening of Sudeten-German identity ensued from clashes between the sober established residents and the expellees. However, within the Sudeten-German community itself, differences soon emerged and tensions arose. In Gersdorf, the other 32 Sudeten-German expellees hailed from northern Moravia, where life had been harder than in the south. These were industrial workers and tended to be more earnest and more reserved, more goal orientated and very industrious. In contrast to their southern Moravian compatriots, with whom they were supposed to share a strong ethnic identification, they were less religiously inclined and their attitude to the church was more critical. Differences also made themselves felt in everyday communication, as the southern Moravians' dialect was close to that of their former Bavarian–Austrian neighbours; the northern Moravians on the other hand spoke a Silesian dialect and Gersdorf's indigenous inhabitants a combination of High German and their own local dialect. Thus there was considerable incompatibility in traditions, customs and dialects, not only between the locals and the expellees, but also within the expelled Sudeten-German community.[7]

Conditions of this kind would have been found all over rural Germany. Within the space of two to three years, the population of Bavaria rose by one quarter.[8] Grave social tension and conflict was no rarity; police intervention – or stern orders from the Allied military authorities – was often necessary to force a native homeowner to take in expellee tenants. With the capacity of private dwellings soon exhausted, schools, public halls, entertainment places, guesthouses, stables, deserted bunkers and even caves had to provide shelter. And as major housing construction did not commence until the introduction of the currency reform in June 1948, hastily built refugee camps were to remain part and parcel of expellee life for years to come. As late as 1949, a Swiss Red Cross worker gave this gloomy account of a camp in the Bavarian city of Augsburg:

> In 1949 our circle of politicians and economists discussed the refugee problem in Bavaria. What a problem! A population of 9.3 million has to swallow a further refugee slice of 2 million. Refugees press into

a state that has itself lost a million of its living spaces through war. The debate moved wholly within the sphere of economic and political considerations. When I then visited the refugee camps in Bavaria, I stood in the middle of reality such as I had not imagined it. And behind the economic and political problem, I saw a human problem. It took my breath away, as my first step into the first camp in Augsburg, into an enclosure or a pen for people, had taken my breath away.

The affliction is no longer hunger or sickness – although these ghosts also remain active – it is overcrowding. On average, a refugee has less than five square meters' living space, while prisoners are required by law to have at least six square meters.

In such a space, whether it be a factory floor or a monastery or a former POW camp, one is hit with the nauseating, sickly sweet air. 'Living spaces' have been set up with shabby bedsteads, pieces of string and rag – it looks like the bivouac of the miserable. There is no fresh cloth; everything is worn out, gray and musty. The kitchen equipment sits on a box; people sit on a stool brought as part of the refugees' belongings. An ill old lady sleeps above, while a child lies below, pale among the uncovered cushions; tomorrow a busy doctor just might put his head in and speak of medicaments, which are not or only with difficulty available. Nobody is hungry; the government provides for food that can be collected at the serving counter somewhere in the cellar. There is butter, occasionally vegetables, conserves with American labels and bread, but the people are hungry for something quite different. The hunger is for home. In every corner here lives a family, whose private life is public, as a string with a rag is not sufficient to provide domestic space. In the smallest spaces people work, eat, sleep, suffer and love. I remember the woman who spoke of her only longing: 'Just once again to be able to comb my hair alone in the morning!' It must not be forgotten that people have now been living in these emergency homes for years; they have had to settle, for a long, long time, into hovels with all the characteristics of provisional arrangements. And nobody knows whether this will end tomorrow, whether it will be another year or even continue for years.[9]

Economically, too, the great hurry with which the expulsions were carried out added further adversity. Rural regions with low population density are characterized by a low level of industrialization, seasonal work being the chief source of employment. Not surprisingly, unemployment among the expellees from Czechoslovakia, with their urban and industrial background, was rampant. As the scarcity of food, fuel and clothing also disadvantaged the new arrivals from eastern Central Europe (among other things, because they had no or only limited access to the black market economy that virtually ran Germany in the immediate post-war years), there was an urgent need – and strong demand – for the expellees to unite and organize, to lift themselves of the doldrums. Regrettably, this option too was closed to them in the early post-war period.

In their eagerness to curtail any attempt on the part of the evicted people to pursue irredentist policies aimed at reversing the Potsdam decisions, the Allies issued a *Koalitionsverbot*, a ban that effectively outlawed political organizations or any other form of expellee association that might evolve into a political pressure group. This step was also motivated by fear that the desperate living conditions might lead to radical action and by an overall concern to eliminate from the outset any reawakening of National Socialism. The *Koalitionsverbot* in the western zones ran counter to the avowed goal of introducing democracy into Germany, but the Allied authorities evidently took the view that Rome was not built in a day either and that sources with the potential to undermine the process of democratization had to be curbed from the start. Thus the refugees and expellees could initially only form organizations that were clearly non-political. The traditional German parties that had just emerged from 12 years of Nazi oppression, most under new names (though the German Social Democrats kept their traditional title), also had no interest in supporting moves that would foster a special political consciousness, which could possibly lead to a separate expellee party. The two major parties, the SPD and the conservative Christian Democrats (CDU/CSU), attempted to win expellee support by advancing party programmes that promised to tackle the grave problems caused by the expulsions. The SPD in particular opposed the creation of a new political party representing the refugees and expellees.[10] It was thus up to the churches and welfare organizations to not only provide moral and material assistance, but also to assist with the creation of the first self-help bodies, for example, emergency associations (*Notgemeinschaften*) such as the 'Auxiliary Committee of Evangelical Sudeten Germans'. These *Notgemeinschaften* were permitted to function at local and regional level as early as 1945, so they were able to present their case for 'equality, justice and equalization of burdens'.[11] As the overwhelming problems ensuing from the forced transfers could not be solved without the participation and cooperation of the expellees, their representatives were included in administrative committees that dealt with refugees' and other war victims' problems; such committees had also been set up on local and regional levels by the end of 1945.

The occupation authorities in the US zone also tolerated expellee groups formed on the basis of occupational, professional or religious interests. These interest groups (*Interessengemeinschaften*), which began to form in 1947, were left relatively undisturbed as long as their mediators refrained from dabbling in politics. The expellees were not permitted to present a united front in the 1947 elections to state assemblies in the US zone, but they could put up individual candidates. Without any organizational backing, a number of these delegates were elected to newly formed diets in Bavaria, Hesse and Württemberg-Baden.[12] Worsening relations between the western Allies and the Soviet Union then led to a tacit abandoning of the *Koalitionsverbot*. Hence, in July 1947 the Sudeten Germans were able to found the *Arbeitsgemeinschaft zur Wahrung sudetendeutscher Interessen* (Working Group for the Protection of Sudeten German Interests). In April 1949 numerous expellee organizations (*Interessengemeinschaften, Notgemeinschaften* and others) in the three western zones, on the initiative of Linus Kater, an East Prussian lawyer from Königsberg who had taken up residence in Hamburg, united to establish the Central Association of Expelled Germans (*Zentralverband der Vertriebenen Deutschen* – ZdV), ostensibly to augment the expellees' political influence and thus to improve their socio-economic conditions.[13] Four months later, in August 1949, Homelands Associations (*Landsmannschaften*) that had been formed in the western tri-zone, for example, the *Landsmannschaft Ostpreussen*, the *Pommersche Landsmannschaft* and the *Landsmannschaft der Oberschlesier*, likewise joined forces to form the United Homeland Association of Eastern Germans (*Vereinigte Ostdeutsche Landsmannschaften* – VOL).[14] After renaming itself *Verband der Landsmannschaften* (VdL) in 1951, this organization was to become politically the most influential pressure group of all expellee movements. The Sudeten-German Home Association (*Sudetendeutsche Landsmannschaft* – SdL), founded in late 1949, was to play the leading role in the VdL. By the time the Federal Republic of Germany (FRG) was constituted in the Rhineland city of Bonn on 7 September 1949, the Allies' say in matters *Vertriebenenpolitik* had practically ended and the *Koalitionsverbot* was officially lifted in the FRG in 1950.

Post-war political developments in the FRG stand in striking contrast to the course of events in the Soviet zone, which in October 1949 became the German Democratic Republic (GDR). Here the *Koalitionsverbot* was never lifted and no independent political life developed. For the first two years after the German capitulation a modest degree of political pluralism was tolerated in the GDR and – as in the western zones – traditional German parties from the days of the Weimar Republic reassembled to face the chaos left by total war. In the East, as in the West, the 3.5 million refugees and expellees fared worse than the original population in terms of access to food and shelter, employment prospects, career and business opportunities.[15] Here too, the *Umsiedler* (resettlers), as the expellees were officially referred to, were seen as intruders and met with widespread hostility.[16] However, with worsening political oppression in the final years of Stalin's rule and the subsequent monopolization of power by the Communist party (from April 1946 the Socialist Unity Party – SED), the Cold War confrontation, the dubious legal foundation of the East German state and the barely surmountable economic obstacles the GDR faced in the late 1940s and early 1950s, the refugee problem was claimed to have been solved and was swept under the carpet. Dissolution of the Central Administration for German Resettlers commenced in 1948 and the whole process of resettling was declared completed by 1950; from then on, references to the term *Umsiedler* were scarce. The operation of the resettlement network's last remnant, the Department for Population Policies (*Abteilung für Bevölkerungspolitik*), was diverted with orders to deal with the growing problem of *Republikflucht* – citizens attempting to escape from the republic.[17] The GDR was in fact the first state to accept the legality of the transfer by entering into a formal reconciliation treaty with Czechoslovakia, which was signed in Prague in June 1950.

Of the 833 000 refugees and expellees who had arrived in the Soviet zone from Czechoslovakia by the end of 1946, 220 000 decided to continue their odyssey, making their way to the western zones by 1950.[18]

It would be a mistake to view the approximately 11 million Germans who lost their *Heimat* at the end of the war in any way as a homogeneous group of people. All were stripped of their homes and possessions and shared, to varying degrees, the humiliating experience of arriving as virtual paupers in a strange land. This aside, there were vast ethnic, linguistic and social differences. A grammar school teacher from the Silesian city of Breslau, for example, would have had little in common with an East Prussian farm labourer. If, in a small Bavarian town, fate brought together a German family from Lithuania and a group of Trans-Sylvanian Saxons expelled from Romania, communication would have been impossible, the two German dialects being vastly different. Similarly, the superficiality of the concept that had formed the basis of the brief and artificial period uniting a supposedly homogeneous *völkisch* community as 'Sudeten Germans' was soon laid bare when that period came to its terrible end in 1945. In the Federal Republic, the diverse cultural and political inheritance of the Bohemian and Moravian Germans sprouted again in no time. All Sudeten-German organizations agreed on one goal – that the transfer be annulled, but there was little unity on the methods to be followed and on the community's place in a future Europe. In a way the political picture returned to that of pre-Henlein days, when there were Social Democrats on the left, Catholics in the centre and nationalists on the right. Of these three strands, the Catholics were the first to regroup after the catastrophe and their programme was the most constructive.

Formed in the Bavarian town of Ingolstadt in January 1947 by a group of former Christian People's Party politicians and members of the Catholic clergy and laity, the Ackermann Community (*Ackermann-Gemeinde*) grew out of post-war Catholic auxiliary movements. Its name derives from a Bohemian late medieval argumentative poem, *Der Böhmische Ackermann* ('The Bohemian Husbandman'), which tells the story of a fellow who loses his young wife and starts to quarrel with Death, cursing the latter and the world's destructive forces. Death defends himself by claiming that he followed God's order, at which point God himself intervenes and settles the dispute by putting everything in its place: death, loss, destruction and catastrophe are all part of the divine world order; responsibility for tragic events in this world lies with divinity, not with the actions of humans.[19] Guided by this connotation, the founding fathers of the Ackermann Community placed emphasis on conciliation and co-operation from the outset. The community's guidelines maintained that the expellees had suffered a terrible injustice and that they would never forego the right to their *Heimat*, but denounced all thought of retribution. Recalling the principles of Catholic universalism, the community branded the obtuse nationalism that had determined the preceding century of European politics a destructive, negative anomaly in humanity, responsible for ruining the continent's ethnic and cultural pluralism:

> If peace and order are to return to the people, the errors must be overcome that led us all into the current misery. Therefore the peoples of Central Europe, Germans, Slavs and Magyars, must recognize that, with their excessive nationalism, for around 100 years, they have destroyed not only the federal basis for their thousand-year coexistence and thereby the conditions for relative prosperity and inner peace for all groups affected, but have also rendered this area a powerless plaything in the arguments of the big powers and have plunged themselves into ruin.[20]

The Ackermann Community played the chief part in the drawing up of the 'Eichstätt Proclamation', issued on the first Advent Sunday 1949 by representatives of all political groupings of the Sudeten Germans.

'Our indisputable demand,' the declaration reads, 'is the return of our *Heimat* in its ethnic and demographic conditions of 1937. At the same time we realize the given historical and geographical situation in Bohemia, in Moravia and in the Carpathian region. We are equally aware of the ancient, fateful interconnection of the Danube peoples. ... At the same time, however, it is essential to create a viable relationship between Germany and her western Slavonic neighbors. Its prerequisite would also be the willingness of the Czechs and the Poles to give the *Heimat* back to the expelled Germans. All these tasks can be resolved only within the framework of an overall federal organization of Europe, which would preclude a position of hegemony of any great power. Our countrymen will understand that their general behavior must be subordinated to these international necessities. Pursuant to this conviction, we desire to work within our national group and with all expellees toward integrating the fight for the regaining of our homes into the great Christian–Humanist struggle for the rebirth of Europe.'

The reference to the Heimat's 'ethnic and geographic borders' (*in den Sprach und Siedlungsverhältnissen*) of 1937 clearly implies a willingness to abandon the political consequences of the Munich settlement and hence the acceptance of a return to the multiculturalism and multinationalism of the Danube monarchy and the First Czechoslovak Republic.[21]

Key principles of the Eichstätt Proclamation, for example, the renunciation of collective guilt and retribution, the acceptance of the traditional historical and geographic conditions of the Bohemian lands and of the principle of a common destiny for the peoples of the Danube nations, and, last but not least, a commitment to a united federal Europe on the basis of a Christian–Humanist rebirth, were incorporated in the 'Charter of the German expellees' unveiled in Stuttgart in August 1950 at a meeting of the ZvD.[22]

Particular attention must be drawn to the publications of one of the Ackermann Community's finest scholars, Eugen Lemberg, formerly a lecturer in sociology at the Charles University in Prague, who became Professor of Sociology and Education at Frankfurt University after the war. As early as 1949, Professor Lemberg argued in lectures and essays that political groups in exile were often afflicted with a condition of stagnation with regard to their historical views. Living abroad in quasi-isolation, they were likely to ignore important changes that had taken place in their homelands since their expulsion and to develop uncompromising patriotic attitudes that sometimes gave rise to extremely passionate, if not grotesque, political ideas. Hence Lemberg urged the Sudeten Germans to reassess their role as an ethnic group before and after the Second World War, keeping in mind that the epoch of nation states, having reached a climax in 1938 with the annexation of Austria and the Sudetenland by Germany, was ending. The dissolution of the German national state in 1945 was accompanied by the expulsions of Germans from eastern European states, leading the peoples of those states to believe that, after decades of struggle, they had achieved new national purity and independence, albeit only briefly, for since then they had all become mere adjuncts to a superpower. In view of this entry into a new historical phase of large, rival power blocks, separate ethnic groups had to assume new roles. Little else but anachronism could result, Lemberg reasoned, from expellee groups reverting to national minority struggles, since, in any case, the lost lands were no longer what they were. A new concept of the traditional homelands must emerge, transforming the image of expellees from that of victims into that of martyrs, from that of the disinherited into that of prophets, from that of expellees into that of pioneers of a new order. This would not eventuate if they looked to past glories; such defensive thinking ought to be avoided:

> Today, the epoch of the Renaissance of nations in Middle and Eastern Europe is past, and the question is one of a new order. We who have been done wrong by the loss of our *Heimat* must proclaim tenets that will still be valid after we have been requited or after we have died and that will do us justice among people.[23]

In Lemberg's view the world had little time for self-pity; if expellees wanted to gain recognition of their rights, they must judge them within the framework of a new order that would guarantee justice for all – that is, for other peoples as well. In particular he admonished his fellow Germans from Bohemia, Moravia and Silesia to modify their views of the Czech people:

> And the third outcome is the new historical concept that we need and that must include the Czechs and other peoples. We must – and this is said with consideration of many accounts, including some now written in exile – we must finally reach a representation of the Czechs that does not see only the bogey man, the hostile enemy, shrewder and perhaps more ruthless than us, and therefore politically always at an advantage, with the confidence of a greater unity, against which we are disadvantaged. This is still the typical image of

the Czechs among Sudeten Germans, an image that takes us nowhere. As the basis of real debate and analysis, we need a flexible image of the Czechs, the Slovaks and other peoples, such as we already have of the English and the French and on the basis of which we are able to engage intellectually with these Western peoples on an equal level. The image to be formed of the Czechs, however, must not only represent the Czech people's multidimensionality, but must also include them in the history that they share with us.

Thus, in relation to our neighbors, a new task faces us in our self-representation and in our interpretation of history. Defensive and apologetic refutation of the opposing side's propaganda can no longer form the purpose and content of our national and historical representations. Of course that too remains necessary, but it is no longer the object of our historiography.[24]

The programme of the second group normally ranked on the moderate wing of Sudeten-German politics lacked specific awareness of the need, whatever Europe's future might hold, to include reconciliation between the expelled Germans from Bohemia and Moravia and the Czech people among its mandatory principles. The Seliger Community (*Seliger-Gemeinde*), which took up the inheritance of the German Social Democratic Party of Czechoslovakia and the London *Treuegemeinschaft*, also began operation in 1947,[25] when expelled Sudeten-German Social Democrats formulated the so-called 'theses of the Seliger Community' at a meeting in the Bavarian city of Regensburg. The organization was named after the first chairman of the DSAP, Josef Seliger, who had died in 1920. After the collapse of the Habsburg Empire, Seliger first firmly advocated the inclusion of German Bohemia into the Reich. When this was ruled out by the Paris peace treaties, Seliger accepted the Czechoslovak state with its historical boundaries, but demanded national autonomy for the German parts on the basis of democracy, self-determination and socialism. In this spirit the theses identified the main task of the *Seliger-Gemeinde* as that of placing 'the *Gedankengut* [body of thought] of Austrian and Sudeten German socialism in the service of a federal reconstruction of Europe' and required that the creation of any transnational community sharing a common destiny must be based on the principle of national self-determination. The realization of national self-determination, however, was to be pursued not in Sudeten-German isolation, but in solidarity with European ethos (*Gesinnung*) and cosmopolitan attitudes (*Weltoffenheit*), and 'spiritual-political and moral' prerequisites were stipulated. As long as the Iron Curtain denied Sudeten Germans the realization of their right of self-determination in their old *Heimat*, they had to rely on their spiritual self-determination (*geistige Selbstbestimmung*) and join the 'spiritual-political fighting fronts of West Germany and West Europe'. In spite of this, the *Seliger-Gemeinde* also advocated a peaceful collaboration with the countries of southeastern Europe and it warned the Europeans against becoming adjuncts of either the American or Soviet superpower. The theses conclude:

> In the spirit of Josef Seliger, the Seliger Community will, in all its work, prove that close connections with the people and socialist loyalty to convictions were and are the basic values of Sudeten German socialism. Out of this orientation it affirms the linked destiny of the displaced Germans and the entire German people. It declares its fraternal association with the German workers' movement, whose strength and influence will have the greatest significance for the future of our freedom. The Seliger Community calls on all Sudeten Germans, in the name of their right to spiritual and intellectual self-determination, to throw their weight behind a strengthening of German socialism and of European democracy.[26]

Whether this high-flown discourse really constitutes a break from the position of the *Treuegemeinschaft*, especially towards a clear denunciation of the terms of the Munich agreement, is open to speculation, in particular as the *Treuegemeinschaft*'s leader, Wenzel Jaksch, became the Seliger Community's first leader.

As so often in twentieth-century European history, it was not the voices of moderation and reconciliation that reached the outside world, but the shriller sounds. On 8 June 1948, 256 Sudeten-German delegates attended a congress at Heppenheim in Hesse. The principal speaker was Dr Lodgmann von Auen, whose paper on 'The basis of the Sudeten German problem in international law and political developments since 1945' insisted that Czech possession of the formerly German parts of Bohemia and Moravia must never be recognized and that steps should be taken to return these lands where they belonged. With the Potsdam declaration, in the speaker's opinion, soon to become a 'dead letter', it was necessary to prepare for restitution and relocation:

> The Germans of the Sudetenland must create the political premise for making the most of the opportunity to cancel out the effects of the Potsdam declaration and to change the status quo that was established

in Europe in 1945. To achieve this they must have prepared not only their plans but also the methods for execution.[27]

Other speakers reminded the audience of the injustices committed at Versailles and St Germain, when the Sudeten Germans were denied their right to national self-determination and were instead, illegally and against their will, incorporated into Czechoslovakia; Munich merely righted this wrong. The fact that Lodgmann von Auen was subsequently elected Chairman of the Sudeten German Homeland Association – a position he held until his retirement on health grounds in 1959 – did not aid the expellees' cause. Abroad it helped to foster the impression that the expellee movement was made up of simple 'revanchists'.[28] An ardent irredentist and one of the chief Negativists of the 1920s, von Auen's reputation for promoting international goodwill and harmony did not improve in later years. In 1938 he wrote in a series of articles for the SdP periodical *Die junge Front* (*The Young Front*) that there should be no hesitation in conducting 'transfers' (*Umsiedlungen*), including those that formed the 'solution' of the 'Jewish question', if this would help take the heat out of the nationality problems that had begun to curse Europe. He referred to expulsions carried out in the Age of Concession (*Konfessionszeitalter*) as an example that could be followed. He also advocated stern action on the part of the Great European Powers in the case of opposition from 'shortsighted unruly elements'.[29]

One of Lodgmann von Auen's first steps as leader of the SdL was to arrange for a rebuttal of the Eichstätt Proclamation. On 25 January 1950 he and his associates issued the 'Detmold Declaration'. The first sentence strikes a new tone: 'The Sudeten German Homeland Association regards itself as the representative of the Sudeten German ethnic groups abroad [*außerhalb der Heimat*] and the latter as an integral part [*Glied*] of the German nation.'[30] Particularly in this time of great hardship, the Sudeten Germans had to be aware of their common destiny (*Schicksalsgemeinschaft*) with Germany. 'The Sudeten German national group,' the declaration continues,

consider as its goal self-preservation within the German nation, preservation of its consciousness of the homeland (*Heimatbewusstsein*) and the legal claim to its homeland, and the bringing of its frontier experiences to the cause of Germandom (*Deutschtum*). Its goal is the regaining of its homeland ... Because it realizes that Germany, and even more the Sudeten German national group, is no longer an active factor in international politics, the Sudeten German group sees educational activities all over the world as its best foreign policy at this time. At any moment propitious to the regaining of its homeland, it wants to stand prepared to decide its future on its own behalf. It therefore rejects all bickering about international political pipe dreams [*Wunschbilder* – a reference to the Eichstätt Declaration], theories and doctrines, as these endanger the unity of the ethnic group and lead inevitably to division.

Clearly the Sudeten-German Homeland Association saw itself not only as predominant, but as the *sole* organization representing the cause of *all* Sudeten Germans. It is also noteworthy that, whereas Eichstätt had referred to a 'common destiny with the Danube peoples', the Detmold Declaration speaks of a 'common destiny with Germany' (*Schicksalsgemeinschaft mit Deutschland*).[31]

The think-tank and motor of the *völkisch* nationalist elements among the Sudeten Germans was the *Witikobund*, established in Munich in May 1948. The association named itself after the hero of a nineteenth-century novel by the Bohemian novelist Adalbert Stifter. Witiko, of Bohemian/ Bavarian origin, in search of his Czech father, eventually finds his destiny in the services of the Přemisliden rulers. Stifter's novel defends the concept of transnational communities and is critical of the growing nationalism of his age. What probably appealed to the founders of the association was the author's ideal of an exemplary state in which justice, law and order would make possible the unimpeded development of gifted, leading individuals – a concept that was also popular with members of the Spann-Kreis in the 1930s.[32] According to its guidelines, the Witikobund constituted:

> a union of people who feel the duty, out of the tradition of the early self-determination struggle in their Sudeten German homeland, to work towards the destiny of those now displaced from their old *Heimat* in all areas of life … It therefore declares itself conscious of the indissoluble bond with its own ethnic group, as well as the common destiny of all those displaced from the homeland. It further recognizes that the questions of the displaced, especially the return of those states that were lost to the German people and thereby to Europe, through violence that went against all human and divine law, cannot be solved by their strength alone, but that the support of the entire German people is necessary.[33]

Furthermore, the *Witikobund* demands a 'creative, open-minded, unbiased and living' community, made up not only of Sudeten Germans, but of the whole German folk, that would be bound together in constructive collaboration and work. Because Bohemia and Moravia had reached cultural fulfillment through integration with the German spirit or 'essence', the Bohemian lands had to be returned to the western world, to become part of a 'convalescing Europe', imbued with an 'occidental spirit' (*abendländischer Geist*). As a scholar of Czech–German relations aptly puts it, 'there is no mention here of the Czechs and the uninformed reader might gain the impression that the Bohemian lands had become an uninhabited desert when they were lost to the German people and hence to Europe'.[34] With the rejection of both the spirit of liberal capitalism and that of Marxist class struggle, human destiny could reach maturity only in the form of a *völkisch* community.

As all this suggests, the *Witikobund* took up the positions of the *Kampfbund* and the SdP. The reference to the *Selbstbehauptungskampf* (self-determination struggle) relates, of course, to the *Volkstumskampf* of the Habsburg days and the First Czechoslovak Republic. Not surprisingly, former Henleinists and ex-Nazis abounded in the *Witikobund*. Leading members included the former SS chief of Belgrade, Karl Kraus and the NSDAP district leader of Prague, Konstatin Höß, the head of the Nazi 'strength through joy' movement in the *Reichsgau*, Viktor Aschenbrenner, the NSDAP district leader of Reichenberg, Franz Böhm, the *Reichsgau* propaganda chief Franz Höller, and such high ranking NSDAP, SS and SD members in *Reichsgau* and the protectorate as Franz Karmasin, Fritz Köllner, Heinz Lange, Rudolf Sander and the leader of the Nazi education system in the Sudetenland, Franz Seiboth.[35]

With the Working Group for the Protection of Sudeten German Interests, the Central Association of Expelled Germans, the Sudeten German Homeland Association, Ackermann and Seliger Communities and the Witikobund, the Sudeten Germans had developed a multiplicity of political organizations, unrivalled by any other expellee group. In the long run, the dualism between the VdL and the ZdV (since 1954 *Bund der Vertriebenen Deutschen* – BvD) and the overall fragmentation among the *Vertriebenenverbände* (expellee organizations) did not assist their cause, but in the early post-war years the common task of easing hardship among compatriots overshadowed everything else.

Reference has already been made to post-war disadvantages experienced by the refugees and expellees in such areas as food procurement, housing and employment prospects. The more enterprising among the Bohemian, Moravian and Silesian Germans started to tackle their desperate situation by setting up trade and crafts shops, even small factories, wherever they could find anything resembling vacant premises. Deserted barracks and labour camps, ammunition depots in remote locations were soon converted to workshops producing all manner of products:

> a conglomeration of articles was produced, most of which would have found no buyer in normal circumstances. A broad range of arts and crafts – paper garlands, straw Christmas stars, ashtrays, hand-carved plates, bowls and lanterns – were made and sold, as well as products made from the remains of military items, such as the oilcloth toilet bag (*Kulturbeutel*). In the many newly established hand-weaving mills, which exchanged their finished products for raw wool from the farmers, cushions, carpets, curtains and small quantities of valuable homespun material for suits and coats were woven by hand. Businesses producing dolls or silver jewelry with artificial gemstones also enjoyed success at that time.[36]

Some of these were to become quite successful. In Bavaria the Haida-Schönhauer glass manufacturer in Vohenstrauss, for example, and the Allgäuer glass, metal and ornaments company in Kaufbeuren employed several hundred workers. All told, by mid-1948 there were 2400 firms operating in Bavaria alone. However, fate was to turn against the new-comers once again. In June 1948 the western zones introduced a major currency reform, putting an end to the *Reichsmark* and introducing the *Deutsche Mark* (DM). This was the first crucial step towards the revitaliza-tion of the West German economy, which was to elevate, within the space of a generation, a war-ravaged, devastated country to one of the most affluent nations on earth. Initially, though, the currency reform did not benefit all and the expellees again fared worst. Increases in the cost of rent, food and other commodities led to a further deterioration of living conditions among people already existing at the most basic level. Lack of capital and of assets and other forms of security, unable to receive credit from banks, most of the newly founded enterprises had to close down again or at least greatly reduce their production.[37] Unemployment tripled among the expellees after the currency reform.[38] Their organizations, in particular the ZvD/BvD and the VdL, thus faced a massive challenge. In addition to the problems of housing and unemployment, household goods and other essentials had to be provided; there was the urgent need to encourage legislation providing financial assistance for economic enterprises and many expellees were in want of legal protection and advice in dealings with the public service. Last but not least, the displaced persons, in their despondency about the lost homeland and embitter-ment about their social isolation and their seemingly meaningless life, also needed moral and spiritual assistance. Predictably, the most vocal demands for a sharing of the burden left by war and the Nazi catastrophe came from leaders of the *Vertriebenenverbände*.

The Allied occupation authorities in the western zones had already instructed the zonal governments in the summer of 1948 to draft a law for the equalization of burden (*Lastenausgleichsgesetz* – LAG), which did result in an initial assistance scheme (*Soforthilfegesetz*) coming into effect in August 1949, just before the first Federal Assembly (*Bundestag*) election. Its economic benefits were small – payments to assist with the purchase of household goods, loans for the self-employed, an increase in housing construction for refugees and expellees and education assistance for young people, all of this on a very modest scale – but at least a start had been made. Also, the elderly and those unable to work were entitled to a pension paid out of *Soforthilfe* funds. The sum was no higher than their previous entitlement (70 DM), but the social stigma of being welfare recipients was removed. Mounting pressure from the expellee movement – leadership and rank and file – forced the Adenauer government to work out a more satisfactory LAG bill, but it was not until 15 May 1952 that a compromise between the divergent interests was reached and the equalization of burden law was passed by the Federal Assembly.

The tax reform law that was finally passed by the Federal Parliament in mid-1952 involved the transfer of 150 billion DM in tax obligations and was thus one of the largest economic and financial transactions in German history. Involving as it did a 50 per cent tax on whatever assets had remained intact at the deadline for the implementation of the currency reform, it appeared to rely comprehensively on this taxpayer segment. But given that the payment of this impost was stretched over thirty years for taxable natives and given that the State pre-financed the taxes to be paid, the tax reform represented a special kind of taxation and, from an economic policy point of view, it was a long-term *bill of exchange*. Because of the economic boom – to which the exiles contributed – this bill of exchange could largely be covered by the redistribution of asset growth, without impinging on the capital assets of the host society. Nevertheless the 10 billion DM that had already been spent between 1949 and 1954 by way of direct aid and tax concessions to the disadvantaged groups (two-thirds of them exiles) that were the intended beneficiaries of the taxation reforms, did represent a substantial supportive measure, bearing in mind that the total budget for 1954 amounted to 24 billion DM. Priority was accorded to assuaging the most pressing needs, such as compensation for lost household goods, veterans' disability pensions, education grants and loans granted to assist with starting a career.

Partial compensation for the loss of former property did not begin until 1957, after an extensive inquiry to establish the value of damages suffered. This did not, however, invalidate claims for compensation against the countries of origin of the exiles. The size of these compensation payments, some of which were only paid to the heirs of the generation that suffered the loss, was established through a compromise between social compensation based on need and personal compensation based on the value of the lost property. Thus compensation was only paid in full for losses up to the value of 4800 DM; greater losses were settled according to a strongly regressive percentage (8 per cent for losses above 1 million DM).[39] By 1979 exiles received an average of only 22 per cent of their – moreover undervalued – asset losses.[40] Hence, for example, more than half of the forced migrants who had owned a house in 1939 could not make up for that loss by 1971, while the proportion of non-exiled homeowners remained constant. Dispossessed farmers fared worse under the LAG. For a farm of 100 acres lost in the east after the war with an estimated value of 30 000 *Reichsmark* a farmer would only receive 15 000 DM, barely enough to purchase a piece of land, let alone a house or new inventory. For a new property of such a size he would have to pay 300 000 – hence compensation effectively amounted to only 5 per cent of his losses.[41]

In the early 1950s LAG payments constituted 2 per cent of the Gross National Product; twenty years later this had dwindled to 0.5 per cent and there certainly was no redistribution of wealth. Of the 350 000 new positions for expellees created between 1950–56 only 48 000 were brought about by *Soforthilfe* and LAG.[42] The remainder was the product of rapid economic growth.[43] All told, equalization of burden made nobody rich and allowances have to be made for the inevitable shortcomings of a project of such magnitude; nevertheless the LAG, 'well beyond its economic significance added strongly to the constituting of a socio-political legitimacy in post-war Germany, [a fact] that because of the disappearance of traditional nationalist forms of integration, has to be ranked of high importance'.[44]

There was, however, discontent among representatives of the expellee organizations who participated in the drafting of the legislation (over the next two decades the Equalization of Burden Law was supplemented by over twenty amendments and modifications) and who played a major role in the LAG's implementation.[45] Complaints in the expellee media concentrated on the inadequacies of the scheme and the slow rate of the restitution process.[46] In fact the chairman of the ZvD/BvD, Linus Kater, was so disheartened by the alleged indifference of the

Adenauer government that he resigned from the CDU in 1954 and joined the 'Union of Expellees and Those Deprived of their Rights' (*Bund der Heimat Vertriebenen und Entrechteten* – BHE),[47] a political party founded in 1950 in Schleswig-Holstein on the initiative of Waldemar Kraft, a farmer of German-Polish origin who had been the managing director for agriculture in the Third Reich between 1940–45. As the name implies, the BHE represented the interests of those whom the founders regarded as the chief losers of the war. With almost a quarter of the votes, the party scored a spectacular success in the 1952 *Landtag* election in Schleswig-Holstein, a state with an even higher percentage of expellees than Bavaria. A year later the BHE received 15 per cent at the Lower Saxony state election and delegates subsequently also entered the state parliaments in Hesse, Württemberg-Baden and Bavaria, where the party came in third at the *Landtag* election. For the 1953 federal election, the name was changed to 'Union of Expellees and Those Deprived of their Rights/All-German Alliance/' (*Bund der Heimat Vertriebenen und Entrechteten/Gesamtdeutscher Block* – BHE/GB), a move that sought to shore up the support of Nazi sympathizers.[48] The Brandenburg Gate was chosen as the Party's emblem. The election, however, was a great disappointment for the BHE/GB. Although the expellees constituted almost 25 per cent of the electorate, only 5.9 per cent gave their vote to the BHE/GB. Nevertheless, this was sufficient to have 27 mandates in the second West German *Bundestag*. In fact Chancellor Adenauer took the party into his coalition government and allocated the Ministry for Refugees to Theodor Oberländer, the deputy chairman of the BHE/GB. Chairman Kraft held a Ministry with no special portfolio.[49] Internal bickering between Oberländer, Kraft and the BHE/GB's spokesman for Foreign Affairs, Frank Seiboth, the president of the *Witikobund* and a leading member of the SdL eroded the party's unity over the next few years. By the mid-1950s Oberländer and Kraft had abandoned their original position on Germany's lost eastern provinces (to achieve a return of the refugees and expellees by winning back the lost homelands) and had taken up a less unrealistic approach (a peaceful regaining of the old *Heimat* as part of a united European Federation west of the Soviet Union), while Seiboth, with the support of the Homeland Association members, insisted on the continuation of hard-line policies, including the possible use of force.[50] Frank and Oberländer left the party in 1955 to join the CDU. When the BHE/GB failed to jump the 5 per cent hurdle at the 1957 federal election and was hence no longer represented in parliament, most MPs followed suit. Seiboth became the new chairman, but his attempt to reinvigorate the party with a particularly aggressive, nationalistic election programme was an abysmal failure. In the 1961 federal election the BHE/GB share of the vote declined to 2.8 per cent. State elections brought similar results and by the mid-1960s the first and only attempt to establish an expellee party on a permanent basis in West Germany's political life had faltered. With the exception of a few left-wing splinter groups, all political parties rejected the consequences of the Potsdam agreement during the 1950s, so the attempts to broaden the BHE/GB's support base by concentrating on nationalist issues were unwise. This error did not help the expellee party's chances, but the real reason for its fumbling performance lay deeper.

The foundation of the Federal Republic in September was a first sign that Germany was recovering from the Nazi disaster. Currency reform, and to a lesser extent Marshall Aid, had begun to revitalize the nation's economy. The Korean War added momentum; in 1953 business was already booming. By the mid-1950s the phenomenal economic success that was to enter the history books as the German Economic Miracle (*Wirtschaftswunder*) was well on its way. The growth rate reached a staggering annual 7.4 per cent throughout the 1950s. Between 1950 and 1955 over 500 000 new houses were built per annum; by 1963 West Germany's share of the world trade was back to one-fifth. Consumption per head had trebled in this time and hourly earnings more than doubled since 1955 – leading to a constant improvement in the standard of living.[51] This exceptional economic performance was not brought about by the enforced immigration of millions of skilled expellees, as is sometimes alleged; on the contrary, the 'refugee problem' initially and temporarily retarded the FRG's economic development.[52] But when the West German economy was able to sustain such solid growth year after year, the fact that the population had increased by 20 per cent added to the momentum. In times of sustained growth, a society of 60 million people obviously achieves a larger GNP than a nation of 48 million people.

The *Wirtschaftswunder* also failed to distribute gains equally between the original established population (*Alteingesessene*) and newcomers. Pictures later painted by politicians, representing the integration process as a smooth and unqualified success, are coloured a few shades too rosy, at least for first-generation expellees. The expellees did well in white-collar jobs and public service positions, where they more or less returned to their pre-war positions. As far as white-collar workers were concerned, expellees' share of the labour market amounted to 21.4 per cent in 1939. By 1955, 20 per cent were again employed in the white-collar professions; this rose to almost 25 per cent by 1961. Corresponding figures for public servants were 7.7, 5.5 and 5.7 per cent respectively.[53] By the mid-1950s, 93 per cent of doctors and dentists were working in their old professions again, although the average income of academically qualified professionals was well below that of their indigenous counterparts. Worst affected by the expulsion was the rural sector. Only 6.3 per cent of independent farmers managed to gain rural properties again and the new holdings were far smaller than their previous properties.[54] Most former farmers were now employed as blue-collar workers: whereas before the war 37.6 per cent of the expellees had been employed as labourers, their share rose to 66.9 per cent by 1956 (although by then this rate was steadily declining).[55] By the late 1950s, the average monthly income of the *Alteingesessene* amounted to 475 DM, that of the expellees to 430 DM, or 10 per cent less. Only 39 per cent of the expellees' families earned more than 500 DM, in contrast to 51 per cent of the indigenous citizens.[56] The second employment category after farmers to see a sharp decline was the self-employed, whose share fell from 33.3 per cent in 1939 to 7.6 per cent in 1956. At this point in time expellees owned only 7 per cent of the plants in the FRG and employed 3 per cent of the workers. Nationwide they captured only 2 per cent of the business volume.[57] It seems, however, that the Sudeten-German self-employed did better. A study of craft shops and businesses owned by expellees in Bavaria shows that their share was twice as high as elsewhere in the Federal Republic.[58] And although the lion's share of new homes and apartments built in the 1950s went to the expellees (about 50 per cent), their housing figures were still well below that of the original West Germans. Whereas by 1956 28 per cent of the latter owned a house or apartment, the figure for the former was only 10 per cent. Thirty-one per cent of the expellees, but only 10 per cent of the natives, still lived in sublet rooms.[59] Even Bavaria, arguably the most successful German state as far as the integration of expelled East Germans and Sudeten Germans is concerned, still had to maintain 445 emergency quarters housing 30 000 expellees and refugees from the GDR as late as 1960.[60]

As these statistics tell, the expellees' share of the Federal Republic *Wirtschaftswunder* cake was smaller than that of the local population. However, they greatly profited from the fact that the cake was constantly growing in size. Housing and employment statistics improved by the year; in other fields too the gaps were narrowing. As far as household and consumer goods were concerned, there was virtually no discrepancy. 'Representative surveys conducted by German polling institutes since 1955 indicate that expellees on the whole own just about as many clothes, motorcycles, sewing machines, radios, and television sets as other West Germans, and that they bought just about as much life insurance, traveled as often and as far on vacation, and generally lost as many hours' sleep over "money matters".'[61]

From this we may conclude that the overall improvement in living conditions eroded the electoral basis of the expellee party. Most expellees who had previously supported the BHE switched their votes to the CDU/CSU coalition, which illustrates the great popularity of and confidence in the Adenauer government's policies. Trying to save the ship from sinking by advocating a particularly rigorous anti-Communist foreign policy had been a step in the wrong direction, as it brought no new voters. As a historian of the expellee problem once remarked about the 1950s:

> Hate of Russia and communism was the binding element of the various political and social groups, of the refugees, the followers of the CDU and SPD, of the churches, of the unions, etc. etc. It was this that gave the new state its identity: to be a bulwark against the East.[62]

Rapid changes in the demographic pattern and a gradual softening of ideological rigidity (which will be covered in the next chapter) removed any chance of the expellee party's revival. Eventually all expellee organizations were to be affected by these long-term trends, but initially the failure of the BHE caused no great harm to the BvD, the VdL or the Homeland Associations. Their cause was assisted by the establishment of scholarly centres that specialized in eastern and southeastern German culture and tradition, such as the *Osteuropa Institut* and the *Collegium Carolinum* in Munich, the *Institut für Ostdeutsche Volkskunde* in Freiburg, the *Osteuropa Institut* in West Berlin and the *Göttinger Arbeitskreis* in Göttingen, to name the major ones. The Homeland Associations also exercised considerable influence over educational matters, especially geography curricula, ensuring that atlases and maps maintained traditional German boundaries.[63]

Among the Sudeten Germans, the SdL consolidated its position by taking over the Sudeten German Council (*Sudetendeutscher Rat* – SdR). This was again the work of Lodgmann von Auen, who in 1955 transformed the 'Working Group for the Protection of Sudeten German Interests' into the SdR, made up of 30 delegates in three groups. The first group of ten was elected by the Federal Assembly of the SdL, a further ten were Sudeten-German Members of Parliament and the final ten were selected by members of the previous two groups.[64] As all delegates to the SdR had to be members of the SdL and as the Sudeten-German Homeland Association had proclaimed itself a kind of Sudeten-German government in exile, the only institution representing all expellees from Czechoslovakia, this body had virtually monopolized the organizational structure of the Sudeten Germans. And with the *Witikobund* holding the majority of seats on the SdR,[65] the Council's future political course was pretty much determined. By the mid-1950s in Bavaria, Sudeten-German companies were also able to present a record of considerable economic achievement, which contributed to the transformation of Bavaria from a chiefly pastoral state into a leading industrial state in the FRG.[66] An astute Bavarian government reciprocated by taking in the Sudeten Germans as Bavaria's 'fourth tribe' (*Baierns Vierter Stamm*);[67] this was a unique occurrence in the history of German expellee integration and assimilation – no other expelled folk group was given the privilege of elevation to the rank of a special *Stamm*. Further evidence of the fact that the Sudeten-German organizers and agitators had lost none of their political skills is seen in the Bavarian government's decision in 1954 to proclaim a patronage (*Schirmherrschaft*) over the Sudeten Germans, bestowing further social and cultural rewards. A grateful Sudeten-German electorate responded by lending solid support to the CSU, Bavaria's ruling party; electorates with a high percentage of expelled Bohemians and Moravians became a solid stronghold for the conservative coalition.

The 1950s were the 'golden years' for expellee politicians. The fight for the aspirations of their compatriots had given them an important position and considerable say in the power structure of the Federal Republic. Their rallies attracted hundreds of thousands of visitors, with the Sudeten-German annual Whitsunday weekend meetings showing the highest attendance figures. Passionate speeches continued to call for further improvements in the new homeland, whilst still advocating the right – and the determination – to return to the traditional *Heimat*.

But, as the decade drew to its close, there were signs of dark clouds on the horizon.

6
In the Forefront

From the beginning of the 1960s there were clear signs that the international political climate or, to use a term that has recently made its way into German works on international relations, the political *Grosswetterlage* (big weather map) was rapidly changing. In the Soviet Union Nikita Khrushchev had further consolidated his position as First Secretary of the CPSU, which enabled him to extend the policy of de-Stalinization from the domestic scene to foreign relations. In contrast to Stalin, Khrushchev sought contact with the West, above all the United States, by advocating a policy of *détente* and 'peaceful coexistence'. Likewise, the newly elected American President John F. Kennedy, supported by his brother Robert and a group of liberal Democrat Party advisers, pursued a political course that was designed to thaw Cold War conditions. This meant that for a decade and a half East–West relations were considerably less antagonistic than those of the confrontationist 1950s and of the second Cold War period of the late 1970s and 1980s. The establishment of a telephone 'hotline' between the Kremlin and the White House in 1963, agreements to restrict the testing of nuclear bombs, the Strategic Arms Limitation Treaty (SALT), the Anti-Ballistic Missile Treaty (ABM), improvement in trade relations between the superpowers and finally the Helsinki Accord are evidence that both sides doubted the logic of piling up huge nuclear arsenals and continuing a massive ideological confrontation, as the only likely outcome emerged as the possible destruction of this globe.[1] Of course it was not always smooth sailing. The construction of US missile bases in Turkey and the subsequent Soviet attempt to build bases in Cuba, leading to the 'Cuban Missile Crisis' that almost pushed the world into war again, the Vietnam War and periodical bouts over spheres of influence in Asia and Africa ensured the failure of any meaningful dialogue that could have brought about a realistic state of 'peaceful coexistence' before 'Afghanistan', 'Reaganism' and 'Thatcherism' reignited the arms race. Despite these stormy waters, though, the 1960s and the first half of the 1970s were times that allowed for intense diplomatic manoeuvring in search of a peaceful future, above all in Europe. The event that was to change the *Grosswetterlage* decisively was the building of the Berlin Wall on 13 August 1961.

The East German government's closure of GDR citizens' last remaining means of access to the West was as much a political and moral triumph for the latter as it was a defeat and major embarrassment for the Soviet Union. On the one hand, the Soviet government loudly proclaimed the achievements, if not superiority, of the socialist system; on the other hand, where people had the choice between capitalism and socialism, they left no doubt about their preference. This was clearly the reason for Khrushchev's desire to have that 'terribly painful tooth'[2] removed. The crux of the matter lay in the fact that, for the Soviets, the post-war set-up with regard to Germany was greatly unsatisfactory. With approximately three-quarters of Germany having become part of the American political and military sphere of influence, Stalin's worst fears during the peace-making process had been realized; under no circumstances would a Soviet government – before the days of Gorbachev – give its consent to a German reunification based on western terms.[3] This in turn meant that the FRG's hard-line policies, in particular the Hallstein doctrine of imposing trade sanctions on countries that recognized the GDR, had become counterproductive, as they were guided by a thorough misconception of the post-war political reality. For even if a GDR government had, hypothetically speaking of course, recognized the futility of attempts to build socialism in the face of insurmountable difficulties and resigned in 1960 or 1961, when people were leaving the state in droves, would a new government – as happened in 1990 – have immediately started negotiations for incorporation into the Federal Republic? Of course not. With hundreds of thousands of heavily armed Soviet soldiers on its soil and millions more on its borders, at the height of the Cold War years such an attempt would have met with a very swift response from the Soviet occupation forces. Events in Hungary in 1956 clearly illustrate the outcomes of a popular uprising against Communism. The East Germans themselves had already experienced the results of meddling with the post-Second World War international set-up when their uprising of 17 June 1953 was crushed by Soviet tanks. The Soviets, to reiterate, would not have given up their hold on the eastern parts of Germany without a satisfactory settlement from their point of view.

Hallstein doctrine and hard-line economic policies had achieved nothing. If anything, conditions for the East Germans had further deteriorated. With a sombre reality slowly setting in again after the traumatic events of August 1961, the need for a new and less antagonistic approach to dealings with eastern Europe was only too obvious. As this was likely to have far-reaching implications for the expelled German communities, the *Vertriebenenverbände* were soon facing a whole new ball game.

By the mid-1950s, leaders of Sudeten-German associations had consolidated their positions. A law passed by the Federal Parliament in 1955 had finally bestowed full German citizenship upon the expellees from Czechoslovakia. Until then their legal status had been dubious. Article 116 of the Federal Republic's Basic Law included in its definition of a German anyone 'who as a refugee or expellee of German nationality... was admitted to the German Reich as of 31 December 1937'. This effectively excluded the Bohemians and Moravians, who, though regarded as 'Germans', did not rank as German citizens. The SdL filed a suit in the Federal Constitutional Court, which ruled in March 1952 that Germans from the former protectorate who became citizens in 1938 and 1939 should not lose their citizen status – a ruling that virtually upheld the validity of the Munich settlement. Moreover, the Preamble to the Constitution reads that 'the whole German nation is urged to fulfill the unity and freedom of Germany in free self-determination'; this too has been interpreted by Sudeten-German spokesmen to include the former German parts of Czechoslovakia. The same goes for the Bundestag's resolution of 14 July 1950, which rejected any validity of the 1950 Prague Treaty between the GDR and Czechoslovakia:

> The German Federal Assembly declares that the [East German] puppet government is neither morally nor politically authorized to make agreements on behalf of the German Nation. The Prague agreement is incompatible with the inalienable right of the Sudeten-German people to live in their own country. The Federal Assembly solemnly protests against the resignation of the right to the homeland of those Germans from Czechoslovakia who now live under the protection [*Obhut*] of the Federal Republic, and declares the Prague agreement invalid.[4]

With the question of legality solved, in the opinion of the SdL, and with the support of the Federal Republic's rapidly expanding economic and political strength, arguments advanced by leading Sudeten-German-politicians grew in assertiveness and confidence. Among the most aggressive and outspoken was Hans Christopher Seebohm, Federal Minister for Transport in the Bonn government from 1949 to 1966. Seebohm's parents owned coalmines in Sokolov,[5] in the Egerland, and he proclaimed himself a Sudeten-German. The fact that he was born in Emmanuelsegen in Upper Silesia, which was part of the German Reich, that he and his parents held (Reichs) German passports and that he received all his education – from elementary to doctorate level – from German schools led his opponents to classify him a 'holiday Sudeten-German'.[6] His crude style knew no uncertainties. 'The German "East" does not end with the frontiers of the Third Reich in 1937', he told a meeting at the Bavarian town of Ansbach on 10 August 1954, 'the all-German problem will not be solved by the restoration of Central Germany [the GDR]. "East" embraces not only the Elbe and Oder, but also Bohemia and all the territories in which Germans have settled in the past.'[7] In Seebohm's view, the world was involved in a double standard of justice, as it failed to recognize the expulsions as crimes. The word 'Lidice' was still given wide publicity as 'the epitome of criminal inhumanity', yet 'who ever mentions Aussig in Bohemia?' where, he claimed, over two thousand men, women and children were shot or drowned in the river Elbe in late August 1945.[8] Frank Seiboth also left no doubt where East lay: 'we must make it clear to the other Germans why the Sudeten-German problem also concerns the citizen in Cologne, Berlin, or Munich. Königsberg and Breslau are betrayed when Reichenberg is not defended. Integration into the Federal Republic is the first step towards a peaceable return to our homeland.'[9] All leading SdL politicians insisted on the validity of the Munich Agreement. Chairman Lodgmann von Auen announced at the 1955 annual Sudeten-German convention, reportedly attended by 470 000 people, that Adolf Hitler had made it clear in 1938 that the 'suppression of Sudeten Germans by sham Czech democracy' would no longer be tolerated. And although the Sudeten Germans had not been asked to vote on the Munich settlement, they had accepted it with great enthusiasm and should not now be ashamed of that decision. Munich, according to Lodgmann, meant 'liberation from foreign oppression'. Subsequent events, that is, the break-up of Czechoslovakia and the establishment of the protectorate, had nothing to do with the Sudeten Germans, he concluded.[10] Similar arguments were advanced by a Sudeten-German legal spokesman, Kurt Rabl, who reasoned, for example, that the transfer of the Sudetenland had been agreed to and legally recognized by the United Kingdom, France and Italy, and effected in accordance with the will of the majority of inhabitants. Hence, later unilateral Allied declarations that annulled the Munich Agreement were not legally valid.[11] And at a meeting of the German Youth of the East (*Deutsche Jugend des Ostens*), the youngsters were told they had to reawaken and prepare for the 'battle of justice [*Rechtskampf*] over the thousand-year-old settlements in Bohemia, Moravia and all the German Eastern Provinces'.[12] *Heimat* must never be deemed lost. An expellee poem concludes:

> Once encircled by the Mongols
> Bulwark of the Christian West
> Stemming Polish greed and hatred
> And a wall to stop the Hussites.[13]

As stated, the Sudeten Homeland Association's approach to the Munich Agreement was not in line with the Federal government's official stand, which spoke of a return to German boundaries as they had existed in 1937, before Hitler started his drive for expansion, and which hence would exclude Austria and the German-speaking parts of the Bohemian lands. Even these foreign policy statements were meant for domestic consumption. Internationally, the three Allied High Commissioners had informed the Adenauer government as early as November 1950 that 'if they [the western Allies] would speak of a re-united Germany, they meant the re-unification of the Federal Republic with the Eastern Zone [the former Soviet Zone] and Berlin, but under no circumstances with any parts east of the Oder–Neisse Line'.[14] There was never any likelihood that the US, British or French governments would change their views on Germany's eastern borders. Rhetoric about the Oder–Neisse Line assisted the Federal government in its aim to achieve the republic's full political and military integration into the West,[15] a goal that was reached in 1955, when Germany joined the North Atlantic Treaty Organization.

The first sign that the FRG's political solidarity on matters expellees might not last forever came in May 1956, when the West German Foreign Minister, Heinrich von Brentano, was asked about his views on the future of the Oder–Neisse Line during an informal gathering of the Foreign Press Association in London. Von Brentano replied that he personally saw the question 'in connection with the reunification of the Soviet Zone with the Federal Republic', but that claims to the Oder–Neisse territories were problematic; hence a partial renunciation might have to be considered to realize reunification with the 17 million East Germans.[16] His statement was followed by furious protests from expellee organizations. He was forced to recant six times in subsequent weeks and tempers did not cool until he declared to the Bundestag on 28 June that 'the right to the homeland, the right of self-determination remain unalterable conditions for the solution of the destiny of all those human beings and nations now living in banishment or in slavery'.[17]

During the von Brentano débâcle, a second incident occurred which particularly aroused the anger of the Sudeten Germans. Speaking in Hanover on 15 May 1956, SPD Bundestag Deputy Otto Greve argued that reunification for the Germans meant the reunification of the four former occupation zones. Having thus affronted all opponents of the Oder–Neisse Line, Greve went on to declare that the Sudetenland was not German, but Czechoslovakian territory. Not surprisingly, the SdL responded by launching a full-scale front-page attack on Greve in the *Sudetendeutsche Zeitung*. This concluded with the comment that it was 'a political irresponsibility without comparable example to label the Sudeten-German expellees' righteous struggle for the assertion of their right to their hereditary homeland as "robbery of foreign state territory", "treason against reunification" or even "agitation for war".'[18] The SPD was forced to issue a major disclaimer expressing the party's regret for the deputy's comments and to hand deliver a letter of apology to the VdL office in Bonn. No sooner had the anger over the Greve affair abated than yet another provocation occurred, which all but resulted in a split of the Sudetens' SPD contingent from that party's ranks. The so-called 'Vanek Affair' shook the Sudeten-German representatives' confidence at the 1956 SPD Party Congress in Munich, in late June 1956, and led to a new vicious press campaign on the part of the SdL and VdL. The SPD had invited Milos Vanek, an expatriate Czechoslovak Social Democrat, to address the party congress. The invitation itself was an affront to each Sudeten-German SPD deputy. Worse still was the fact that Vanek had been a member of the Czech National Front, which had participated in the 1945–46 expulsion. After weeks of hammering the Social Democrats, the *Sudetendeutsche Zeitung* finally pledged to do all in its power to ensure that the SPD would pay for its treacherous steps at the ballot boxes.[19]

Verzichtspolitiker, 'renunciants' or 'denunciators', as dissenting politicians were scornfully called, were not confined to the Socialists. On 21 January 1957, the President of the Bundestag, Kurt Sieveking, in his capacity as Leader of the Christian Democrats, was invited to address the Foreign Press Club in Bonn. In his speech he too advocated an end to the 'illusions' harboured by expellees and suggested that the government should start talking to the Eastern Bloc. Frontier settlements, he argued, should be indefinitely postponed. 'Germans must be aware of the fact that even if there have to be corrections on the frontiers, the Polish eastern frontier ... is to a great extent settled'. And negotiations concerning Germany's other borders 'must take realities into consideration' when they occur.[20] The CDU, to avoid a fate similar to the one dished out to its chief opposition party, quickly extinguished the fire by having the Party's Expellee Committee Chairman, Uwe von Hassell, repudiate Sieveking's speech in its entirety within 24 hours.[21]

The steadily growing list of *Verzichtspolitiker* included notable citizens outside the political parties. When the much respected president of the German Evangelical Church in Hesse and one of the presidents of the Church's Ecumenical Council, Pastor Niemöller, explained after a visit to Poland that 'no illusions' should be held concerning 'the recovery of the East', he was sternly rebuked for 'having put everything in its shade that has so far been said about Germany's eastern problem'.[22] The disdain poured upon 'denunciators' did not stop at the FRG's borders, eastern or western. Western statesmen such as Charles de Gaulle, newspapers such as *The Times* and scholars or journalists who raised doubts about the expellees' historical rights faced a barrage of condemnation. Emotions peaked with the publication of Elizabeth Wiskemann's book *Germany's Eastern Neighbours* in 1956. BHE leader Linus Kather told a meeting held at the Bonn market place that the 'Royal-British Society for International Questions' [*sic*] that had commissioned this study was the same Society that in the year 1936 had welcomed Konrad Henlein as its guest'. According to Kather, it was all too convenient that 'in the year 1938 Frau Wiskemann went in and out of Herr Henlein's Prague office, where she gathered a large part of that wisdom she came out with in her first book. One can only ever say, "God protect us from the fascism of the anti-fascists" (bravo, applause).'[23]

Yet the problems caused by *Verzichtspolitiker* refused to go away. In 1956 the Polish Foreign Minister Adam Rapacki advanced a plan for the establishment of a nuclear-free zone in Central Europe, which hinted that the Warsaw government might be interested in establishing diplomatic relations even if the Federal Republic had not formally recognized the Oder–Neisse Line. The Rapacki Plan constituted a platform for foreign policy debates in sections of the media and in parliament, enabling a move towards a more conciliatory approach that could eventually lead to a decline in international tension.[24] Suggestions of this kind, which in any case were not acceptable to the Federal German Government, met with unanimous disapproval from the expellee organizations. In 1959 all political parties voted in state assemblies and in the Bundestag to support the expellees' right of national self-determination and to their homeland and to reject the permanence of the Oder–Neisse border. As far as the Sudeten Germans were concerned, the Bonn government acknowledged, during the 1959 Geneva Conference of Foreign Ministers, that some dispute remained regarding the validity of the 1938 Munich Agreement. It maintained that it did not hold 'any territorial claims against Czechoslovakia', but that this did not rule out the German government's obligation to uphold the Sudeten Germans' right to national self-determination.[25]

If the *Vertriebenenverbände* had hoped that the Federal Government's official position would silence the *Verzichtspolitiker*, they were again mistaken. In the Federal Parliament a group of 'denunciators' had gathered around the SPD Vice-President of the Bundestag, Carlo Schmid, known for his colourful parliamentary speeches. Schmid had already made a name for himself as a convinced *Verzichtspolitiker* and was quoted in the German media in May 1959 as claiming:

> Only a madman can believe that the Sudetenland has a chance of being restored to Germany. Except for the few years of the Third Reich, that territory never even belonged to Germany.[26]

Clearly the knives were now being sharpened. In the Sudeten-German Homeland Associations the *völkisch* nationalist hawks around the *Witikobund* had compounded their prominent position in the SdL and had rid themselves of anything resembling moderation. Transport Minister Seebohm's speeches, which promulgated in ever shriller tones the responsibility of the Treaty of Versailles and of the Czechs for the outbreak of the Second World War and which insisted on the German boundaries as of 1938 and not 1937, caused such uproar that calls for his resignation as Chairman of the SdL came even from members of his own organization. The Bavarian State Labour Minister, Walter Stain, appealed to the Germans to muster their courage and 'highlight the best of their history'. For only then could they create a new force whose sole task would be to bring all Germans, expellees and West German alike, into a united front of irredentists – 'All of Germany must become a frontier; all Germans have to be trained to the kind of ideas which frontier Germans must learn in their trades.'[27] And BHE chief Seiboth made statements that at times were reminiscent of his Nazi past:

> We must focus our attention on overcoming our population density. We cannot aim at throttling our population number because the East is already threatening to crush us biologically. Religious and moral considerations also speak against that strategy. Nor is emigration a suitable way to overcome that future dilemma, because efficient emigrants would only help other nations to become even more efficient

in competing with us in the global markets. ... Given the existing situation, no-one in the world can take it amiss that we want to regain the land that is, by right, ours alone. The German East was not only the granary of the Reich in the past. It will have to become that again, as well as having to receive German people, so that we should not suffocate in the confines of half a Germany.[28]

There is no evidence that such extremist views were widely shared among the expelled Bohemian and Moravian Germans; in fact there is no evidence that the majority of the Sudeten Homeland Association members (estimated at around 340 000 at that time) supported the radical tactics of the *Witikos*. On the other hand, it would be a mistake to set such sentiments aside as the rumblings of an extremist fringe group. The *Witikobund* virtually monopolized the expellee media scene, estimated to have had a circulation of 1.4 million.[29] So, again, it was not the quiet contemplations of the Ackermann Community that reached the outside world. Contributions to that community's periodical *Der Neue Ackermann* revealed a growing realization that the expellees faced an almost insoluble riddle, trying on the one hand to preserve not only the Sudeten Germans' right but also their compatriots' desire to return to their *Heimat* and, on the other hand, confronting the reality of the situation in the FRG, where continuous economic success was rapidly creating a meaningful existence, if not indeed a new permanent home, for the great majority of Germans expelled from the East. *Der Neue Ackermann* was forced to close down for economic reasons in 1958 and was later replaced by a bimonthly newsletter with a relatively small number of subscribers. The *Seliger-Gemeinde*, which faced the additional problem of having to adjust its identity in light of the SPD's official realignment as a 'people's party' rather than a workers' party (decided in the Bad Godesberg Programme of 1959), also reached few people apart from its members and subscribers.[30] It was the *Witikos* who made the running. Tensions between the latter and the moderate members of the Sudeten-German Homeland Association continued to grow, reaching breaking point at the SdL Executive Conference held alongside the 1961 Whitsunday Annual Meeting. Ackermann and Seliger representatives, intellectuals and other moderate members had drafted the following article as part of a new Sudeten-German manifesto:

In the year 1938 the Sudeten Germans were merely the objects of big power politics, just as they were at the end of the World War. Hitler had unconscionably toyed with the fate of the Sudeten Germans and forced the development toward the Munich Agreement.[31]

The word 'force' in relation to the Munich Agreement angered the members of the *Witikobund*, as it eroded their claim that Munich 1938 was a binding international agreement, ceding most of the German-speaking parts of the Bohemian lands to the German Reich in a perfectly legal manner. Nor did the *völkisch* nationalist wing of the SdL appreciate the claim that the Munich Agreement was the product of illegal manipulation; they moved that the reference to force be deleted, a motion that was passed by 25 votes to 23. This in turn led to the resignation of all moderate members from the SdL's Executive Committee. Chairman Seebohm needed all his organizational skills to find a compromise that salvaged the article in its original form. The incident illustrates clearly – and contrary to Homeland Association claims – that the radical views expounded by the SdL in public were not those of all Sudeten Germans; in fact the claim made in an angry letter to the *Sudetendeutsche Zeitung* that the *Witikobund*'s nationalist, irredentist policies would be supported by at most 15 per cent of the Czechoslovakian expellees is probably an accurate assessment.[32] The 'Whitsunday Manifesto of 1961', however, failed to bring about a change in the executive's policies, where the influence of *Witiko* remained as predominant as ever.

On 14 June 1961, *Seliger-Gemeinde* President Wenzel Jaksch presented the Bundestag with the findings of the 'Committee for Relations with the East' that he had chaired for the preceding three years. Frequently interrupted by 'thunderous applause', Jaksch called upon the Adenauer administration to uphold its rejection of the Oder–Neisse Line. A resolution that the Federal Government, together with its allies, implement an eastern policy that would 'restore' the whole of Germany (*Gesamtdeutschland*) as a free country (of course Jaksch's vision included the Sudetenland) was passed unanimously. This was the last time that all political parties, the *Bund der Vertriebenen/Vereinigte Landsmannschaften und Landesverbände* (BdV) (the VdL and BvD having merged in 1959 to form the BdV) and all Homeland Associations voted with one accord[33] on the issue of the expellees' *Heimat*.

An initial softening of the Hallstein doctrine occurred in 1962 when the newly appointed Foreign Minister Gerhard Schröder modified the original content by declaring that it only applied to states that had already established diplomatic relations with Bonn. Schröder asserted that the Federal Government could not pursue a policy of retribution towards Eastern Europe, instead advocating the establishment of diplomatic relations with the Eastern Bloc. 'Our aim', he declared at the CDU Party Congress in Dortmund in July 1962, 'is a just and new European order based on peaceful agreements, in which all nations may live freely together as good neighbors. The nations of the Warsaw Pact also belong to Europe.'[34] In 1963 West Germany established official trade missions in Warsaw, Budapest, Bucharest and Sofia. On 5 October 1963 Konrad Adenauer resigned as Federal Chancellor. His successor, Ludwig Erhardt, father of the highly successful West German social market policy, declared in his first speech as chancellor on 18 October 1963 that, with Germany having succeeded to establish peaceful relations with the West, his government was ready to take the same path of reconciliation with her eastern neighbours. Six months later, on 22 May 1964, Transport Minister Seebohm, in his capacity as spokesman for the SdL, told the Whitsunday gathering that the rights of the Sudeten Germans to their homeland and to self-determination were not based on any treaties made this century, but on basic human principles. This meant 'that the lands that had been stolen from the Sudeten Germans had to be returned'.[35] Chancellor Erhardt made the following reply, at the New York Council of Foreign Relations on 11 June:

> The Munich Treaty was torn to pieces by Hitler in 1938. The Federal Government has no territorial claims whatsoever with regard to Czechoslovakia and clearly distances itself from declarations that suggest otherwise.[36]

Massive protests from SdL and BdV led to a Joint Declaration by the Chancellor and the Sudeten-German Council that renunciation of territorial claims against Czechoslovakia did not preclude Sudeten Germans' rights to the homeland or to self-determination and that the solution of problems caused by the illegal expulsion were still a matter for the entire German people. However, the course had been set. In early December 1966, the centre-right coalition that had governed the Federal Republic since its beginnings was replaced by a 'Grand Coalition' of the two largest parties, the CDU/CSU and the Social Democrats. The new chancellor, Kurt Georg Kiesinger (CDU), again in his first speech, stressed the need to come to terms with Eastern Europe. As far as Czechoslovakia was concerned, he repeated Erhardt's dictum that Munich 1938 was invalid, giving four reasons. Firstly, it had been concluded under duress. Secondly, the treaty had never been ratified by the ČSR's political institutions and, thirdly, Munich had violated existing treaties. Finally, it was rendered invalid by the German invasion of Czechoslovakia. *Ostpolitik* had now started in earnest. An impatient foreign minister, SPD leader Willy Brandt, was to become its chief executor.

Major changes in West German foreign policy were one key factor working against the expellee associations, but not the only one.

Equally, if not more significant, were far-reaching demographic and social changes that had become clearly visible by the mid-1960s. A whole new generation had grown up knowing their old *Heimat* only from stories told by their parents and grandparents. Population surveys in 1961 had already shown that 22 per cent of all 'expellees' had been born after 1946 and 50 per cent were younger than 35 years of age.[37] The great majority of young expellees, almost from the time of their arrival, married West Germans,[38] a fact likely to reduce the desire to return. Their children would know only their new home, which to them was not only a *zu Hause*, a place of settlement, as it had been to their parents, but was likely to become their *Heimat*. Here were their friends, their peer groups, their schools and their social lives. The *Heimat* in distant Czechoslovakia was something to be preserved and cherished, because it was the land of their ancestors, but it is doubtful that many second-generation expellees were ardent to return to their fathers' lands in Bohemia or Moravia. The numbers of those still longing for their old *Heimat*, chiefly the older people, reduced as the years passed. Life was taking its natural course. This had obvious results. Membership in expellee organizations declined both in overall numbers and in percentage rates. In 1949 in Bavaria, 26.7 per cent of all expellees from Czechoslovakia belonged to an expellee organization; this had declined to 15 per cent by 1963. In the Federal Republic at large, of the population aged 16 to 29, only 5 per cent belonged to a *Vertriebenenverband*. Opinion polls conducted in 1963 found the number of expellees willing to return as low as 7 per cent.[39] Continuously rising living standards would have contributed to this trend, as would political considerations. As a West German historian argued at a time when *Ostpolitik* was dividing German society, 'It remains to be asked whether the much-cited right to *Heimat* may not have to be modified, inasmuch as life in a civil society in which one finds oneself may be preferable to living in a *Heimat* which fails to effectively guarantee individual rights.'[40] Reports from the annual gatherings mentioned that, increasingly, these were meaningful only to the elderly, while young people present were chiefly interested in exploring the host city once the ritualistic tasks had been completed.[41]

Adding to the expellee officials' malaise was a broad change in public opinion on the lost eastern lands and on Germany's relations with its eastern neighbours. Acceptance of the reality created by Potsdam was no longer confined to a few *Verzichtspolitiker*, but was now widely proclaimed by influential liberal newspapers and periodicals, such as the *Süddeutsche Zeitung*, *Der Stern* and *Der Spiegel*. A particular blow to the leaders of the BdV and the Homeland Associations was the change in outlook of the German Evangelical Church – the nation's largest church, which had started to criticize the one-sided representations of the events of 1945 and 1946, because these neglected the injustices done to the non-German people of eastern Central Europe. A 'Memorandum of the German Evangelical Church' published in 1965 joined the chorus calling for conciliation between West Germany and the Eastern European countries.[42]

Beleaguered from all sides, the *Vertriebenenverbände*, with the SdL in the forefront, rose to one last massive campaign. Transport Minister Seebohm led the charge again. 'We are the pioneers in the foremost frontline,' he is quoted as claiming, 'to throw off the yoke of Bolshevik colonialism over Europe'. According to him, the brave stance of the expellees made 'a far bigger contribution to saving the world from Bolshevism than the blood of the American soldiers shed in Korea and Vietnam'.[43] At the Sudeten-German Whitsunday Meeting held in Munich in 1966, Seebohm announced that the right to *Heimat* was a hereditary right to be bequeathed to their children and children's children.[44] After Seebohm's death in September 1967, his successor as Secretary of the SdL, Walter Becher, warned his compatriots of the 'rabies coming from the East'. He declared he would accept a 'fourth or fifth partition of Poland'[45] if this would prevent Breslau from remaining Polish. With such statements, he soon gained a reputation as an 'ultra-rightwing' politician.[46] Yet Becher was moderate in comparison with Seebohm's personal consultant and secretary of the 'German Society for the Promotion of the Sudeten-German Ethnic Group', Albert Karl Simon, who had this to say about the Munich Treaty:

This national and international enactment did not only define Greater Germany, it also amended the treaty-complex of Versailles and St Germain and elevated the principle of self-determination to the defining principle in Central Europe. What was the real significance of 1938?

Having regained its strength, the German people in the German Reich and its Leader and Chancellor [Adolf Hitler] strove to reunite all Germans in one realm on the basis of national self-determination. In line with his 'Ostpolitik', the Leader and Chancellor also aimed at elimination of the Czechoslovak Republic, a satellite of the Soviet Union and of France ...

The Sudeten Germans did not only view the 'Anschluss' as a victory for self-determination, but also as a historic achievement of the Leader and Chancellor, who had peaceably succeeded in completing the historic events of 1866, 1871 and 1918, in the sense of creating a German Reich that includes all Germans in a contiguous territory of settlement. This view needs to be understood in terms of the conditions extant in 1938, when it was fully justified. For all these reasons the Munich Agreement remains for the Sudeten Germans a decisive pact for legitimizing their rights of domicile.[47]

By the mid to late 1960s, the SdL was the only organization, other than the newly formed far-right German Nationalist Party (NPD), that still upheld the validity of the treaty. As one of its newspapers, *Der Sudetendeutsche*, sums it up: 'We Sudeten Germans – in contrast to the Federal Government – still hold territorial claims towards Czechoslovakia.'[48] Attacks on *Verzichtler* and *Aufgeber* (those who 'surrendered') journalists who criticized the aggressive and militant tirades published in the expellee media continued to be spiteful and vicious:

> According to the *Volksbote* newspaper, 'The Left defends its monopoly.' 'A privileged caste of monopolists' could 'throttle' the people at any time and 'pro-forma democracy' is unable to defend the people against this 'terror'. 'The monopolists and fellow travelers defend the license-holders' privileged position that was created by the Morgenthau regime.' 'A greasy journalistic clique, afraid of losing its dominant position, terrorizes and befuddles the entire nation in the name of press "freedom" and "the right of the public".'[49]

The federal election of October 1969 marked the end of the 'Grand Coalition' and the beginning of a centre-left government headed by Willy Brandt. Although Kiesinger had been keen on a policy of *rapprochement* with the East, as the election drew nearer he had developed cold feet, as opposition mounted against too radical or too hurried foreign policies. This pressure had come from the ranks of the CDU and, in particular, from its Bavarian wing, the CSU. Supported by his Liberal Foreign Minister, Walter Scheel, and his close personal consultant, Egon Bahr, the new chancellor embarked on a forceful foreign policy that within four years led to treaties with the Soviet Union, Poland, the GDR and the Czechoslovak Socialist Republic (ČSSR), as Czechoslovakia was named from 1960. This impressive *tour de force* brought Brandt enormous international prestige, prizes as statesman of the year and, of course, the Nobel Prize for Peace. *Ostpolitik* significantly changed the political map of Europe in the short term and was one of the factors working towards the disintegration of the Soviet Bloc in the long term.

Although with student radicalism on the left and the NPD on the far right, there were already signs of political polarization before 1969, neither before nor after was West German society so deeply divided as during the years of Willy Brandt's Chancellorship, which ended with his resignation on 6 May 1974. His chief antagonists, the BdV and the Homeland Associations, received solid support from the CDU/CSU opposition. Many Conservative parliamentarians opposed *Ostpolitik* because they too believed that the government *Verzichtler* were pursuing an intolerable sell-out policy. Just as many, if not more, hoped that blocking reconciliation with the Communist world would return them to the government benches. However, they underestimated the public support Brandt's policies enjoyed; opinion polls towards the end of the 1960s indicated a clear majority acceptance of the post-Second World War reality on the part of the West German populace. In November 1971 Brandt again went to the polls to have his policies confirmed by the electorate – and won. The signing of the Prague Contract, a treaty between the FRG and the ČSSR, completed Brandt's remarkable foreign policy record.

Of all the treaties with Eastern Bloc countries, the FRG-ČSSR 'Neighbourhood Treaty' required most time for finalization. Negotiations between Bonn and Prague were the last to commence and by far the last to conclude. Relations between West Germany and Czechoslovakia had remained inimical for the best part of two decades after the expulsion. In 1960 the ČSSR government had countered the Geneva 1959 statement on the FRG's foreign policies with a hostile response:

> The circumstances which led to the conclusion of the Munich Treaty leave no doubt that this Treaty was null and void from the beginning… Equally null and void are all subsequent agreements stemming from the Munich Treaty… The Government of the Federal Republic of Germany, the only government that so far has not dissociated itself from the criminal Munich dictate, has clearly indicated that she regards the so-called Munich Treaty as valid in order to use it as the basis for her vengeful policies.[50]

Chancellor Erhardt's speech of 11 June 1964 brought a major change in the Federal Government's official position on the Munich Treaty. The treaty was still deemed initially valid, but Hitler's annexation policies, which led to the destruction of Czechoslovakia, subsequently made it invalid. This was a clear acceptance of the territorial *status quo*, but the new course failed to improve relations with the ČSSR, which insisted on the invalidity of the Munich Treaty from the begininning – *ab initio*. Prague thus missed out on the first round of West German trade missions established in Eastern Europe in 1963 and 1964. Kiesinger's strongly worded statement of 13 December 1966, that the Munich Treaty, 'brought about by the threat of force, is not valid anymore today', improved the situation and did lead to the establishment of a trade mission. However, the ČSSR government's continued insistence on a declaration of Munich and all its consequences as null and void *ab initio*, and, furthermore, its demands that Bonn fully recognize the GDR and abandon its claim on West Berlin, foiled attempts to prepare the way for full-scale diplomatic relations.[51]

The crushing of the Prague Spring by troops of the Warsaw Pact also temporarily stalled further talks, but the election of Willy Brandt as chancellor immediately restarted the process of *détente* with the socialist East. In his policy statement of 28 October 1969, Brandt told the Bundestag that 'the German people need peace in the full sense of the word, with the states of the Soviet Union and with all countries in eastern Europe. We are prepared to make an honest attempt to reach an understanding, so the legacy of the misery that a criminal clique bestowed on Europe can be overcome … [This includes] … our preparedness to reach agreements with our direct neighbor Czechoslovakia that will put a seal on the past.'[52]

As far as Munich 1938 was concerned, the SPD Party Convention held the previous April in Dortmund had already passed the motion that the 'Munich Treaty, which was unjust from the beginning and is invalid, should be extinguished through contractual agreements, which will once and for all rule out a policy directed at the destruction of the Czechoslovak Federation'.[53]

At the same time, the Soviet Union was also keen to stabilize Europe's political climate, and negotiations between Brandt's State Secretary, Egon Bahr, and the Soviet Foreign Minister Gromyko began in January 1970. Agreement was soon reached that an FRG–Soviet Union treaty renouncing the use of force be accompanied by similar treaties with Poland, the GDR and the ČSSR. Talks between the Bonn and Prague governments commenced on 13 October 1970. Diplomatic delegations from both countries met over the next 18 months at five meetings, before further negotiations were called off indefinitely. No measurable progress towards an agreement had been made and neither the Czechoslovak nor the West German government seemed in any hurry to resume talks. Discussion at all five meetings dealt with only one problem – the legal status of the Munich Treaty. The Czechoslovak position remained, as it always had, that Munich had no validity at all, that it was null and void from the beginning, *ab initio* or, in legal terms, *ex tunc*. As stated, the Federal Government maintained that Munich was originally valid, but that it was destroyed by Hitler's subsequent policies; hence it was later made invalid, legally *ex nunc*.

This debate is as old as the Munich Pact itself and the legalist arguments on both sides have long since shot their bolt. The invalidity of the Munich Pact was derived from the argument that the Czechoslovak Republic was not a party to it and that it was thereby a pact to the detriment of a third party and thus inadmissible in international law. According to the counterargument, the Munich Pact merely laid down provisions and conditions for the cessation of the Sudetenland, while agreement to the actual cession was reached via an exchange of notes between Britain, France and Czechoslovakia between 19 and 21 September 1938, so that Czechoslovakia had in fact been a participant. The fact that agreement to the pact was reached by threats of violence speaks for its invalidity. It remains debatable, however, whether the invalidity of a treaty agreed to under the duress of threatened violence, as determined by the Vienna Convention on treaty law on 3 May 1969, was already applicable by treaty law extant at the time. Proponents of the invalidity thesis argue that the Czechoslovak constitution required the Czechoslovak parliament to legitimize boundary changes and that it had not done so. Opponents claim that infringements of domestic constitutional law do not necessarily invalidate an international pact. They point out that the Munich Pact was actually implemented and that the Czechoslovak government participated in the implementation. That, however, does not answer questions as to the legal basis of the pact.[54]

Ex tunc was unacceptable to the West German government, as it would have meant accepting the Czechs' justification of the expulsion of the German-speaking population from Czechoslovakia. It would also have rendered expellees, as former Czechoslovak citizens, liable to charges of high treason or murder. In reality the Czechoslovak government did not expect any change to the *de facto* legal situation, that is, the Reichs citizenship of the former *Reichsgau* Sudetenland population.[55] As compensation claims were also not an issue and as the validity of civil matters conducted between 1938 and 1945, such as marriages, inheritances and the like, also went unchallenged by the Czech negotiators, the question of what caused the intransigence of the ČSSR government has puzzled analysts since the days of the negotiations. Part of the explanation, Czech historian Radko Břach has recently argued, might lie in the dilapidated state of the Husák government after the 1968 débâcle and the pressure from the hard-line Ulbricht government in the GDR, with whom the ČSSR conservative Communists had formed a close liaison after the crushing of the Prague Spring. But above all, Břach points to psychological and moral reasons to explain the somewhat irrational stance of the Czechoslovak negotiators: 'the [new] treaty should erase (*tilgen*) the Munich Treaty, to alleviate the trauma that it caused; to tell the world that one does not do such things, a proper proclamation should free Czechoslovak–German relations from this historical burden'.[56]

Soviet pressure on Prague led to resumption of talks in April 1973. As stated, the Brezhnev government wanted the Czechoslovak–German treaty as part of an overall arrangement in Eastern Europe. Treaties that confirmed the existing frontiers in Europe and renounced the use of force as a means to achieve political ends had already been concluded between the Soviet Union and West Germany, and between Poland and West Germany. A *Grundlagenvertrag* (Basic Treaty) with the GDR to formalize relations between the two Germanies had also been signed and passed. Normalization of relations with Hungary and Bulgaria were to follow the completion of the ČSSR–FRG *Nachbarschaftsvertrag*. Walter Ulbricht had already become a casualty of the *détente* process and was replaced as first secretary of the East German Socialist Unity Party on 3 May 1971. On 20 June 1973 the final draft of the Neighbourhood Treaty was handed to the foreign ministers of the two countries. Article One stated that the Czechoslovak Socialist Republic and the Federal Republic of Germany regarded the Munich Treaty of 29 September 1938 as *nichtig* in the German version and *nulitný* in the Czech. *Nichtig* and *nulitný* translate as invalid, null or void. The word was clearly chosen to avoid reference to *ex tunc* or *ex nunc*. In reality, however, the term *nichtig* or *nulitný* does not exist in international law; if something is invalid, it is *ex tunc*. Hence the choice of the term *nichtig* appears to be a concession to the Czechoslovak position that the Treaty was invalid *ab initio*. Article Two, however, defines the conditions of the invalidity declaration, that is, the rejection of legal claims against natural or juridical persons for the time between September 1938 and 9 May 1945 and the requirement that laws governing questions of citizenship in both states remain untouched and that the Treaty not entitle the ČSSR to lodge claims for material compensation against the Federal Republic.[57]

Thus the nullity was valid only under the conditions laid down in Article Two – hence, *ex nunc*. As this was probably the only occasion in international law that a contract was at the same time *ex nunc* and *ex tunc*, either side could impose its own interpretation. The remainder of the Neighbourhood Treaty renounced the use of force in the two countries' future relations, recognized the existing boundaries and declared the partners' willingness to foster further economic cooperation and to establish contacts in the fields of science, the arts, sport and environmental matters. The final signing of the contract was delayed for several months over questions concerning the legal status of West Berlin, again settled only with Soviet intervention;[58] it was not until 11 December 1973 that Chancellor Brandt, Foreign Minister Walter Scheel and their Czech counterparts signed the *Nachbarschaftsvertrag* in Prague.

Predictably, *Ostpolitik* and Czechoslovak–German negotiations in particular, met with sharp criticism from the Sudeten-German Homeland Association and the *Witikobund*. SdL Secretary Becher still viewed the Sudetenland as under temporary Czechoslovak administration:

> The glasses we drink from in a guesthouse are ours while we are drinking, but they remain the property of the owner. Likewise, those who live in our houses now, in our *Heimat*, are the occupants. But we, who have been illegally expelled, remain the owners.[59]

Chairman Franz Böhm added 'that the [Munich] Treaty only confirmed the rights of the German State to the territory that had become temporarily part of Czechoslovakia; the real rights of the Sudeten Germans are much older. They belong to the much bigger realm of the moral law of nature, which is not governed by [petty factors such as] "Munich".'[60] For the *Witikobund*, Brandt and his ministers had finally become fellow travellers of Soviet imperialism. Because the negotiations were watched worldwide – with Brandt's policies receiving full international approval – his opponents, the SdL in particular, also received widespread media coverage. Pictures of angry protest rallies denouncing *Ostpolitik* and the SdL's claim to speak for all expellees from Czechoslovakia led to the impression abroad that all Sudeten Germans were incorrigible irredentists. This, of course, was not the true state of affairs. The *Seliger-Gemeinde* supported the policies of the Brandt government, including the *Nachbarschaftsvertrag*, and expressed its hope that the treaty, after all the suffering of the past, would lead to reconciliation between Czechs and Germans.[61] The *Ackermann-Gemeinde* also supported the policies of the Federal Government in principle, but expressed regret that the treaty only mentioned the injustice of Munich and failed to include the harshness of the expulsion.[62]

In summary, the Czechoslovak–German Neighbourhood Treaty was a further step towards normalization in Europe. It brought no tangible results in the short term, but it formed a basis for future cooperation between the two countries. Chancellor Brandt's comment that the treaty, 'like the agreements reached with Moscow and Warsaw or the Basis Treaty with the GDR, did not give away anything that had not been lost long ago',[63] is difficult to refute. In the long run *Ostpolitik* removed the grounds for claims that hardline policies (and hardline regimes) were needed to counter 'West German Revanchism'. This was to become an important factor in the mid to late 1980s, when the Soviet system started to falter.

The Sudeten-German Homeland Association's attempt to have the Federal Constitutional Court overturn the Prague Treaty failed,[64] as did its submission to the United Nations. Complaints filed by a well-funded organization from one of the most affluent countries on earth did not carry as much persuasion as did the case of the Palestinians. Hopes that CSU chief Strauss might reverse the tide were dashed when the 1978 federal election again returned an SPD/FDP coalition. The SdL had lost its battle. It was not that they had been fighting a lost cause, but the methods they pursued were bound to fail.

7
Lest We Forget

In May 1984 the annual Whitsunday meeting of the Sudeten-German Homeland Association in Munich was a special occasion – it marked the thirtieth anniversary of Bavaria's patronage declaration, which had officially bestowed upon the expellees from the Bohemian lands the honour of being the state's 'Fourth Tribe'. This was also celebrated with a 17-day exhibition entitled 'Bavaria's Fourth Tribe – The Sudeten Germans'. A lengthy brochure was published, listing many of the chief characteristics of Bavarian–Bohemian relations, past, present and future. The foreword confirms that, although forty years had passed since the expulsion and although Sudeten Germans had dispersed all over Germany and, indeed, all over the world, thanks to the obliging benevolence of the Free State Bavaria, they had still managed to maintain their common identity. The text includes a copy of the original patronage document which states that:

> In the light of the century old historical and cultural bonds between the Bavarian and Bohemian lands and the family ties of the Old Bavarians, Franconians and Swabians to the Germans in Bohemia, Moravia and Silesia, and as a sign of recognition on part of the Free State Bavaria and the Bavarian people for the contributions made by the fellow citizens from the Sudetenland, the State government of Bavaria has used the occasion of the fifth Sudeten-German Whitsunday meeting 1954 in Munich to confer its patronage over the Sudeten-German folks group.[1]

In 1962 this was supplemented by a certificate handed to the SdL spokesman Hans-Christoph Seebohm by the Bavarian Prime Minister

Hans Erhardt:

By bestowing this patronage the Bavarian state Government wants to visibly express its gratitude for the valuable contribution made by the expelled Sudeten Germans to the political, cultural and social reconstruction of the Free State Bavaria, and for proving themselves as a reliable pillar of our liberal democratic order.

The Bavarian government regards the Sudeten-German folks group as a Bavarian tribe. She commits itself to fully support the Sudeten Germans' right to return to their homeland and to self-determination. She will always attempt to support the Sudeten Germans' *völkisch* identity and she will financially back all institutions that foster the political, cultural and social traditions of the Sudeten-German folks group.[2]

The brochure also includes numerous extracts from speeches and articles by leading Bavarians and Sudeten Germans over the years, for example, Prime Minister Franz Josef Strauss's address to the 1979 Whitsunday gathering in Munich, in which he praises the Sudetens for having foiled Stalin's plot to subvert the whole of Europe through Communist imperialism. There is a quote from SdL Chairman Walter Becher referring to the *Glück im Unglück* ('stroke of luck in the midst of misfortune', suggesting things could have been much worse) the Sudeten Germans had in finding their new home in Bavaria. Becher continues:

They came to a related motherland; the Bavarians took in an industrialized people, a sensible supplement to their own agrarian society! The integration that was subsequently to develop constitutes an exemplary, historically unique process.[3]

The Bavarian government was certainly not stingy. Cultural contributions in the mid-1980s included the maintenance of the *Haus des Ostens* in Munich, the *Egerland Kulturhaus* in Markredtwitz and the Sudeten-German Gallery in Regensburg. The Sudeten-German Archive and the *Collegium Carolinum* in Munich, the Sudeten-German Council, the *Institutum Bohemicum* of the Ackermann Community, the Institute for Reformation and Church History of the Bohemian Lands and the Sudeten-German Academy for Science and the Arts are all either fully or largely financed out of the Bavarian State budget. So is the SdL and its various sub-organizations, such as the Working Community of Sudeten-German Educators (*Arbeitsgemeinschaft Sudetendeutscher Erzieher*), the Sudeten

German Social Assistance Society (*Sudetendeutsche Sozialwerk*) and the *Adalbert-Stifter-Verein*, as well as numerous other associations and institutions. The impressive 'Sudeten-German House', situated in the centre of Munich near the Isar river, was largely financed by state funds, as was the reconstruction of the Hohenberg Castle on the River Eder and that of the *Heiligenhof* in Bad Kissingen, both used by the *Sudetendeutsche Sozialwerk*, and the *Haus Sudetenland* in Waldkraiburg, a centre for the Sudeten-German Youth Movement. This is by no means the full list.

Backslapping and self-congratulations aside, the expellees from Czechoslovakia did make a remarkable contribution to the Free State's economy. By the mid-1980s expellee initiatives had led to the establishment of over 4000 new enterprises in Bavaria, mainly in the glass, furniture, jewelry, clothing and textile industries, as well as in metal processing and the production of musical instruments. Neugablonz, near Kaufbeuren, ranks as Germany's largest jewelry centre. The industrial giant Siemens established a household goods factory in Traunreut, where the population is largely of Sudeten-German origin, employing 4000 workers. There are also clothing and precision instrument factories in Traunreut. Waldkraiburg is another large industrial centre in Bavaria founded on the initiative of the new settlers. A 1984 study lists over 50 major Sudeten-German industrial centres, surrounded by around 70 smaller settlements.[4] Many expellees from the Bohemian lands had, then, acquired considerable wealth again; the great majority would have enjoyed the Federal Republic's high living standards and all but a few were well housed and able to enjoy West Germany's advanced and generous social services, not to mention its free and liberal political life. Clearly the 'Fourth Tribe' had settled in well. For the observer, this raises the question of how the leaders of the expellee organizations expected to reconcile the successful integration that had been achieved by the 1980s in their new homeland with the avowed aim of re-gathering what had been stolen from them and again living in their old *Heimat*, freely and according to the principle of national self-determination. It is scarcely possible to reside in Bavaria as a member of one of the state's four tribes and at the same time to repopulate the Sudetenland with German settlers. Nevertheless, a 14-point manifesto issued by the SdL and the Sudeten-German Council in 1979 reiterates the right of self-determination for all peoples and ethnic groups, in particular to those, like the Sudeten Germans, who 'through centuries of peaceful work' had cultivated their country 'not with the soldier's sword, but with the plough of the farmer, as peaceful miners, citizens, craftsmen and merchants'.[5] United Nations Resolution Number 3236 of 22 November 1974, which acknowledged the Palestinians' right to return to their homes and to the restitution of their property, was viewed as supporting their cause.[6] The final point of the 1979 declaration maintains that 'A new Europe built on the basis of justice and freedom will include the lands of our ancestral homes, and will, above all, give the young people a chance of transforming the Sudetenland once again into a flourishing part of the center of our continent.'[7] It is hardly plausible that the spokesmen of the SdL and the SdR really believed that the expellees' children and grandchildren would pack up their bags, leave their residences and return *en masse* to their ancestral homes. The combination of membership of Bavaria's fourth tribe and full citizenship of the former German-speaking parts of Czechoslovakia could only be achieved if the Sudetenland were to become part of Bavaria. Hence, statements like the 1979 Manifesto encouraged charges that the SdL had still not overcome the spirit of the Henlein days, that is, the view that the lands ceded by the ČSR in the Munich Treaty of September 1938 belonged to Germany.

Patronage was – and still is – based on a system of *Patenschaften* ('godparenthoods'). This involves the adoption for patronage of a town, city or whole district of the former German-speaking parts of Bohemia or Moravia by a town or city in the FRG. By the mid-1980s, 150 of these *Patenschaften* had sprung up all over Germany, most of them, predictably, in Bavaria. Unlike city partnerships or twin town arrangements in the West, which aim to foster cultural and social links between communities in different countries, Sudeten-German *Patenschaften* seek to maintain the 'cultural inheritance' of the expellees and their descendants. The Württemberg town of Geislingen/Steige, for example, has bestowed its godparenthood on southern Moravia, which means that the town administration has established a *Heimatmuseum* and archives displaying memorabilia of the old homeland. Southern Moravians apparently travel 'home to Geislingen/Steige' for their annual meetings. Contact with places of origin in the ČSSR was specifically discouraged and there was little hope for the Czechs of a change in this policy unless the latter issued 'a clear renunciation of the crime of expulsion'.[8]

With attitudes like these, the Sudeten-German Homeland Association and the Sudeten-German Council were nationally and internationally isolated, the Federation of Expellees being their only ally. Despite SdL refusal to re-establish contact with its former homeland, though, as many as one-quarter of the expellees and their descendants had visited Czechoslovakia on their own initiative by the mid-1980s. 'Homesickness Tourism' (*Heimweh-Tourismus*) is said to have taken the place of *Heimatpolemik* and meetings with the new owners in the Germans' old homes occurred in a friendly and conciliatory manner.[9] The Ackermann and Seliger Communities, the *Adalbert-Stifter-Verein* and the *Collegium Carolinum* had also begun to establish links across the border well before the curtain went up. Politically, too, there were no signs of encouragement for the SdL and SdC. Hopes had run high that the return of a conservative government might signal a reversal from *Ostpolitik*. The Bavarian Prime Minister Franz Josef Strauss had been a particularly vociferous supporter of expellee demands. 'I have not been fighting against this *Ostpolitik* for 13 years', he declared in 1982, 'only to announce its continuation in year 14.'[10] However, when the CDU/CSU emerged victorious from the 1982 federal election, he soon surprised political observers by arranging a one billion DM loan for the much maligned other German state. Further generous loans and trade concessions for the GDR – which was, financially, in dire straits – soon followed, leading to tangible results for East Germany's citizens, even before the Wall came down. Chancellor Helmut Kohl had already announced in 1981 that the 'lost unity, as it was in the old German national state, cannot be restored'.[11] None of this, however, seemed to dampen the enthusiasm of the expellee spokesmen – now commonly referred to as *Berufsvertriebene* ('professional expellees') – to advocate a return of their people to their former homes. At a 'First Sudeten-German People's Congress' in 1987, the SdL declared itself the sole democratically elected representative of the Sudeten Germans.[12] Whether this 'People's Congress' really constituted a legitimate source of authority is questionable. A public opinion survey in 1985 showed that 90 per cent of expellees from Czechoslovakia, or their descendants, saw themselves as fully integrated into the Federal Republic.[13] Claims that SdL membership was still over 100 000 have also been queried.[14] Circulation of the *Sudetendeutsche Zeitung* had declined to 25 000 by 1970.[15] Figures for the 1980s are not available, but are unlikely to have seen an increase. All told, the SdL's claim to speak for all Sudeten Germans has to be regarded as dubious.

With the advent of Mikhail Gorbachev to the position of First Secretary of the Communist Party of the Soviet Union, the international *Grosswetterlage* again changed decisively. Whilst he attempted to solve the USSR's political and economic malaise with *glasnost* and *perestroika*, oppositionists and reformers in the People's Republics had also set to work. In Poland the anti-communist Catholic 'Solidarity' movement, under Lech Walesa, had been challenging rigid one-party rule since the early 1980s; in Hungary reform communists began to tackle the system's inflexibility from within. In fact it was Gyula Horn and his Hungarian reformers who tested the new climate by lifting the Curtain and thereby breaking fraternal socialist solidarity. The exodus that had been dammed in 1961 by the building of the Wall could now freely resume through Hungary. The GDR, as unable in 1989 to cope with an open border as she had been 28 years earlier, disintegrated within seven months. Politically and economically the key country in Eastern Europe outside the Soviet Union, the GDR was followed by the People's Republics and their masters, who collapsed like a stack of cards. After decades of massive spending for military and ideological purposes – to save the world from either Communism or Capitalism – the Cold War had come to a farcical end.

Jubilation over the end of socialism was highest in East Germany and Czechoslovakia. Support for the SED had always been limited in the GDR and the Czechoslovak Communist Party had lost its credibility during the events of 1968. Whereas reformed and renamed Communist Parties in Poland and Hungary were re-elected to government within the space of a couple of years – and continue to play influential roles in these countries' political lives, the Party of Democratic Socialism (PDS), which succeeded the SED, has not been able to attract more than one-fifth of the vote in post-1989 elections. The Communists in Czechoslovakia initially fared even worse. Here the 'Velvet Revolution' elected Václav Havel, a playwright and distinguished Czech dissident, as president of the newly constituted Federal National Assembly in December 1989.

The fact that 23 political parties, covering the full spectrum from left to right, contested the June 1990 election to the Assembly illustrates that 40 years of Communist rule had failed to wipe out Czechoslovak democratic tradition and political diversity. Havel, already internationally respected as a scholar and humanist, soon lived up to his reputation. Encouraged by the aura of goodwill and conciliation that marked the end of the oppressive system in Eastern Europe, the Czech president in particular set out to heal the division between Czechs and Germans. Shortly after his election to the Presidency, Havel wrote a letter to the German President, Richard von Weizsäcker, in which he stated that he personally – like many of his friends – condemned the expulsion of the Germans after the war. 'I have always considered it the greatest immoral deed', the letter read, 'which caused not only the Germans but possibly to an even greater degree the Czechs themselves moral and material damage.'[16] Havel repeated his condemnation over subsequent months and an official apology for the crimes and injustices committed during the expulsions was handed to President Weizsäcker during his state visit to Prague on 15 March 1990 (the 51st anniversary of the German invasion of Czechoslovakia).

By this time, however, it had become clear that, in the view of the Bavarian government and the SdL, goodwill and conciliation entailed acceptance of the Sudeten-German Homeland Association's demands. By December 1989 Prime Minister Max Streibl had already called on the new government in Prague to apologize to the Sudeten Germans and to start negotiations with the SdL about future Czechoslovak–German relations.[17] The Czechoslovak ambassador to Germany did indeed attend the 1990 annual Sudeten-German Whitsunday meeting in Munich, where Association Chairman Franz Neubauer thanked Havel for his rejection of the theory of collective guilt and his condemnation of the expulsion; this aside, Neubauer reiterated the association's traditional demands for restitution and the right to resettle in the former *Heimat*. Other Sudeten spokesmen were more strident, demanding unlimited sovereignty for Sudeten Germans in their homeland[18] and rejecting 'any claims on the Sudetenland by a Czechoslovak state'.[19] Such policy statements did not assist the re-establishment of cordial relations between Czechs and Germans. With the large majority of the Czech population still maintaining that the expulsion of the German population after the war was justified,[20] Havel's apology had been a brave step; the media releases coming out of Bavaria soon had the Czechoslovak media up in arms again. Claims that 'revanchism' was in the air and that the Sudeten Germans were stabbing the newly won democracy in the back made the front pages, as they had done in the past, and at the end of 1990 only three political parties, the Slovak Christian Democratic Movement, the Slovak Democratic Party and the Beer Lovers' Party, supported President Havel's apology.[21]

German foreign policy, however, was not made in Munich, but in Bonn and, quarrels over Sudeten-German issues aside, the governments of both states continued to work towards a bilateral agreement. In February 1990 Foreign Ministers Jiri Dienstbier and Hans-Dieter Genscher set up the Czech–German commission of historians to investigate relations between the two peoples throughout modern history and to seek explanations for events of the catastrophic decade from the mid-1930s to the mid-1940s. In April 1991 Genscher and Dienstbier issued a list of ten mutual foreign policy priorities, the so-called 'Prague Theses'. The ten points were aimed at establishing a Friendship Treaty that would break the 'vicious circle of injustice and counter-injustice' and turn attention towards the future.[22] 'The states of Central and Eastern Europe should find their stability and place in Europe within the framework of pan-European institutions and on the basis of bilateral agreements'.[23] This future Europe was not to be subjugated to the 'dictates of individual interest groups':[24]

The Bonn government understood that future Czechoslovak membership in the EU would render concepts such as *Recht auf Heimat* superfluous, because purchasing property and settling in Bohemia should be as easy as doing so in Denmark, England and Bavaria. Thus, the government's approach to the Sudeten Germans' demands was simply to bracket restitution and resettlement issues from the Friendship Treaty and to let these issues solve themselves in the future within the multilateral framework of European institutions.[25]

A first draft of the envisaged Friendship Treaty was initialed by the two foreign ministers on 7 October 1991, but pressure from the CSU delayed the official signing into the new year; in the end Chancellor Kohl announced that he would not tolerate any further bickering within the coalition government and that the treaty would be signed in February without alteration.[26] Hence President Havel and Chancellor Kohl officially signed the Czechoslovak–German Treaty on Good Neighbourly Relations and Friendly Cooperation on 27 February 1992 in Prague. The treaty was then ratified by the Czechoslovak Federal Assembly on 22 April, by the *Bundestag* on 20 May and the *Bundesrat* (the Chamber of Germany's Federal States) on 26 June. Of the 16 German states, only Bavaria voted against the treaty. The initial two articles of the treaty confirmed that relations between the two states were based on respect for human rights, basic freedom, democracy and the rule of law, as well as peace, security and cooperation in Europe at large. Article Three stated that neither side had any claim to territory of the other, that there was mutual respect for each other's borders and that each state would respect the other's sovereignty and territorial integrity. Subsequent articles addressed economic development and improved co-operation at a regional level. Article Ten formally expressed Germany's support for Czechoslovakia's entry into the European Union.[27] Issues not addressed were compensation for Nazi war crimes and the Sudeten-German question. Not surprisingly, SdL Chairman Neubauer announced on 25 May that the treaty was 'not only a slap in the face for the 3.5 million Sudeten Germans who were robbed and expelled after the war, but also a dangerous precedent for all those pursuing similar plans for expulsion in Croatia, Serbia, Bosnia and elsewhere'.[28] This statement, together with Bavaria's defiant vote against the treaty in the *Bundesrat*, so angered the Czechoslovak government that Prime Minister Petr Pitthart cancelled his scheduled visit to a symposium in Bavaria on regional participation.[29] On 1 January 1993, when Czechs and Slovaks again took separate paths and formed two distinct nations, dialogue between the Czech Republic and Germany went from bad to worse. The two new states agreed to maintain all treaties, but legally new signatures were required. Therefore, when the Czech Republic was again to sign a treaty of friendship and good neighbourliness, sections of the political communities on both the Czech and German sides took the opportunity to seek redress for omissions they felt had been made from the 1992 treaty.

In February 1993, the German foreign minister in the Kohl government, Klaus Kinkel, visited Prague. During his visit Kinkel raised the issue of compensation for Czech victims of Nazism. In reply his Czech counterpart Josef Zieleniec indicated that he supported compensation through the establishment of a foundation. Prime Minister Václav Klaus joined the discussion, stating that although the Czech Republic was ready for dialogue, any Sudeten-German claims were unacceptable to his government. This drew a reciprocal statement from the Sudeten-German Homeland Association, that compensation for Czech victims of Nazism should be rejected. At the Sudeten-German Whitsunday gathering in Munich in 1993, the Bavarian Premier Edmund Stoiber again called on the Czech government to include the Sudeten Germans in bilateral talks. At this stage the response from Prague was positive, with the ruling coalition agreeing to the establishment of a working group to commence dialogue with the SdL. At a meeting with Chancellor Kohl on 1 June 1993, Havel suggested the formation of a Czech parliamentary delegation to negotiate with the SdL. This was followed by several weeks of disagreement and lack of progress on the establishment of such an initial working party. In a 30 June letter to Stoiber, Prime Minister Klaus regretted that statements made at the last Whitsunday meeting would negatively affect further plans. He also stressed that it was unacceptable that the construction of an oil pipeline to link Ingolstadt in Bavaria with central Bohemia was conditional on a change in the Czech government's attitude towards the SdL. In September 1993, Chancellor Kohl joined the chorus demanding that the Czech Republic's admission to the EU be jeopardized if it failed to include the Sudeten Germans in talks. No solution was reached by the end of 1993 and in 1994 disagreement over the question of compensation for Czech victims of Nazism added to the stalemate. A sum of DM 34.5 million from the German government was to be distributed among victims, but Klaus insisted on referring to this money as a humanitarian gesture rather than compensation. At the 1994 Whitsunday Congress, CSU representatives from the Federal German and the Bavarian governments again called for the abolition of the Beneš decrees, while at the same time continuing to support the establishment of dialogue with the Czech government. From Prague there were hostile reactions to these speeches and the reconciliation process was hampered, although Czech Foreign Minister Josef Zielenic suggested for the first time that the Czech–German past remained open from legal and political points of view.[30]

A low point was reached in November 1994, when the SdL tried to internationalize the Sudeten-German question by linking Czech entry to the European Union with its resolution. Again it was Havel who tried to break the deadlock. On 17 February 1995 he gave the first in a series of lectures at the Charles University, seeking ways for Czechs and Germans to develop a new understanding. Havel recalled the two people's centuries of coexistence, which ended so violently with the Nazi occupation of Bohemia and Moravia and the subsequent expulsion of three million Germans from Czechoslovakia. He admonished both Czechs and Germans to come to terms with the past and put an end to mutual recriminations:

> if we, that is, the Czechs, are able to recognize our share of responsibility for the end of the Czech–German coexistence in the Czech lands, we have to say, for the sake of truth, that we let ourselves become infected by the insidious view of the ethnic concept of guilt and punishment, but that it was not us who brought that view, at least not in its modern destructive form, into this country.[31]

Both sides agreed to work out a joint parliamentary declaration. To minimize obstacles, the nature and content of negotiations were to be kept secret and it was hoped that the declaration would be completed by the end of 1995. But progress was slow and difficult. On 8 March the Czech Constitutional Court rejected a proposal to abolish Beneš's decree on the confiscation of enemy property, leading to a renewed declaration on the part of SdL Chairman Neubauer that Czech membership of the EU was unacceptable. This argument was repeated by Otto Habsburg, son of the last Austro-Hungarian emperor and a CSU member of the European Parliament, in an interview with the Czech newspaper *Právo*.[32] Throughout the year there was a bitter battle of words, with accusations of nationalism over the role of German musician Gerd Albrecht as Chief Conductor of the Czech Philharmonic. There was some improvement in Czech–German relations in the summer months, when the cities of Berlin and Prague signed a sister city agreement, pledging political, economic and cultural cooperation. There were also proposals by the opposition parties in the Bundestag, the SPD and Alliance 90/Greens, for recognition without preconditions of Czech victims of Nazism's claims for compensation. On 30 October, President Havel and his German counterpart Roman Herzog attended a session of the joint Czech–German Historians' Commission in Dresden. Havel was evidently impressed that the historians were working in a friendly atmosphere and had found 'a common language'.[33] The two presidents also announced the establishment of annual Czech–German youth meetings and of a German library in Reichenberg, which would include Sudeten-German literature. This was to be built on the site of a synagogue razed to the ground by the Nazis during *Kristallnacht* in 1938.

By the end of 1995, completion of the joint parliamentary declaration was as distant as ever. This led a group of 95 Czech intellectuals to demand from the government a condemnation of the expulsion and an admission of their 'former fellow citizens' to the negotiating table. This view, however, was shared by only a small percentage of the Czech population. Only 7 per cent of people interviewed for a public opinion poll said they would vote for a party that intended to apologize to the Germans for the expulsion.[34] Confrontation between supporters and opponents of the SdL reached a new high – or low – during the 25–6 May 1996 Sudeten-German Whitsunday meeting in Nuremberg, when Bavarian Premier Edmund Stoiber spelt out four fundamental conditions for CSU approval of the declaration – establishment of direct dialogue between the Czech government and the Sudeten Germans, condemnation of the post-war expulsion as an iniquity, recognition of Sudeten-Germans' right to homeland and dissociation from expulsion-related laws and decrees.[35] CSU Chairman and Federal Finance Minister Theo Waigel told the meeting that Prague 'should confess the crime' and call it by its right name. 'It was an expulsion', Waigel told the jubilant audience, and a word of regret 'would bring the Czech Republic a step closer to European standards of justice'.[36] These statements were not only rejected by the Klaus government, but also drew a chorus of protest from Germany's liberal media, accusing the Bavarian leaders of unwarranted strong-arm tactics. By the end of 1996 the impasse over terminology was finally breached. As the Czech term *Vyhnání* was as unacceptable to the Czechs as was the word *Odsun* to the Sudeten Germans, the word finally chosen for the joint declaration was *Vyhánění*, 'expelling' rather than 'expulsion', a less accusatory term to the Czechs.[37] Thus, with all obstacles finally cleared, Chancellor Kohl and Czech Prime Minister Klaus signed the 'Czech–German Declaration on Mutual Relations and their Future Development'. A fine piece of international statesmanship that well deserved the praise and prestigious prize referred to at the beginning of this book, the key points are worth quoting:

> The governments of the Czech Republic and the Federal Republic of Germany, mindful of the Treaty between the Czech and Slovak

Federative Republic and the Federal Republic of Germany on good neighborliness and friendly cooperation made on 27 February 1992, in which the Czechs and Germans offered each other their hands, appreciative of the long history of fruitful and peaceful coexistence of Czechs and Germans, during which time a rich cultural heritage was formed and still endures, aware that the Federal Republic of Germany fully supports the acceptance of the Czech Republic into the European Union and NATO, in the conviction that it is in the common interest, recognizing the need for trust and openness in bilateral relations as a condition for reconciliation that is permanent and aimed towards the future, jointly declare:

I

Both sides are aware of their commitment and responsibility in further developing Czech–German relations in the spirit of good neighborliness and partnership and thus contributing to the creation of a uniting Europe. The Czech Republic and the Federal Republic of Germany today share common democratic values, respect human rights, basic freedoms and norms of international law, and are dedicated to the principles of a legal state and a policy of peace. On this basis they are resolved to work together in a friendly and close manner in all areas important to the development of relations. Both sides are also aware that the joint path to the future requires a clear statement about the past, and that in this, cause and effect in the course of events cannot be overlooked.

II

The German side admits Germany's responsibility for its role in the historical development that led to the Munich Agreement of 1938, to the flight and expelling of people from the Czechoslovak border areas, and to the breakup and occupation of the Czechoslovak Republic. It regrets the suffering and wrongs inflicted on the Czech people by the National Socialist crimes of the Germans. The German side pays homage to the victims of violence perpetrated by the National Socialist government and honors those who put up resistance to this violence. The German side is also aware that the National Socialist policy of violence towards the Czech people helped prepare the ground for the postwar flight, expelling and forced resettlement.

Point Three expresses the Czech side's regret, referred to above,[38] Point Four the intention of both sides not to burden their relations with political and legal questions arising from the past. Point Five confirms the Treaty on Good Neighbourliness and Friendly Cooperation of 27 February 1992. Six deals with economic matters, Seven with the establishment of a Czech–German fund for the future. To conclude with Point Eight,

> Both sides agree that the historical development of relations between Czechs and Germans, especially in the first half of the 20th century, requires joint examination, and therefore undertake to continue the hitherto successful work of the Czech–German Committee of Historians. Both sides also consider the maintenance and care of the cultural heritage which links Czech and Germans to be an important contribution to the building of bridges to the future. Both sides will arrange for the establishment of a Czech–German discussion forum, which will be financed mainly from the Czech–German Fund for the Future and which, under the aegis of both governments and with the participation of all circles with an interest in close and good Czech–German partnership, will cultivate Czech–German dialogue.

The Bundestag passed the Czech–German declaration on 30 January 1997 with an overwhelming majority. Of the 621 delegates present when the vote was taken, 578 voted in favour of the declaration, 22 against and 23 abstained from voting.[39] Most votes against came from the CSU, yet the majority of CSU members supported the resolution. The Czech Chamber of Deputies passed the declaration of 14 February, with 131 of the Lower House's 200 deputies voting in favour. The joint parliamentary declaration was bitterly attacked by the SdL, the BdV and all other Homeland Associations. A year later, the Federal Election returned a Red–Green coalition; among the first steps taken by the newly appointed Chancellor Gerhard Schröder was the assurance of his Czech counterpart Miloš Zeman, also a Social Democrat, who had succeeded Klaus at the end of 1997, that the expellee organizations' demands would no longer impede Germany's foreign policies. Both premiers also declared that neither government would burden bilateral relations with property issues arising from the Second World War.[40] This policy has since been reaffirmed by Schröder and by the foreign minister in his government, Joschka Fischer. During Havel's presidential visit to Berlin on 10 May 2000, he and German President Johannes Rau again declared that the Beneš decrees would not burden Czech–German relations in the future. An attempt on the part of the SdL to challenge this policy by lodging a complaint with the United Nations Human Rights Commission at Geneva has been shelved.

The intransigence of the Sudeten-German Homeland Association has puzzled political analysts for a long time. In the mid-1990s an American observer argued that property restitution was not the real issue dogging Czech–German relations, but rather the Czech government's refusal to ease legal restrictions on the right of foreigners to buy property in the republic; disagreement between the Federal German government and the Bavarian government is said to have arisen over the timing of such legal revisions. 'Whereas Bonn expected Prague to set clear goals in order to achieve, in the future, legal conditions for European integration, Munich demanded the immediate creation of such legal conditions.'[41] However this may be, demands for restitution can scarcely be ruled out as a major motive behind SdL policies. Opinion polls conducted in 1996 found that 85 per cent of Sudeten-German expellees, or their descendants, had 'finished with the subject of Sudetenland'. Asked whether they wanted restitution for lost property, 75 per cent answered 'no'.[42] This still leaves a fair number of people who do not regard the matter as closed, possibly those who lost most in the expulsion. There are no suggestions that the new century might see a significant change in SdL policies on the restitution issue. Immediately after his election as successor to SdL Chairman Neubauer in February 2000, the President of the Bavarian Diet, Johann Böhm, announced that he would take the Federal Government to court over Chancellor Schröder's statement of March 1999 that restitution questions between Germany and the Czech Republic were closed. At the same time, Sudeten Germans living in the United States were said to be preparing for class action under United States law against insurance companies that profited from the collective expropriation of the Sudeten Germans.[43]

The battle for recognition of grievances is not confined to the political level. Since its inception in 1990, the joint Czech–German Historians' Commission has published six books, as well as a summary of its findings[44] on the chief themes of the two countries' difficult recent past. Most contributions are of excellent academic quality and although not all points of contention have been cleared up – nor could this be expected, a great deal of progress has been made. Gone is the antagonism and the relentless subjectivity that marked so many previous historical works; a clearer and much more objective picture of Czech and German modern history is becoming visible. Because many of the arguments advanced in these publications run counter to the SdL's historical accounts, it did not take long for writers representing the Homeland Association to go on the offensive again. In particular the downward correction of the number of people who perished during or as a direct result of the expulsion from the earlier 250 000 or so to about a tenth of this figure angered SdL historians, who countered by raising the death toll to 400 000.[45] At the same time the number of Czech people expelled from the Sudetenland after its incorporation into the Reich was reduced to 40 families.[46] With no new evidence to support these claims in any way, such allegations are not likely to be taken seriously.

Statements made in the mid-1990s by the then UN High Commissioner José Ayala Lasso, that the right not to be expelled from one's homeland was a fundamental human right, and a draft declaration of the UN Commission on Human Rights, made in 1997, that every person has the right to return 'voluntarily and in safety and dignity, to the country of origin' and moreover 'to adequate remedies, including restoration of properties of which they were deprived ... as a result of population transfers', are geared to lead to a more peaceful and harmonious twenty-first century than the preceding one was. They do not constitute a legal basis to overturn or reverse international decisions made more than half a century ago on the conclusion of the most devastating war in human history. For this reason it might be more useful for the professional Sudeten-German expellee politicians to turn their considerable skills towards a more co-operative approach. The chairman of the Upper Silesian Homeland Association, Herbert Hupka, for example, during the 1970s and 80s a leading warrior against the *Verzichtler*,[47] made a major commitment to the economic reconstruction of his former hometown Ratibor, which gratefully awarded him with an Honorary Medal. Since the mid-1990s, Hupka and other representatives of the expellees from Poland have been received at the highest level in this country. Böhm's comment at the 2000 Whitsunday gathering that demands for territorial autonomy were not likely to succeed and that they could not be implemented in a meaningful way even if successful, but that personal autonomy for anyone wishing to return was still an important aim, does suggest that a more realistic course on the part of the SdL might not be too far away after all.

Since the collapse of the Eastern Bloc, Germany is very much in a league of its own in Europe, west of the former Soviet Union. In terms of population it is by far the largest in Europe, in terms of economic strength second in the world only to the United States. Czechoslovakia, on the other hand, is no more, and with a population of around ten million, the Czech Republic has joined the ranks of the smaller European states. Nevertheless, both the Kohl and Schröder governments have treated relations with their southeastern neighbour with sensitivity and tact and there is no reason to believe that this policy will change in the future, that is, that Bonn will demand that Czech entry into the EU be conditional on meeting demands of the SdL. Opposition here might come from Austria, where Jörg Haider's neo-right Freedom Party forms part of the government. Haider's support for the Sudeten-German Homeland Association has occasionally been reported; still, few observers believe that the Austrian government would seriously block Czech entry. In any case the spectre of exclusion from the EU is not likely to haunt either the Czech government or the population. The Czech government has stated repeatedly that the Beneš decrees are no longer valid. However, just as German governments have rejected demands to declare the Munich Treaty of September 1938 *ex tunc* (because of the theoretical risk of massive Czechoslovak compensation demands for the damage inflicted upon the country during the years of Nazi occupation), Czech governments cannot be expected to declare the Beneš decrees invalid *ab initio*, as this would open the gates to a flood of SdL demands.

Economically the Czech Republic has managed to build up a steady record since the Velvet Revolution. For all its misdemeanors, the Communist government did not leave its successors a mountain of debts, which made it possible to pursue policies that circumvented the massive inflation and spiraling unemployment characteristic of all former socialist countries in the early 1990s. After a period of economic decline between 1989 and 1993 (amounting to 17 per cent), the republic achieved growth rates of around 4 per cent in the mid-1990s. There was a renewed decline in 1997 when a series of scandals unsettled the republic's economic and political stability. Allegations of embezzlement involving leading politicians, including Klaus, forced the latter from his position as premier in November 1997, although charges against him could not be substantiated. There were also irregularities with donations to political parties.[48] Since then positive growth has again been attained, with the 2002 financial year expecting a figure of about 3 per cent. Unemployment was comparatively low throughout the 1990s – between 4 and 6 per cent, but reached about 8 per cent by the turn of the century. As the Czech economy leads those of the EU applicants as far as GDP and Foreign Direct Investment are concerned, it is not surprising that the republic is being ranked as 'the least problematic of the prospective entrants in economic and political terms, being highly industrialized, with only a relatively small agricultural sector, and relatively wealthy'.[49] (The agricultural sector accounts for only 12 per cent of the Czech economy, while corresponding figures are 19 per cent for Hungary and 21 per cent for Poland.)

In 2000, 70 per cent of all foreign trade was with the EU,[50] Germany being the Czechs' main trading partner. Buoyed by its reputation as the most successful free market economy among the post-communist countries,[51] the Czech Republic conducts its affairs with the Brussels EU negotiators in a confident manner. The Czechs achieved a considerable reduction in the 'opt out' time preceding new member states' free access to the European Union's labour market. Václav Klaus, minister for finance from 1989 to 1992, prime minister from 1992 to 1997 and leader of the ODS, has been decidedly critical of attempts to rush the Czech Republic into the EU. On the other side of the political spectrum, one of the successor parties to the former Communist Party of Czechoslovakia, the Communist Party of Bohemia and Moravia, which in the late 1990s took the lead in political opinion polls,[52] has also been reticent on the issue of EU membership. The Communists propose a plebiscite approval as a condition for entry. Most Czech people remain in favour of entry, but protracted negotiations and rigid demands have cooled earlier enthusiasm. Average wages and consumer costs in the Czech Republic are far lower than those in the EU and many Czechs fear that it will be prices that rise first on the republic's way to reaching EU standards. Prices for houses, property and land are still a fraction of those in EU member states, in particular in many of the former German-speaking parts of the Bohemian lands. In 1991 questionnaires conducted in Czech border regions found that 45 per cent of those surveyed did not believe that Sudeten Germans wanted to return in large numbers. The shrill sounds of the SdL's professional expellees meant that four years later only one-fifth of those surveyed did not expect a larger influx of Sudeten Germans.[53] Shortly before the turn of the century, news circulated that a poll conducted in Germany found that 400 000 Sudeten Germans intended to take advantage of the cheap land prices in the Czech Republic – said to be one-tenth of those in Germany – and would wish to return to family homes and towns.[54] The real figure would, of course, not be anywhere near 400 000, but stories like this readily cause concern on the Czech side of the border.

To avoid wealthy westerners snapping up vast swathes of the country, the Czech government has requested a derogation period of seven years, while the EU prefers a two-year 'opt out' period; negotiations are still proceeding. Previous admission of new member states has shown that no lengthy derogation period is necessary; an unrestricted real estate market constituting an important part of the free market economy, the earlier restrictions are lifted the better.

With the Nice summit having virtually given the green light to the first round of admissions from the former socialist bloc, the Czech Republic will become part of the EU by 2004,[55] a valuable addition given the Czechs' proud history of cultural and political tradition. This will mean that, in addition to those not expelled after the Second World War, new Germans will again arrive in the Bohemian lands. Some of the expelled Germans or their descendants will indeed return to the old *Heimat*, while other Germans or Austrians will settle here, attracted by the beauty of the landscape, by quiet unspoiled nature or, indeed, by low land prices. All this will contribute to the creation of the multicultural and transnational community a united Europe is setting out to achieve. After all the animosity, the horror and bloodshed that occurred between 1914 and 1945, French and Germans, Danes and Germans, Dutch and Germans, Austrians and Italians have grown together and have learned to live together harmoniously in western Europe in the second half of the last century. There is no reason to doubt that such a spirit of good-will and reconciliation will also be achieved in Germany's relations with her eastern neighbours in this new century.

Notes

Introduction

1 There were occasional geographical references to this region as *'Sudetenland'* or *'Sudetengebiet'* before 1918, but these were rare.
2 R. Ohlbaum, *Baierns vierter Stamm, die Sudetendeutschen: Herkunft, Neubeginn, Persönlichkeiten* (Munich: Aufstieg-Verlag, 1980) pp. 13–4.

1 The Lands of the Weceslav Crown

1 P. Moraw, 'Das Mittelalter' in F. Prinz, *Deutsche Geschichte im Osten Europas. Böhmen und Mähren* (Berlin: Siedler Verlag, 1993) p. 26.
2 Ibid.
3 F. Seibt, *Deutschland und die Tschechen. Geschichte einer Nachbarschaft in der Mitte Europas* (Munich: Piper, 1993) pp. 57–8.
4 F. P. Habel, *Die Sudetendeutschen* (Munich: Herbig, 1992) p. 19.
5 Seibt, p. 60; Moraw, pp. 46–7.
6 Moraw, p. 115.
7 G. Barraclough, *The Origins of Modern Germany* (Oxford: Basil Blackwell, 1966) pp. 341–2.
8 Ibid., p. 356.
9 Weceslav was King of Germany from his father's death until 1400, when rival factions managed to dispose of him; Sigismund, his half-brother took up the office again in 1410 and was also crowned Emperor, Sigismund II, in 1433. Weceslav remained King of Bohemia until his death in 1419; because of the Hussite wars Sigismund was not able to take full posession of his hereditary lands until 1436 (see pp. 6–7).
10 The more well-known cases include the Cathars in the tenth century. Joachim of Fiore advocated millenarian ideas in the twelfth century in the Calabrian region; around the same time the Albigenses were accused of heresy in the Provence region of France. The origins of Walldensian in Piedmont and the surrounding Swiss Alps also date to the twelfth century.
11 Seibt pp. 148–9 firmly supports the traditional claim; for a less committed approach Moraw (p. 156) claims that there is no conclusive evidence on this topic.
12 The Fourth Lateran Council confirmed the doctrine of transubstantiation, i.e. during the communion the bread and the wine is transformed into the body and blood of Christ. In the Catholic church the community takes the bread but only the priest can perform the function of drinking the wine.
13 The Council of Basle (1431–49) followed the Council of Trent. Again the problems of heresy and reform were the chief items on the agenda.
14 In the Prague *Kompaktat* lay communion was tolerated on a regional basis in some parts of the realm but elsewhere the traditional practice was restored.

The Pope refused to accept this agreement and revoked the *Kompaktat* in 1462.

15 Seibt, p. 155.
16 For the first position: Moraw pp. 161–5; on the role played by Bohemia's Germans: Seibt, pp. 155–62.
17 Alliance of protestant German princes formed in 1538 at the town of Schmalkalden to uphold Lutheran principles and to provide resistance against the Emperor Charles V.
18 Seibt, pp. 174–5.
19 Note e.g. E. Wiskemann, *Czechs and Germans* (Oxford: Oxford University Press, 1938) p. 10; H. Seton-Watson, *Eastern Europe between the Wars 1918–1941* (New York: Harper and Row, 1967) p. 28: R. A. Kann, *A History of the Habsburg Empire 1526–1918* (Berkeley, CA: University of California Press, 1975) p. 51.
20 For a recent criticism: I. Cornejová, 'Wie finster war die "Finsternis"', in ' "Unsere Geschichte": Die tschechisch-deutsche Vergangenheit als Interpretationsproblem', *Bohemia*, **35** (1994) 384–7.
21 See pp. 13–14.
22 E. Winter, *Barock, Absolutismus und Aufklärung in der Donau-Monarchie* (Vienna: Europa Verlag, 1971) pp. 33–56, 109–32, 195–218; Kann, pp. 384–8, Prinz, pp. 267–94.
23 Seibt, p. 185.
24 For a summary: M. S. Anderson, *Europe in the Eighteenth Century 1713–1783* (London: Longmans, 1963) pp. 324–5.
25 Ibid. p. 125.
26 H. E. Strakosch, *Austria. An Imperial Destiny* (Adelaide: Rigby, 1973) p. 38.
27 W. Menzel, *Die nationale Entwicklung in Böhmen, Mähren und Schlesien. Von der Aufklärung bis zur Revolution von 1848* (Nuremberg: Helmut Preußler Verlag, 1985) pp. 55–84.
28 R. W. Seton-Watson, *A History of the Czechs and Slovaks* (London: Hutchinson, 1943) p. 177.
29 J. Kořalka, 'Nationsbildung und nationale Identität der Deutschen, Oesterreicher, Tschechen und Slowaken um die Mitte des 19. Jahrhunderts', in H. Mommsen and J. Kořalka (eds), *Ungleiche Nachbarn. Demokratische und nationale Emanzipation bei Deutschen, Tschechen und Slowaken (1815–1914)* (Essen: Klartext, 1993) p. 47.
30 Ibid.
31 B. R. Anderson, *Imagined Communities: reflections on the origin and spread of nationalism* (London: Verso, 1983) p. 60; this was considerably less than the number of persons who actually spoke French at the beginning of the French nation in 1789, which was estimated at 50 per cent (although only 12–13 per cent were said to have spoken French 'correctly' (ibid.)
32 Prinz, p. 346.
33 H. Slapnicka, 'Die Ohnmacht des Parlamentarismus gegüber der nationalistischen Übermacht', in F. Seibt (ed.), *Die Chancen der Verständigung. Absichten und Ansätze zu übernationaler Zusammenarbeit in den böhmischen Ländern 1848–1918* (Munich: R. Oldenbourg, 1987) pp. 151–65.
34 Prinz, p. 351, 355; J. Křen, 'Nationale Selbstbehauptung im Vielvölkerstaat: Politische Konzeption des tschechischen Nationalismus 1890–1938', in

J. Křen, V. Kural and D. Brandes, *Integration oder Ausgrenzung. Tschechen und Deutsche 1890–1945* (Bremen: Donat & Temmen, 1986) p. 16, n. 3, pp. 57–8. On von Schönerer, see pp. 46–7.

35 K. E. Franzen, *Der Prager Vertrag vom 11. Dezember 1973 im Sudetendeutschen Urteil* (Cologne: self published MA thesis, 1995) p. 1.

36 Z. A. B. Zeman, *The Making and Breaking of Communist Europe* (Oxford: Basil Blackwell, 1991) pp. 35–6; for a brief summary of industrialization in the Bohemian lands note N. M. Wingfield, *Minority Politics in a Multinational State. The German Social Democratic Party, 1918–1938* (New York: Columbia University Press, 1989) pp. 3–5.

37 For a critical analysis of their interpretations of nationalism note H. Mommsen, 'Die mitteleuropäische Sozialdemokratie im Konflikt zwischen Internationalismus und nationaler Loyalität', in Mommsen and Kořalka, pp. 91–106.

38 E.g. M. Scharrer, *Die Spaltung der deutschen Arbeiterbewegung* (Stuttgart: Cordeliers, 1983) pp. 14–50.

39 Mommsen, pp. 100–06.

40 J. Galandauer, 'Tschechische Sozialdemokraten zwischen Internationalismus und Nationalismus (1889–1914)' in Mommsen/Kořalka, pp. 113–17.

41 Prinz, pp. 331–2, Zeman, *Making and Breaking*, pp. 27–41, G. B. Cohan, *The Politics of Ethnic Survival: Germans in Pragues 1861–1914* (Princeton: Princeton University Press, 1981) pp. 153–5.

42 Radical Czech nationalist parties recieved only 4 out of 62 seats; radical German nationalist 20 out of 55: J. Křen, 'Nationale Selbstbehauptung' p. 27; for the Badeni crisis see p. 22.

43 E. Kovaccs, 'Die katholische Kirche im Spannungsfeld von Nationalismus und Patriotismus zwischen 1848 und 1918', in Seibt, *Chancen*, p. 59.

44 Note e.g. G. Otruba, 'Das Kapital. Zusammenarbeit aus Sachzwang anstelle sachfremder Integration?', ibid. pp. 63–86.

45 P. Heumoos, 'Interessensolidarität gegen Nationalgemeinschaft. Deutsche und tschechische Bauern in Böhmen 1848–1918', ibid. pp. 87–100; and 'Mythos, Aufklärung, Identität' in "Unsere Geschichte": Die tschechisch–deutsche Vergangenheit als Interpretationsproblem', *Bohemia*, **35** (1994) 415–21.

46 R. Luft, 'Die Mittelpartei des mährischen Großgrundbesitzes 1879–1918. Zur Problematik des Ausgleichs in Mähre und Böhmen', in Seibt, *Chancen*, pp. 187–244.

47 L. Höbelt, 'Deutschösterreich und die Sudetendeutschen', in H. Lemberg und P. Heumoos, *Das Jahr 1919 in der Tschechoslowakei und in Ostmitteleuropa* (Munich: Oldenbourg, 1989) p. 166.

48 Slapnicka, pp. 160–74.

49 Luft, pp. 230–36.

50 Among others: A. J. P. Taylor, *The Habsburg Monarchy 1809–1918* (London: Hamish Hamilton, 1972) pp. 228–32, Kann, pp. 517–20, V. S. Mamatey, 'The Establishment of the Republic', in V. S. Mamatey and R. Luža, *A History of the Czechoslovak Republic 1918–1948* (Princeton: Princeton University Press, 1973) pp. 23–5, C. A. Macartney, *The Habsburg Empire 1790–1918* (London: Weidenfeld and Nicholson, 1968) pp. 747–809.

51 D. Blackbourne and G. Eley, *The Peculiarities of German History. Bourgeois Society and Politics in Nineteenth Century Germany* (Oxford: Oxford University

Press, 1984); for a summary of the debate: R. J Evans, *Rethinking German History. Nineteenth Century Germany and the Origins of the Third Reich* (London: Allen and Unwin, 1987) pp. 93–120.

52 W. Doyle, *The Old European Order 1660–1800* (Oxford: Oxford University Press, 1978) pp. 357–78.

53 Note e.g. R. Magraw, 'Socialism, Syndicalism and French Labour before 1914', in D. Geary (ed.) *Labour and Socialist Movements in Europe before 1914* (Oxford: Berg, 1989) pp. 49–100.

54 For a stimulating discussion: J. Remak, 'The healthy invalid: how doomed was the Habsburg Empire?', *Journal of Modern History*, **41** (1969) 127–43.

55 However distasteful Magyarization might have been for Slavonic nationalists, it did enjoy considerable support among the Slovaks (see pp. 35–6). And the Magyar oligarchy had to compromise with nationalities that managed to find cohesion and politically organize themselves, like the Croatians (Z. A. B. Zeman, *The Break-Up of the Habsburg Empire 1914–1918*, (London: Oxford University Press, 1961) p. 250.

56 Křen, 'Nationale Selbstbehauptung', pp. 19–38, p. 58, n. 5.

57 Zeman, *Break-Up*, p. 20.

58 R. Luža, *The Transfer of the Sudeten Germans. A Study of Czech–German relations 1933–1962* (London: Routledge and Kegan Paul, 1964) pp. 6–10.

59 Zeman, *Break-Up*, pp. 250ff, *Making and Breaking*, pp. 34ff.

2 Czechoslovakia

1 Křen, 'Nationale Selbstbehauptung', p. 38.

2 Cited in Zeman, *Break-Up*, pp. 43–4.

3 Ibid., p. 44.

4 Ibid.

5 See Friedrich Naumann's *Mitteleuropa*, published February 1915, in T. Nipperdey (ed.), *Friedrich Naumanns Werke*, vol. 4, *Schriften zum Parteiwesen und zum Mitteleuropaproblem* (Cologne: Westdeutscher Verlag, 1964) pp. 485–767.

6 The National Socialists were a non-Marxist workers' and middle-class party led by Vacláv Klofáč, like Kramář an ardent Russophile; in the pre-war years this party was distinguished by its strong anti-militarism.

7 On Thomas Masaryk's political background, see Z. A. B. Zeman, *The Masaryks. The Making of Czechoslovakia* (London: I. B. Tauris & Co, 1990) pp. 36–59.

8 Testing 'western opinion' primarily meant establishing contact and arranging meetings with the editor of *The Times* newspaper, Wickham Steed, and the historian Robert Seton-Watson, both convinced and leading advocates of an end to the Habsburg Empire. (Zeman, *Break-Up*, pp. 77–81).

9 Mamatey, 'The Establishment of the Republic', p. 14. According to Mamatey, Štefanik was a scientist, astronomer, meteorologist, traveller, and, since the war, an officer in the French airforce (p. 13).

10 Following an unconvincing peace offer made on 1 December 1916 by the German Chancellor Bethmann-Hollweg, the US president, six days later, addressed an enquiry to all war faring nations as to their aims in pursuing the war.

11   Zeman, *Break-Up*, p. 117.
12   Ibid., pp. 126–7.
13   Ibid., pp. 132–3.
14   The United States had already declared war against Germany on 6 April 1917.
15   Zeman, *Break-Up*, p. 178.
16   For a summary of Wilson's position, see M. Trachtenberg, 'Versailles after Sixty Years', *Journal of Contemporary History*, **17** (1982) 487–506.
17   Zeman, *Break-Up*, p. 215.
18   D. Newton, *British Policy and the Weimar Republic, 1918–1919*, (Oxford: Clarendon Press, 1997) p. 140.
19   Trachtenberg, p. 489.
20   Newton, pp. 147–58.
21   Ibid., p. 185.
22   P. Krüger, 'Die Friedensordnung von 1919 und die Entstehung neuer Staaten in Ostmitteleuropa', in H. Lemberg and P. Heumoos, *Das Jahr 1919 in der Tschechoslowakei und in Ostmitteleuropa* (Munich: Oldenbourg, 1993) p. 109.
23   Zeman, *Break-Up*, ch. vii, 'The Life of Edvard Beneš, 1884–1948' (Oxford: Clarendon Press, 1997) p. 29.
24   Zeman, *Break-Up*, p. 192.
25   Ibid., p. 215.
26   United States Foreign Relations (*USFR*), 1918, supplement 1, vol. 1, p. 824, cited in Zeman, *Break-up*, p. 215.
27   J. K. Hoensch, 'Tschechoslowakismus oder Autonomie. Die Auseinandersetzung um die Eingliederung der Slowakei in die Tschechoslowakische Republik', in Lemberg and Heumoos, *Das Jahr 1919*, p. 131.
28   Ibid., p. 130.
29   Hoensch, 'Tschechoslowakismus', pp. 144–57; J. Felak, 'Slovak Considerations of the Slovak Question: The Ludak, Agrarian, Socialist and Communist Views on Interwar Czechoslovakia', in J. Morison, *The Czech and Slovak Experience* (New York: St. Martin's Press – now Palgrave Macmillan, 1991) pp. 136–62.
30   Throughout the country there had been demonstrations on this day against the Prague government's refusal to let German-speaking people in Bohemia and Moravia participate in the Austrian election; in some towns Czech soldiers and policemen resorted to force. Czech historians claim that this was brought about by attacks on Czech army barracks (Luža, *Transfer*, p. 34). Fifty-four of the victims were Germans; two were Czechs (V. Zimmermann, *Die Sudetendeutschen im NS-Staat. Politik und Stimmung der Bevölkerung im Reichsgau Sudetenland* (Essen: Klartext, 1999) p. 35.
31   L. Hoebelt, p. 160.
32   J. W. Brügel, 'The Germans in Pre-War Czechoslovakia, in Czechoslovakia', in Mamatey and Luža, p. 169.
33   Ibid., p. 169; Wingfield, p. 15.
34   Brügel, 'The Germans', p. 179.
35   P. Burian, 'Der Staat und seine neue Verfassung', in Lemberg and Heumoos, *Das Jahr 1919*, pp. 204–14.
36   R. Hilf, *Deutsche und Tschechen* (Opladen: Leske & Budrich, 1986) p. 68.
37   Seibt, *Deutschland*, pp. 280–3; R. Jaworski, *Vorposten oder Minderheit. Der sudetendeutsche Volkstumskampf in den Beziehungen zwischen der Weimarer Republik*

und der ČSR (Stuttgart: Deutsche Verlagsanstalt, 1977) pp. 37–40; Brügel, 'Germans', 185–6.

38 C. Boyer, *Nationale Kontrahenten oder Partner. Studien zu den Beziehungen zwischen Deutschen und Tschechen in der Wirtschaft der* ČSR (Munich: Oldenbourg, 1999); 'Die Vergabe von Staatsaufträgen in der ČSR – ein Vehikel zur Ruinierung der sudetendeutschen Wirtschaft?' in J. K. Hoensch and D. Kováč, *Das Scheitern der Verständigung: Tschechen, Deutsche und Slowaken in der Ersten Republik 1918–1938* (Essen: Klartext, 1994) pp. 81–118.

39 Jaworski, pp. 37–40.

40 Seibt, *Deutschland*, p. 279; Luža, *Transfer*, pp. 42–4; Brügel, 'Germans', pp. 183–4.

41 M. Alexander, *Der Deutsch-Tschechoslowakische Schiedsvertrag von 1925 im Rahmen der Locarno-Vertrage* (Munich: Oldenbourg, 1970) p. 141.

42 Ibid., pp. 141–2; Brügel, 'Germans', pp. 184–5.

43 P. Burian, 'Die nationalen Minderheiten in Parliament und Regierung', in H. Lemberg, *Ostmitteleuropa zwischen den Weltkriegen 1918–1938* (Marburg: Verlag Herder, 1997) pp. 231–5; Seibt, *Deutschland*, pp. 277–95.

44 C. Brenner, 'Die Geschichte der böhmischen Länder und die Geschichte des tschechischen Volkes: eine Geschichte oder zwei?', in *Unsere Geschichte*, p. 378.

45 D. Loeber, 'Die Minderheitenschutzverträge – Entstehung, Inhalt und Wirkung', in Lemberg, *Ostmitteleuropa*, p. 191.

46 J. Kučera, *Minderheit im Nationalstaat. Die Sprachenfrage in den tschechisch-deutschen Beziehungen 1918–1938* (Munich: Oldenbourg, 1999) p. 38, n. 131.

47 J. W. Brügel, *Tschechen und Deutsche* (Munich: Nymphenburger Verlagshandlung, 1974) pp. 43–6. Brügel cites an extensive extract from Masaryk's 22 December 1918 speech: 'As far as the Germans in our states are concerned, our programme has long been known; the area settled by the Germans is our territory and remains so. We have created our state, we have maintained it, we are reconstructing it; I would like to think that our Germans would work with us on this – that would be a better policy than their current doubtful efforts. However, I understand and take into account that they are in a difficult situation; they unfortunately embraced the pan-Germanic anti-Czech expansionist programme all too willingly, they did not understand the world situation, they were carried away by the first appearances of success; our Germans became victims of the false, deceitful Austrianism and the short-sighted Habsburgers. It is psychologically understandable that it is an unpleasant awareness they now bear, of how tragically they were mistaken and that we were and are right. I repeat: we have created our state; through it the position in national law of our Germans is determined, the Germans who originally came into the country as emigrants and colonists. We have full rights to the wealth of our territory, which is imperative for our industry and that of the Germans among us. We do not want to and cannot sacrifice our significant Czech minorities in the so-called German territory. We are also convinced that the economic advantages of our Germans will transfer to and be shared with us. It is up to them to adopt the right attitude to us. They might just like to remember that, together with us, they asked the Emperor to have himself crowned King of Bohemia. I honestly hope we can reach agreement as soon as possible. I concede that it is difficult for us to forget

that our Germans and the Germans in general in Austria accepted the inhuman terrors of the Austrian and Hungarian gang of soldiers without protest. It is very hard to forget that our Germans formed the most fanatical contingent of pan-Germanism. Despite that, we accept them willingly, if they decide on cooperation. Nobody can blame us if we are cautious after so many bitter experiences, but I give my assurance that the minorities in our state will enjoy full national rights and equal citizenship rights. The American Republic preferred to allow itself to get involved in a civil war rather than permit the secession of its South. We will never countenance the secession of our mixed North. In the setting up of a truly democratic self-administration, we have appropriate means of resolving the nationality question. A straight linear division is not possible, due to the extensive and particular mixture, and the problem is not only a national one, but also, and to a great extent, a social one ...' (p. 44).

48 Kučera, p. 53.
49 Ibid., p. 30.
50 United States Department of State, Papers relating to the Foreign Relations of the United States. '1919 The Paris Peace Conference', vol. XIII (Washington, 1947) pp. 811–15, cited in M. Cornwall, 'Edvard Beneš and Czechoslovakia's German Minority, 1918–1943', in Morison, *The Czech and Slovak Experience*, p. 194.
51 Kučera, pp. 57–61.
52 Ibid., p. 309.
53 V. Kural, 'Die Tschechoslowakei als Nationalstaat? Das sudetendeutsche Problem', in J. K. Hoensch and D. Kováč, *Das Scheitern der Verständigung: Tschechen, Deutsche und Slowaken (1918–1938)* (Essen: Klartext, 1993), p. 66; Gemeinsame deutsch–tschechische Historikerkommission: *Konfliktgemeinschaft, Katastrophe, Entspannung. Skizze einer Darstellung der deutsch–tschechischen Geschichte seit dem 19. Jahrhundert* (Bonn: Bundeszentrale für politische Bildung, 1998) p. 16.
54 These were said to be the Agrarians, Social Democrats, National Democrats, National Socialists and the Peoples' Party.
55 See pp. 50–4.
56 J. Steele, *Why Switzerland?* (Cambridge: Cambridge University Press, 1978) pp. 53–97.

3 The *Reichsgau Sudetenland* and the Protectorate of Bohemia and Moravia

1 For a compact analysis, see R. Bessel, 'Why did the Weimar Republic collapse?' in I. Kershaw, *Weimar: Why Did German Democracy Fail?* (New York: St. Martins – now Palgrave Macmillan, 1990) pp. 126–7: 'the incessant din about the injustices heaped upon a defeated Germany, allegedly undefeated on the field and stabbed in the back at home, in effect served to reinforce an idea that things would be normal, if only the external burdens imposed by the Allies could be lifted ... the constant – indeed ritual – complaints about Versailles served to disguise the extent to which the War really had impoverished Germany. Germany was a poorer place not because she had lost the war

but because she had fought it. These illusions were dangerous [because] ... as long as the truth about the War, its causes and consequences, remained excluded from the political discussion, it was impossible to face harsh economic and political realities ... Responsible politics remained a hostage to myths about the First World War, and Weimar democracy eventually had to pay the price.'

2 P. S. Wandycz, 'Foreign Policy of Edvard Beneš, 1919–1938' in Mamatey and Luža, pp. 216–38.

3 Wingfield, pp. 101–5; Seibt, *Deutschland*, pp. 318–19; Zimmermann, pp. 38–9; Gemeinsame Historikerkommission, p. 18.

4 Boyer, *Vergabe, passim*.

5 Quoted in Jaworski, *Die Sudetendeutschen*, p. 35.

6 The term *völkisch* developed in the latter half of the nineteenth century. *Völkisch* ideologies aimed to protect and foster German ethnic and cultural traditions; they were inherently anti-democratic, anti-liberal, anti-semitic and anti-Slav. Organizations and movements that embraced *völkisch* ideas were also prone to xenophobic and aggressive tendencies. Note R. M. Smelser, *The Sudetenproblem 1933–1938. Volkstumspolitik and the Formulation of Nazi Foreign Policy* (Middletown: Wesleyan University Press, 1975) pp. 5–8.

7 C. E. Schorske, *Fin-de-siècle Vienna. Politics and Culture* (New York: Knopff, 1979) p. 128, cited in I. Kershaw, *Hitler. 1889–1936. Hubris* (Penguin: 1998) p. 33.

8 Kershaw, ibid.; see also Luža, *Transfer*, pp. 47–9.

9 There is no synonym for the term *Volkstum* in English; Ronald Smelser's translation 'Germandom' renders the meaning well. Like *völkisch*, it stands for German culture and tradition, which is seen and presented by proponents of *Volkstumspolitik* or *Volkstumskampf* ('struggle for Germandom') as the apex of human civilization.

10 B. Hamann, *Hitlers Wien. Lehrjahre eines Diktators* (Munich: Piper, 1996) p. 389.

11 Cited in Luža, *Transfer*, pp. 37–8.

12 J. K. Hoensch, p. 27; Luža, *Transfer*, p. 37.

13 Jaworski, 'Die Sudetendeutschen', pp. 36–7.

14 Zimmermann, p. 41.

15 Zimmermann, pp. 43–5; Smelser, pp. 60–1.

16 Zimmermann, p. 55.

17 Gemeinsame Historikerkommission, p. 17.

18 Alexander, *Schiedsvertrag*, p. 136.

19 Ibid., pp. 160–4; Brügel, *Tschechen*, p. 212.

20 E. Kubů, 'Die brüchigen Beziehungen, Die Weimarer Republik und die Tschechoslowakei' in Hoensch and Kováč, pp. 22–8.

21 V. Mastny, *The Czechs under Nazi Rule. The failure of national resistance* (New York: Columbia University Press, 1971) p. 11.

22 Kershaw, *Hubris*, p. 63.

23 Seibt, *Deutschland*, pp. 320–1, see also n. 563, pp. 455–6; Luža, *Transfer*, p. 49, n. 11. Allegedly recorded by the president of the Gdansk Senate, Hermann Rauschnigg, and published under the title *Gespräche mit Hitler* (*Hitler Speaks*), they have been found to lack any authentity (Kershaw, *Hubris*, p. xiv).

24 Boyer, 'Vergabe'. p. 111; Brügel, *Tschechen*, pp. 309–13, Wingfield, pp. 151–3; H. Slapnicka, 'Die böhmischen Länder und die Slowakei', in K. Bosl, *Handbuch der Geschichte der Böhmischen Länder, vol. iv, Der Tschechoslowakische*

Staat im Zeitalter der Modernen Massendemokratie und Diktatur (Stuttgart: Anton Hiersheim, 1970) p. 79.

25 Brügel, *Tschechen*, p. 311, n. 20, p. 597; Zimmermann, p. 185.
26 Quoted in V. Kural, 'Die Tschechoslowakei als Nationalstaat? Das sudetendeutsche Problem', in Hoensch and Kováč, p. 68.
27 Zimmermann, pp. 49–57.
28 Brügel, *Tschechen*, p. 332.
29 I. Kershaw, *Hitler 1936–45. Nemesis* (London: Allan Lane, 2000) pp. 46–9; Smelser, pp. 207–8.
30 A. J. P. Taylor, *The Origins of the Second World War* (London: Hamish Hamilton, 1961), pp. 132.
31 Ibid., p. 133.
32 Luža, *Transfer*, pp. 119–20; D. Brandes, 'Die Politik des Dritten Reiches gegenüber der Tschechoslowakei', in M. Funke, *Hitler, Deutschland und die Mächte. Materialien zur Außenpolitik des Dritten Reiches* (Düsseldorf: Droste, 1978) pp. 517–8.
33 Zimmermann, p. 60.
34 *Die Tagebücher von Joseph Goebbels, Teil 1, Aufzeichnungen 1923–41* (Munich: Elke Fröhlich, 1993–8) vol. 7, p. 80, cited in Kershaw, *Nemesis*, p. 100.
35 Ibid., p. 101. 'Case Green' was originally designed by the German army in 1937 to launch a pre-emptive strike against Czechoslovakia in case of war with France in the west.
36 Wingfield, p. 169.
37 Boyer, 'Vergabe' p. 113.
38 On 16 May, 1935, Czechoslovakia had signed an alliance treaty with the Soviet Union. However, the treaty stipulated that in order to render the obligation of mutual military assistance between the ČSR and the Soviet Union effective, France must first accord aid to the party that fell victim to the attack. Also, in order to compel the French government to act against the aggressor, it was necessary to obtain the unanimous recommendation of the Council of the League of Nations, following the definition under Article 16 of the Covenant.
39 Kershaw, *Nemesis*, p. 92.
40 H. Goscurth, *Tagebücher eines Abwehroffiziers 1938–1940*, ed. H. Krausnick and H. C. Deutsch, (Stuttgart: Deutsche Verlagsanstalt, 1970) pp. 111–12 (4 September 1938) in Kershaw, *Nemesis*, p. 88.
41 B. Celovsky, *Das Münchener Abkommen 1938* (Stuttgart: Deutsche Verlagsanstalt) p. 332.
42 Kershaw, *Nemesis*, p. 89.
43 G. E. R. Gedye, *Fallen Bastions. The Central European Tragedy* (London: Golloncz, 1939) p. 396, cited in Kershaw, *Nemesis*, p. 871, 167.
44 Taylor, pp. 174–86.
45 P. Calvocoressi, G. Wint and J. Pritchet, *Total War. Causes and Consequences of the Second World War* (Harmondsworth: Penguin, 1989) pp. 82–3.
46 Mastny, p. 17.
47 K. Eubank, 'Munich', in Mamatey and Luža, p. 243.
48 G. L. Weinberg, *Germany, Hitler and World War Two* (Cambridge: Cambridge University Press, 1995) pp. 109–20, 'Reflections on Munich after 60 years' in I. Lukes and E. Goldstein, *The Munich Crisis 1938. Prelude to World War Two*

(London: Frank Cass, 1999) pp. 1–12; E. Goldstein, 'Neville Chamberlain, The British Official Mind and the Munich Crisis', in Lukes and Goldstein, pp. 276–92.

49 Kershaw, *Nemesis*, p. 106.

50 B. W. Memming, 'The Munich Crisis in Light of Soviet War Planning and Military Readiness' unpublished conference paper, cited in M. Hauner, 'The Quest for the Romanian Corridor: the Soviet Union and Czechoslovakia during the Sudeten Crisis of 1938' in F. Taubert, 'Mythos Müchen', forthcoming (Munich: Oldenbourg 2003); M. Hauner, 'Zrada, sovítizace, nebo historicky lapsus? Ke kritike dvou dokumentú k éeskoslovensko-sovítskym vztahum z roku 1938', *Soudobé díjiny*, vi/4/1999, pp. 545–71; H. Ragsdale, 'Soviet Military Preparation and Policy in the Munich Crisis: New Evidence', *Jahrbücher für Geschichte Osteuropas*, **47**, 2 (1999), pp. 210–26.

51 G. R. Ueberschär, *Generaloberst Franz Halder, Generalstabsched, Gegner und Gefangener Hitlers* (Göttingen: Muster-Schmidt, 1991) pp. 33–4; H. B. Gisevius, *Bis zum bitteren Ende, Bd. II: Vom Münchener Abkommen biz zum 20. Juli 1944* (Zürich: Fretz und Wasmuth Verlag, 1946) p. 326, cited in Kershaw, *Nemesis*, p. 123, 879, n. 408.

52 For details see Mastny, p. 66.

53 *Der Spiegel*, 30 August 1947, p. 4.

54 Zimmermann, pp. 63–5.

55 P. Heumoos, *Die Emigration aus der Tschechoslowakei nach Westeuropa und dem Nahen Osten 1938–1945* (Munich: Oldenbourg, 1989) pp. 15–17, J. Gebhart, 'Migrationsbewegung der tschechischen Bevölkerung in den Jahren 1938–1939. Forschungsstand und offene Fragen' in D. Brandes, E. Ivaničkova und Jiří Pešek, *Erzwungene Trennung. Vertreibung und Aussiedlung in und aus der Tschechoslowakei 1938–1947 im Vergleich mit Polen, Ungarn und Jugoslawien* (Essen: Klartext, 1999) pp. 14–19.

56 Seibt, *Deutschland*, pp. 339–40.

57 Gebhart, pp. 18–19.

58 Zimmermann, pp. 79–82.

59 Ibid., pp. 90–108.

60 Ibid., pp. 142–57.

61 Ibid., pp. 134–5, pp. 172–3.

62 Ibid., pp. 183–4.

63 Ibid., pp. 212–25

64 Ibid., pp. 193–209.

65 For the *Reichsgau*: Zimmermann, p. 280. For all the former German regions in Bohemia and Moravia: J. Macek, 'Zur Problematik der Geschichte der abgetrennten Gebiete besonders des sogenannten Sudetenlandes in den Jahren 1938–1945', in D. Brandes and V. Kural, *Der Weg in die Katastrophe: deutschtschechoslowakische Beziehungen 1938–1947* (Essen: Klartext, 1994) p. 58.

66 Macek, pp. 59–60; Zimmermann, pp. 296–305, p. 351.

67 In Luža, *Transfer*, p. 189, 'Assimilierung des Tschechentums, d.h. Aufsaugen etwa der Hälfte des tschechischen Volksteile im Deutschtum'.

68 Ibid.

69 Zimmermann, pp. 329–34. See p. 67.

70 Ibid., p. 353.

71 Ibid., pp. 353–6.

72 J. Macek, pp. 68–71; Zimmermann, pp. 406–12.
73 Macek, p. 73.
74 Celovsky, p. 472.
75 Mastny, p. 24; these included the organization of a Nazi party and a German education system ranging from primary to university level.
76 *DGFP*, D, IV, 99–100, No. 81, cited in Kershaw, *Nemesis*, p. 162.
77 Kershaw, *Nemesis*, p. 165.
78 Mastny, p. 29.
79 Mastny, p. 30.
80 Kershaw, *Nemesis*, p. 169.
81 Decree of 16 March, 1939, *DGFP*, D, IV, pp. 283–6, cited in Mastny, pp. 50–1.
82 D. Brandes, 'Nationalsozialistische Tschechenpolitik im Protektorat Böhmen und Mähren", in Brandes and Kural, pp. 49–50.
83 Gemeinsame Kommission, p. 22; Mastny's estimate of Jewish victims of the Holocaust in the protectorate is 90 000 (p. 192).
84 Brandes gives a figure of 2000 ('Nationalsozialistische Tschechenpolitik', p. 40); Mastny speaks of 'several thousands' (p. 106); Luža lists the figure of arrested persons as high as 8000 (*Transfer*, p. 205)
85 See pp. 59–60.
86 J. Miltová, 'Die NS-Pläne zur Lösung der tschechischen Frage', in Brandes, Ivaničkova and Pešek, pp. 34–5.
87 Brandes, 'Nationalsozialistische Tschechenpolitik', p. 46.
88 *Czechoslovák*, 28 October 1942 (a London weekly), cited in Luža, *Transfer*, p. 191.
89 Miltová, p. 35.
90 Mastny, p. 180.
91 Ibid., p. 191.
92 Kershaw, *Nemesis*, p. 519.
93 Brandes, 'Nationalsozialistische Tschechenpolitik', p. 47. Mastny gives the number of victims sentenced by summary courts as 1331 (p. 220).
94 Mastny, pp. 220–1; Gemeinsame Kommission, p. 22.
95 Czech terms for the resistance movement: covering resistance organizations at home as well as the government and army in exile and their activities.
96 V. Kural, 'Tschechen, Deutsche und die sudetendeutsche Frage während des Zweiten Weltkriegs' in Brandes, Ivaničkova and Pešek, pp. 73–6; R. Luža, 'The Czech Resistance Movement' in Mamatey and Luža, pp. 348–53; Zeman, *Beneš*, pp. 180–1.
97 J. K. Hoensch, 'Grundzüge und Phasen der deutschen Slowakei-Politik im Zweiten Weltkrieg', in Brandes and Kural, pp. 236–7.
98 Kural, 'Tschechen, Deutsche', p. 75.
99 G. Rhode, 'Das Protectorat Böhmen und Mähren', in E. Lemberg and G. Rhode, *Das deutsch–tschechische Verhältnis seit 1918* (Stuttgart: Kohlhammer, 1969) pp. 60–1.
100 Brandes, 'Nationalsozialistische Tschechenpolitik', p. 49.
101 Frank managed to escape to the American occupation zone but was returned to Czechoslovakia. He was sentenced to death by a Czechoslovak court and executed on 27 May 1946.
102 Mastny, p. 224.
103 S. Hoffmann, 'Collaborationism in France during world War II', in *Journal of Modern History*, **40** (1968), 375.

104 Mastny, p. 225.
105 G. Hirschfeld and P. Mann, *Collaboration in France. Politics and Culture during Nazi Occupation, 1940–1944* (Oxford: Berg, 1989); W. Benz, J. Houwink ten Cate, G. Otto, *Die Bürokratie der Okkupation. Strukuren der Herrschaft und Verwaltung im besetzten Europa* (Berlin: Metropol, 1998); note also G. Hirschfeld, 'Zwischen Kollaboration und Widerstand – Europa unter deutscher Besatzung', in *Brockhaus Bibliothek Weltgeschichte*, Vol. 5, X, 3 (1999) 639–40.
106 Luža, *Transfer*, pp. 192–3.
107 Ibid., pp. 194–6.
108 V. Urban, *Hitler's Spearhead* (London: Trinity Press, 1945) p. 42; Theodor Schieder, *Die Vertreibung der Deutschen Bevölkerung aus der Tschechoslowakei*, Part IV/1 of the series *Dokumentation der Vertreibung der Deutschen aus Ost/Mitteleuropa* brought out by the German Federal Ministry for Expellees, Refugees and War Victims (Berlin: Heyne's Erben, 1957) states that a large number of people working in the arms production industries of the protectorate and in the protectorate' administration were Sudeten Germans (p. 17, n. 3). Zeman claims that the 'German administration and security services employed the Sudeten Germans in large numbers, so there would be no mistake as to who the new masters of the province were' (*Making and Breaking*, p. 156); according to Brandes, however, so far, and with the exception of Frank, there has been no investigation into the influence of Sudeten Germans in the protectorate, *Der Weg zur Vertreibung 1938–1945. Pläne und Entscheidungen zum 'Transfer' der Deutschen aus der Tschechoslowakei und aus Polen* (Munich: Oldenbourg, 2001) p. 116. The Czech–German Historians' Commission states that the question of Sudeten-German participation in the running of the protectorate needs further research (Gemeinsame Kommission, p. 25).
109 L. L. Whetten, *Germany's Ostpolitik. Relations between the Federal Republic and the Warsaw Pact Countries* (London: Oxford University Press, 1971) p. 170; according to the Gemeinsame Kommission it has not been possible so far to accurately assess the ČSR's wartime material damage (p. 30).
110 Luža, *Transfer*, p. 199.
111 P. Skorpil, 'Probleme bei der Berechnung der Zahl der tschechoslowakischen Todesopfer des nationalsozialistischen Deutschlands', in Brandes and Kural, pp. 161–4.
112 Kural in Kren, Kural and Brandes, pp. 90–1, 'Zum tschechisch–deutschen Verhältnis', pp. 116–18; Luža, *Transfer*, pp. 260–1.
113 Kren, 'Zum tschechisch–deutschen Verhältnis', p. 117.
114 33 419 died here, 86 934 were send to extermination camps. A. Suppan, 'Soziale und wirtschaftliche Lage im Protektorat Böhmen und Mähren', in R. G. Plaschka, H. Haselsteiner, A. Suppan and A. A. Drabek (eds) *Nationale Frage und Vertreibung in der Tschechoslowakei und Ungarn 1938–1945* (Vienna: Oesterreichische Akademie der Wissenschaften, 1997) p. 23.
115 K. E. Franzen, *Die Vertriebenen. Hitlers letzte Opfer* (Berlin–Munich: Propylaen, 2001).

4 Expulsion and Forced Resettlement

  1 Benešův archiv (BA), *druhá světová válka*, box 95, cited in Zeman, *Beneš*, p. 144.

2   Hubert Ripka's introduction to E. Beneš, *Tři roky druhé světové války, projevy a dokumenty 1938–1942* (London, n.d.) p. 6, cited in Zeman, *Beneš*, p. 141.
3   Ibid., pp. 148–9.
4   Ibid., pp. 155–6.
5   A. J. P. Taylor, p. 153.
6   BA, 2SV, k. 278a, cited in Zeman, *Beneš*, p. 179.
7   Brandes, *Weg zur Vertreibung*, pp. 5–6. The first plan attempted to solve the Czech–Sudeten-German problem with the introduction of a nationality status (April 1938), while the second plan (July 1938) offered the creation of national diets, plan four (August 1938) of three German districts and plan four (September 1938) of a German federal state (See pp. 53–4).
8   Ibid., p. 6.
9   Kural, 'Tschechen, Deutsche', p. 85; 'Zum tschechisch–deutschen Verhältnis', pp. 101–3; Brandes, *Weg zur Vertreibung*, pp. 68–9.
10 Brandes, *Weg zur Vertreibung*, pp. 39–41.
11 Ibid., pp. 11–13; Kural, 'Zum tschechisch–deutschen Verhältnis', pp. 98–9.
12 Brandes, *Weg zur Vertreibung*, p. 12.
13 Ibid., p. 34: 'die Autonomieforderungen scharf herausarbeiten, um nach Ablehnung durch die Tschechen unsere Operationsfreiheit wiederzugewinnen'.
14 According to Kural, his turnaround was tactical and not sincere ('Zum tschechisch–deutschen Verhältnis' n. 8, pp. 98–9); this view is not shared by Brandes, *Weg zur Vertreibung*, p. 39, n. 109.
15 Kural, 'Tschechen, Deutsche', pp. 85–6; 'Zum tschechisch–deutschen Verhältnis' pp. 103–6.
16 Kural, 'Tschechen, Deutsche', pp. 87–8; 'Zum tschechisch–deutschen Verhältnis' pp. 107–8.
17 Kural, 'Tschechen, Deutsche', p. 88.
18 Kural, 'Zum tschechisch–deutschen Verhältnis' pp. 110.
19 Brandes, *Weg zur Vertreibung*, pp. 76–81. Headed by the chairman of the German Miners' Union in Czechoslovakia, Josef Zinner, about one-third of the DSAP left the party in a split over Jaksch's policies in October 1940. This 'Zinner Group' supported the National Council's policies.
20 Kural, 'Tschechen, Deutsche', p. 91.
21 E. Taborsky, 'Politics in Exile', in Mamatey and Luža, p. 333; Zeman, *Beneš*, p. 184.
22 Leman, Beneš, p. 186; Taborski, p. 336; E. Beneš, *Memoirs of Dr. Eduard Beneš* (London: George Allen & Unwin,1954) pp. 193–5.
23 Luža, *Transfer*, p. 246; Brandes, *Weg zur Vertreibung*, pp. 299–301; Kural, 'Tschechen, Deutsche', p. 91.
24 Luža, *Transfer*, p. 247.
25 *Foreign Relations of the United States. The Conference of Berlin 1945.* I, p. 648, cited in Luža, *Transfer*, pp. 247–8.
26 M. Hauner, 'Září 1938: kapitulovat či bojovat?', *Svědectví*, **13** (1975) 151–68, cited in H. Ragsdale, 'Soviet Military Preparations and Policy in the Munich Crisis: New Evidence', *Jahrbücher für die Geschichte Osteuropas*, **47** (1999) 210.
27 Department of State, *Foreign Relations of the United States. Diplomatic Papers.* Vol. 3, 1941 (Washington: United States Government Printing Office, 1959) pp. 360–1.

28   Brandes, *Weg zur Vertreibung*, p. 275.
29   See p. 86.
30   Kershaw, *Nemesis*, p. 577, n. 82, p. 983.
31   W. Benz, 'Vierzig Jahre nach der Vertreibung. Einleitende Bemerkungen', in
     W. Benz, *Die Vertreibung der Deutschen aus dem Osten. Ursachen, Ereignisse,
     Folgen* (Frankfurt: Fischer, 1995) p. 8; 'Fremde in der Heimat: Flucht-
     Vertreibung-Integration', in K. J. Bade, *Deutsche im Ausland – Fremde in der
     Heimat* (Munich: C. H. Beck, 1992) pp. 375–9.
32   V. A. Isupov, *Demografîcheskie katastrofy i krisizy v Rossii v pervoi polovine XX
     veka* (Novosibirsk: Academician Polyakov, 2000) p. 195; O. Bartov, *The Eastern
     Front, 1941–45 German Troops and the Barbarisation of Warfare* (Basingstoke:
     Macmillan – now Palgrave Macmillan, 1996) pp. 106–41; D. Wolkogonow,
     Stalin. Triumph and Tragedy (London: Weidenfeld and Nicholson, 1991)
     p. 505, estimates total human losses of the Soviet Union in the Great Patriotic
     War to have been between 25 and 27 million; note also S. G. Wheatcroft,
     'Ausmaß und Wesen der deutschen und sowjetischen Repressionen und
     Massentötungen 1930 bis 1945' in D. Dahlmann and G. Hirschfeld, *Lager,
     Zwangsarbeit, Verteibung und Deportation. Dimension der Massenverbrechen in
     der Sowjetunion und in Deutschland 1933–1945* (Essen: Klartext, 1999)
     pp. 67–109.
33   Zeman, *Making and Beaking*, p. 120.
34   The 'Interdepartmental Committee on the Transfer of German Populations'
     was formed in December 1943 (Brandes, *Weg zur Vertreibung*, pp. 245–73).
35   In a last submission to the British Foreign Office before his return to
     Czechoslovakia in March 1945, Beneš's figure for those remaining was
     894 000, Brandes, *Weg zur Vertreibung*, p. 308.
36   V. Konopka, *Živé tradice* (Prague: Nase Vojsko, 1959) pp. 201–2; International
     Military Tribunal, *Trials of the Major War Criminals before the Nuremberg
     International Military Tribunal. Nuremberg 1945–46* (Nuremberg: 1947–9) Vol.
     XXXVI, pp. 88–9.
37   D. Brandes, *Die Tschechen unter deutschem Protektorat. Part Two, Besatzungspolitik,
     Kollaboration und Widerstand im Protektorat Böhmen und Mähren vonHeydrichs
     Tod bis zum Prager Ausfstand* (Munich/Vienna: Oldenbourg, 1975) pp.
     113–26.
38   Cited in Urban, pp. 43–4; note also V. Buben, *Šest let okupace Prahy* (Prague:
     1946) pp. 263–4.
39   Seibt, *Deutschland*, pp. 352–3.
40   T. Staněk, '1945 – Das Jahr der Verfolgung. Zur Problematik der außerg-
     erichtlichen Nachkriegsverfolgung in den böhmischen Ländern' in Brandes,
     Ivaničkova and Pešek, pp. 128–33; E. Hrabovec, *Vertreibung und Abschub.
     Deutsche in Böhmen und Mähren* (Frankfurt: Peter Lang, 1995) pp. 84–93.
41   Hrabovec, pp. 96–103.
42   V. Kaiser, 'Das Ende des Krieges und die Vertreibung der Deutechen aus dem
     Aussiger Gebiet', in Brandes, Ivaničkova and Pešek, pp. 209–13.
43   Hrabovec, p. 63.
44   L. Němec, 'Solution of the Minorities Problem', in Mamatey and Luža, p. 417.
45   H. Slapnicka, 'Die rechtlichen Grundlagen für die Behandlung der Deutschen
     und Magyaren in der Tschechoslowakei 1945–1948', in R. G. Plaschka,
     H. Haselsteiner, A. Suppan and A. A. Drabek (eds) *Nationale Frage und*

Vertreibung in der Tschechoslowakei und Ungarn 1938–1945 (Vienna: Oesterreichische Akademie der Wissenschaften, 1997) p. 185.

46 A. Suppan, 'Soziale und wirtschaftliche Lage im Protektorat Böhmen und Mähren', in Plaschka, H. Haselsteiner, A. Suppan and A. A. Drabek, p. 27; Němec, p. 418.

47 Hrabovec, pp. 106–7; Luža, *Transfer*, p. 273, Němec, p. 419.

48 Staněk, pp. 138–42.

49 As part of the overall *Flüchtlings- und Vertriebenenliteratur*, a bibliography compiled in 1982 already lists 1135 titles (Stiftung Ostdeutscher Kulturrat (ed.), *Bestandsverzeichniss der deutschen Heimatvertriebenenpresse* (Munich: Saur, 1982); Gertrud Krallert-Sattler's *Kommentierte Bibliographie zum Flüchtlings- und Vertriebenenproblem in der Bundesrepublik Deutschland, in Oesterreich und in der Schweiz* (Vienna: Braunmueller, 1989) extends into close to one thousand pages. Further monographs not – or only partly – cited so far in this work in chronological order: W. Turnwald, *Dokumente zur Austreibung der Sudetendeutschen* (Munich: Arbeitsgemeinschaft zur Wahrung sudetendeutscher Interessen, 1951), *Dokumentation der Vertreibung der Deutschen aus Ost/Mitteleuropa* issued by the German Federal Ministry for Expellees, Refugees and War Victims (Vols 1–5, Berlin: Heyne's Erben, 1954–60) and edited by T. Schieder; E. Franzl, *Sudetendeutsche Geschichte. Eine volkstümliche Darstellung* (Munich: Kraft, 1958), *Die Vertreibung. Sudetenland.1945/46* (Landshut: Aufstieg Verlag, 1967); A. Bohmann, *Das Sudetendeutschtum in Zahlen* (Munich: Sudetendeutscher Rat, 1959), Ziemer, G. *Deutscher Exodus. Verteibung und Eingliederung von 15 Millionen Ostdeutschen* (Stuttgart: Seewald, 1973); A. Bohmann, *Bevölkerung und Nationalität in der Tschechoslowakei* (Cologne: Verlag Wissenschaft und Politik, 1975); DeZayas, Alfred M., *Nemesis at Potsdam: the Anglo-Americans and the expulsion of the Germans; background, execution, consequences* (London: Routledge & Kegan Paul, 1979); F. Grube and G. Richter, *Flucht und Vertreibung: Deutschland zwischen 1944 und 1947* (Hamburg: Hoffmann and Campe, 1980); G. Böddeker, *Die Flüchtlinge. Die Vertreibung der Deutschen aus dem Osten* (Munich: Herbig, 1980); R. Mühlfenzl, *Geflohen und Vertrieben. Augenzeugen berichten* (Königstein/Taunus: Athenäum, 1981); W. Arndt, *Ostpreußen, Westpreußen, Pommern, Schlesien, Sudetenland 1945/6. Eine Bild-Dokumentation der Flucht und Vertreibung aus den deutschen Ostgebieten* (Friedberg: 1982); H. Nawratil, *Vertreibungsverbrechen an Deutschen. Tatbestand, Motive, Bewältigung* (Munich: Universitätsverlag, 1982); W. Ahrens, *Verbrechen an Deutschen. Dokumente der Vertreibung* (Arget: Ahrens, 1984); M. Frantzioch, *Die Vertriebenen: Hemnisse, Antriebskräfte und Wege Ihrer Integration in der Bundesrepublik Deutschland* (Berlin: Reimer, 1987); K. J. Bade (ed.), *Neue Heimat im Westen: Vertriebene-Flüchtlinge-Aussiedler* (Münster: Westfälischer Heimatbund, 1990); A. Wagnerowa, *1945 waren sie Kinder. Flucht und Vertreibung im Leben einer Generation* (Cologne: Kiepenheuer und Witsch, 1990); A. Lehmann, *Im Fremden ungewollt zuhaus: Flüchtlinge und Vertriebene in Westdeutschland 1945–1990* (Munich: Beck, 1991); R. Streibel (ed.), *Flucht und Vertreibung. Zwischen Aufrechnung und Verdrängung* (Vienna: Picus 1994); Sudetendeutsches Archiv, *Odseun. Die Vertreibung der Sudetendeutschen* (Munich: Verlagshaus Sudetenland, 1995); D. Hoffmann, M. Kraus, M. Schwartz, *Vertriebene in Deutschland. Interdisziplinäre Ergebnisse und Forschungsperspektiven* (Munich: Oldenbourg, 2000).

50 E. Wiskemann, *Germany's Eastern Neighbours* (London: Oxford University Press, 1956) p. 61. This book was viciously attacked in the Federal Republic (note, for example, K. Rable, 'Zur Frage der Deutschenvertreibung aus der Tschechoslowakei', *Bohemia*, 2 (1961) 417–8, n. 10; H. W. Schoenberg, *Germans from the East. A study of their migration, resettlement, and subsequent history* (The Hague: Martinus Nijhoff, 1970) p. 359.

51 For a summary see M. Alexander, 'Die Diskussion über die Vertreibung der Deutschen aus der Tschechoslowakei', in Streibel, pp. 158–73.

52 T. Staněk, 'Vertreibung und Aussiedlung der Deutschen 1945–8', in Brandes and Kural, p. 185.

53 See pp. 57–61, 106–9.

54 During the Cold War years the validity of the Potsdam agreement was repeatedly challenged, in particular by historians and lawyers in the Federal Republic of Germany (note J. Foschepoth, 'Potsdam und danach – die Westmächte, Adenauer und die Vertriebenen', in Benz, *Vertreibung*, pp. 86–113). The governments of the signatories at Potsdam, however, left no doubt about the agreement's full legality, as was shown again by the finalization of the German borders ratified by the former Allies after the collapse of the Soviet Union.

55 Slapnicka, *Grundlagen*, pp. 157–63.

56 Cited in Turnwald, p. 549.

57 Staněk, '1945', pp. 125–6.

58 Cited in Gemeinsame Kommission, p. 55.

59 Franzen, *Die Vertriebenen*, p. 183.

60 Ibid., p. 184.

61 Schieder, *Dokumentation*, vol. IV/1; Statistisches Bundesamt, *Die deutschen Vertreibungsverluste* (Wiesbaden: Kohlhammer, 1958); Bohmann, *Sudetendeutschtum in Zahlen*; G. Reichling, *Die deutschen Vertriebenen in Zahlen* (Bonn: Kulturstiftung der deutschen Vertriebenen, 1986) part 1.

62 Luža, pp. 293–300.

63 J. Kucera, 'Statistische Berechnungen der Vertreibungsverluste – Schlußwort oder Sackgasse', in Brandes and Kural, pp. 187–200; 'Statistik auf dem Holzweg. Einige Bemerkungen zur Berechnung der Sudetendeutschen Vertriebenenverlust', in Plaschka, Haselsteiner, Suppan and Drabek, pp. 145–54; R. Overmanns, ' "Amtlich und wissenschaftlich erarbeitet." Zur Diskussion über die Verluste während der Flucht und Vertreibung der Deutschen aus der CSR' in Brandes, Ivaničkova and Pešek, pp. 149–77.

64 Overmanns, pp. 176–7.

65 Zeman, *Making and Breaking*, pp. 241–2.

66 M. Walker, *The Cold War* (London: Vintage, 1993) pp. 26–7.

5 Expellee Politics

1 Schieder, IV/2, p. 465.

2 Seibt, *Deutschland*, p. 356.

3 Recent German literature on the topic of post-Second World War expulsion and integration uses the terms 'Zwangsaussiedlung' and 'Zwangsassimilation'; note T. Grosser, 'Die Integration der Vertriebenen in der Bundesrepublik

Deutschland. Annäherungen an die Situation der Sudetendeutschen in der westdeutschen Nachkriegsgesellschaft am Beispiel Baiers', in H. Lemberg, J. Křen and D. Kováč, *Im geteilten Europa. Tschechen, Slowaken und Deutsche und ihre Staaten 1945–1989* (Essen: Klartext, 1998) pp. 41–94.

4 By the end of 1946 approximately 833 000 expellees from Czechoslovakia were living in the Soviet Zone and close to 1 500 000 in the American Zone. The French Zone (Rhineland-Palatinate, South Baden and Württemberg-Hohenzollern) refused to take any refugees or expellees because France had not been part of the Potsdam agreement. This did change with the foundation of the Federal Republic in 1949. The British Zone, which covered the north and north-west of Germany took in most expellees from the former German eastern parts (Grosser, pp. 80–1).

5 In the early post-war years not much difference in terminology was made between *Flüchtlinge* (refugees) and *Vertriebene* (expellees).

6 P. Ther, *Deutsche und polnische Vertriebene. Gesellschaft und Vertriebenenpolitk in der SBZ/DDR und in Polen 1945–1956* (Göttingen: Vandenhoek & Ruprecht, 1998) pp. 136–8; the Soviet authorities from the beginning insisted on the use of the term *Umsiedler* (transferrees) which is far weaker than *Vertriebene*. The former expression was – and still is – virtually unanimously rejected in West Germany.

7 K. Kurz, 'Der Wandel des Dorfes Gersdorf, Kreis Herzfeld, durch das Einströmen der Heimatvertriebenen', in E. Lemberg and L. Krecker, *Die Entstehung eines neuen Volkes aus Binnendeutschen und Ostvertriebenen* (Marburg: N. G. Elwert Verlag, 1950) pp. 32–43.

8 F. Neumann, *Der Block der Heimatvertriebenen und Entrechteten 1950–1960. Ein Beitrag zur Geschichte und Struktur einer politischen Interessenpartei* (Marburg: 1966), p. 2.

9 M. Kornrumpf, *In Baiern angekommen. Die Eingliederung der Vertiebenen. Zahlen-Daten-Namen* (Munich: Günter Olzog, 1979) pp. 46–7.

10 M. Wambach, *Verbändestaat und Parteienoligopol. Macht und Ohnmacht der Vertriebenenverbände* (Stuttgart: Ferdinand Enke, 1971) pp. 33–5.

11 Schoenberg, p. 73.

12 Ibid., p. 136.

13 For the foundation and first years of the ZvD: L. Kather, *Die Entmachtung der Vertriebenen. Die entscheidenden Jahre* (Munich/Vienna: Günter Olzog, 1964) vol. 1.

14 This is not to be confused with the colloquial terms East Germans or East Germany that started to circulate after the foundation of the German Democratic Republic (GDR) in 1949, and that became quite common after the construction of the Berlin Wall in 1961.

15 P. Ther, pp. 139–41; Ziemer, pp. 227–8. Authorities in the Soviet Zone there were more rigorous as far as housing policies were concerned, which favoured the expellees but by 1948 the available pool of living space available had dried up (Ther, pp. 206–11).

16 Ibid., pp. 283–93.

17 Ibid., pp. 230–40; M. Schwartz, ' "Vom Umsiedler zum Staatsbürger". Totalitäres und Subversives in der Sprachpolitik der SBZ/DDR', D. Hoffmann, M. Kraus, and M. Schwartz, *Vertriebene in Deutschland. Interdisciplinäre Ergebnisse und Forschungsperspektiven* (Munich: Oldenbourg, 2000) pp. 135–66;

M. Wille, 'Die Vertriebenen und das politisch-staatliche System der SBZ/DDR', in Hoffmann, Kraus and Schwartz, pp. 203–18.

18   Grosser, pp. 80–1.

19   Seibt, *Deutschland*, p. 359.

20   E. Nittner, *Dokumente zur Sudetendeutschen Frage 1916–67* (Munich: Ackermann Gemeinde, 1967) p. 319, cited in E. Hahn, 'Die Sudetendeutschen in der deutschen Gesellschaft: ein halbes Jahrhundert politischer Geschichte zwischen "Heimat" und "Zuhause" ', in Lemberg, Křen and Kovač, p. 118.

21   Hahn, p. 125; note also B. Celovský, 'The transferred Sudeten-Germans and their political activity', in *Journal of Central European Affairs*, **17**, 2 (1957), 133–5; full text in Habel, *Dokumente*, p. 311.

22   Cited in E. Nittner, 'Traditionen der Sudetendeutschen', in R. Schulze, D. Von der Brelie-Lewien and H. Grebing, *Flüchtlinge und Vertriebene in der westdeutschen Nachkriegsgeschichte* (Hildesheim: August Lax, 1987) pp. 93–4; also Schoenberg, p. 162.

23   E. Lemberg, 'Die Sudetendeutschen im Exil,' Sudetendeutsche rufen Europa (Munich: Volksbote, 1950), Schriftenreihe der Ackermann Gemeinde, 2, p. 35.

24   Cited in E. Nittner, *Die Ackermann Gemeinde. Bilanz und Auftrag* (Munich: Kultur-und Bidungswerk der Ackermanngemeinde, 1978) pp. 20–1; E. Lemberg, 'Bemerkungen zu einem Geschichtsbild', *Der neue Ackermann*, 2, 4 (1954) pp. 28–37.

25   Officially the Seliger Gemeinde did not constitute itself until November 1951, Franzen, 'Prager Vertrag', p. 19.

26   Ibid., pp. 17–18; Hahn, pp. 119–20; Habel, *Dokumente*, p. 300; note also Celovský p. 137.

27   *Der Sudetendeutsche*, 6 April 1950.

28   Celovský, *passim*; A. Snejdárek, 'Über die Anfänge des sudetendeutschen Revanchismus in Westdeutschland', *Wissenschaftliche Zeitschrift der Karl-Marx Universität Leipzig*, Sonderband IV, 1964, pp. 140–52.

29   Wiskemann, *Eastern Neighbours*, pp. 179–90.

30   Cited in Seibt, *Deutschland*, p. 365.

31   Celovský p. 135; Hahn, pp. 125–6; Seibt, *Deutschland*, pp. 372–3; Habel, p. 314:

32   See p. 49.

33   Seibt, *Deutschland*, p. 363.

34   Hahn, p. 121; E. Hans and W. Brand, *Der Witikobund. Weg-Wesen-Wirken* (Munich: Eigenverlag des Witikobundes, 1969).

35   Hahn, pp. 121–2.

36   M. Imhof, 'Die Vertriebenenverbände in der Bundesrepublik Deutschland. Geschichte, Organisation und Gesellschaftliche Bedeutung', Inaugural-Dissertation, Philipps-Universität Marburg, 1975, pp. 230–58.

37   Riemer, p. 143.

38   K. Gatz, 'East-German and Sudeten Germans Expellees in West Germany 1945–1960', unpublished PhD thesis, Indiana University, 1989, p. 41 and p. 301.

39   Ibid., p. 39.

40   Grosser, p. 64.

41   H. Neuhoff, 'Der Lastenausgleich aus der Sicht der Vertriebenen', in H. J. von Merkatz, *Aus Trümmern wurden Fundamente. Vertriebene/Flüchtlinge/Aussiedler. Drei Jahrzehnte Integration* (Düsseldorf: Walter Rau, 1979) p. 147.

42   Riemer, p. 166.

43 W. Abelshauser, 'Der Lastenausgleich und die Eingliederung der Vertriebenen und Flüchtlinge – eine Skizze', in Schulze. Breslie-Lewien and Grebing, p. 234.

44 P. Lüttinger, *Integration der Vertriebenen. Eine empirische Analyse* (Frankfurt/Main: Campus Verlag, 1989) p. 167.

45 R. Schillinger, 'Der Lastenausgleich', in Benz, *Vertreibung*, p. 240.

46 M. Wambach, pp. 67–9.

47 H. J. Gaida, *Die offiziellen Organe der ostdeutschen Landsmannschaften*, (Berlin: Duncker & Humblot, 1973) pp. 242–4; note also Neumann, pp. 71–3.

48 L. Kather, *Die Entmachtung der Vertriebenen. Die Jahre des Verfalls* (Munich/Vienna: Günter Olzog, 1965) Vol. 2, pp. 21–37; 'those deprived of their rights' were mainly the victims of the post-war de-Nazification process. Nazis who had compromised themselves and lost their positions and/or had their civil rights temporarily suspended. The great majority of the party's supporters were expellees and refugees.

49 Schoenberg, pp. 135–8.

50 For a brief summary of the GB/BHE: H. Weiß, 'Die Organisation der Vertriebenen und ihre Presse', in Benz, *Vertreibung*, pp. 251–3. On Seiboth, see p. 121.

51 A. J. Ryder, *Twentieth Century Germany* (New York: Columbia University Press, 1973) p. 517.

52 Abelshauser, p. 229.

53 Schoenberg p. 53.

54 Grosser, p. 65; Schoenberg pp. 56–8.

55 Schoenberg, p. 53.

56 G. C. Paikert, *The German Exodus. A selective study of the post World-War II expulsion of German populations and its effects* (The Hague: Martinus Nijhoff, 1962) p. 27.

57 Schoenberg pp. 55–6.

58 P. Strenkert, 'Eingliederung der Vertriebenen und Flüchtlinge in Bayern. Erfolge und Aufgaben', unpublished report of the Minister for Work and Social Security of 11 February 1963, p. 5.

59 Schoenberg, p. 55.

60 Strenkert, p. 3.

61 Schoenberg, p. 55.

62 Foschepoth, p. 110.

63 Note the contributions in volume 3 of E. Lemberg and Edding.

64 Franzen, *Prager Vertrag*, pp. 36–7.

65 Ibid., pp. 32–3; Weiß, pp. 253–5.

66 Abelshauser pp. 235–6; see p. 140.

67 The other tribes were said to be the 'Old Bavarians', the 'Franks' and the 'Swabians'.

6 In the Forefront

1 For a summary: E. Hobsbawm, *Das Zeitalter der Extreme. Weltgeschichte des 20. Jahrhunderts* (Munich: Deutscher Taschenbuch Verlag, 1998) ch. 8, 'Der Kalte Krieg', pp. 285–323.

2 F. Roberts, 'The Berlin Crisis', *Politics and Society in Germany, Austria and Switzerland* (1989), Vol. 1, 2, p. 9.

3 Note the author's 'Causes, Course and consequences of the Division of Germany. An Essay on Cold War and Post Cold War Policies', in A. Bonnell,

G. Munro and M. Travers Power, *Conscience and Opposition. Essays in German History in Honour of John A. Moses* (New York: Peter Lang, 1996) pp. 387–404.

4 Čelovský, pp. 144–5; Hahn, p. 115, p. 124; Habel, *Dokumente*, p. 315.
5 A. Snejdárek, p. 151.
6 *Der Spiegel*, 2 September 1953, p. 35.
7 K. Bittel, *Der Revanchismus*, cited in Eberle, p. 482.
8 Mitteilungs-und Informationsdienst für Vertriebenen-, Flüchtlings-und Kriegsgeschädigtenfragen (MID) (Bonn), 6 March 1955 (Eberle 171).
9 Cited in Celovský, p. 146.
10 *Sudetendeutsche Zeitung*, 4 June 1955.
11 Schoenberg, pp. 222–3.
12 Ibid., p. 176.
13 Ibid., p. 177.
14 Foschepoth, p. 107.
15 Ibid., p. 110.
16 *The Times*, 2 May 1956; Schoenberg, pp. 273–4.
17 *VdL Information*, 21 May 1956, p. 2, cited in Eberle pp. 492–3.
18 26 May 1956 p. 2.
19 Eberle, pp. 494–5.
20 *Die Welt*, p. 18.
21 Eberle p. 498.
22 Naumann, p. 189.
23 Kather, vol. 2, p. 128. 'Her first book' is a reference to Wiskemann's book *Czechs and Germans* (London: Oxford University Press, 1938).
24 Schoenberg, pp. 278–9; Eberle, pp. 488–9.
25 Schoenberg, p. 281.
26 *Sudetendeutsche Zeitung*, 24 May 1959.
27 Cited in Eberle, p. 601.
28 Cited in Naumann, pp. 181–2.
29 Eberle, pp. 137–42.
30 Franzen, *Prager Vertrag*, pp. 15–16.
31 Cited in Eberle, p. 602.
32 Právo, 10 April 1961; membership in the 1950s according to SdL figures was 340 000 (Wambach, p. 47) of whom not all would have supported radical nationalism. Note also Eberle, pp. 602–5.
33 As with so much concerning expellee terminology the word '*Gesamtdeutschland*' could be interpreted in various ways. It could mean both East- and West-Germany (which would be acceptable to the *Verzichtspolitiker*), or Germany in the borders of 1937, or it could include all Germans.
34 Schoenberg, p. 282.
35 ADG cited on p. 41 in Franzen, *Prager Vertrag*.
36 ADG, 11 June, 1964, cited in Franzen, *Prager Vertrag*, p. 41.
37 Schoenberg, p. 63.
38 Eberle, pp. 519–20.
39 Schoenberg, p. 294.
40 P. Burian, 'Der Transfer und seine Konsequenzen', in K. Bosl, *Das Jahr 1945 in der Tschechoslowakei* (Munich: Oldenbourg, 1971) p. 215.
41 Ganz, p. 455.
42 Eberle, pp. 638–9.

43   Cited in D. Strothmann, ' "Schlesien bleibt unser": Vertiebenenpolitiker und das Rad der Geschichte', in W. Benz, *Die Vertreibung der Deutschen aus dem Osten. Ursachen, Ereignisse, Folgen* (Frankfurt: Fischer, 1995) p. 274.
44   E. Weick, 'Gibt es einen Rechtsradikalismus in der Vertriebenenpresse?' in I. Fetcher (ed.), *Rechtsradikalismus* (Frankfurt/Main: Europäische Verlagsanstalt, 1967) p. 105.
45   Strothmann, p. 274.
46   E.g. *Der Spiegel*, 12 April 1971, p. 26.
47   Weick, pp. 112–13.
48   17 June 1966.
49   Weick, pp. 115–16.
50   Cited in Habel, *Dokumente*, p. 340.
51   Franzen, *Prager Vertrag*, pp. 43–4.
52   Bulletin des Presse- und Informationsamtes der Bundesrepublik, Bonn, Nr. 132, 29 October 1969, cited in ibid. p. 44.
53   Cited in Habel, *Dokumente*, p. 370.
54   R. Břach, 'Die Bedeutung des Prager Vertrags von 1973 für die deutsche Ostpolitik', in H. Lemberg, J. Křen and D. Kováč, p. 175.
55   Ibid., pp. 177–8.
56   Ibid., pp. 178–84.
57   Břach, p. 185. Full text in Franzen, pp. 150–1.
58   Břach, pp. 186–9.
59   Cited in Franzen, *Prager Vertrag*, p. 64.
60   *Sudetendeutsche Zeitung*, 4 June, 1971, p. 2 cited in ibid., p. 60, p. 57.
61   Franzen, Prager Vertrag, pp. 55–6, 67, 137–8.
62   Ibid., p. 141.
63   Ibid., p. 130.
64   Benrather Kreis, *Der Prager Vertrag vor dem Bundesverfassungsgericht* (Düsseldorf: Arbeitsgemeisnschaft für Deutschland, 1977).

7   Lest We Forget

1   U. Reichert-Flügel (ed.), *Unter dem weißblauen Schild. 30 Jahre Schirmherrschaft Bayerns über die Sudetendeutschen* (Munich: Verlagshaus Sudetenland) p. 5.
2   Ibid., p. 15.
3   Ibid., p. 19.
4   F. Prinz, 'Heimatvertriebene als Industriepioniere. Der Beitrag der Sudetendeutschen zu Bayerns Wirtschaft', pp. 63–5; G. D. Roth, 'Ein Wirtschaftpotential in Bayern. Sudetendeutsche Siedlungen', *Bayerland Impressum*, **4** (1978) 37–42; Benz, Vertreibung, (1985 edition) pp. 170–1.
5   Cited in F. P. Habel, *The Sudeten Question. Brief Exposition and Documentation* (Munich: Sudeten German Council, 1984) p. 28.
6   Ibid., p. 29.
7   Ibid., p. 30.
8   H. Haun, 'Die Patenschaften als Stützenpfeiler der Schirmherrschaft', in Reichert-Flügel, pp. 88–9.
9   Strothmann, p. 267; Seibt, *Deutschland*, p. 398.
10   Cited in Strothmann, p. 272.

11 Ibid., p. 273.
12 Hahn, p. 128.
13 Grosser, p. 76.
14 Strothmann, p. 267.
15 Wess, p. 205.
16 CTK News Agency, 'Profile of the Sudeten German Problem', 31 May 1995, p. 1.
17 E. Nagengast, 'Coming to terms with a European Identity: the Sudeten Germans between Bonn and Prague', *German Politics*, 5, 1 (1996) 86.
18 H. Hochfelder, 'Über die Ziele sudetendeutscher Politik', in R. Eibicht (ed.), *Die Sudetendeutsche und ihre Heimat. Erbe-Auftag-Ziel* (Wesseding: Gesamtdeutscher Verlag) pp. 50–9.
19 R. Schnürch, 'Konsequenzen sudetendeutscher Heimatpolitik', in Eibicht, p. 83.
20 V. Houvièka, *Betrachtungen zur Sudetendeutschen Frage* (Prague: Foreign Ministry of the Czech Republic, 1999), p. 6.
21 Nagengast, p. 89.
22 *Frankfurter Allgemeine Zeitung*, 13 April 1991, cited in ibid., p. 91.
23 Ibid.
24 'Schlußstrich unter Vergangenheit', *Süddeutsche Zeitung*, 12 April 1991.
25 Ibid., p. 91.
26 Ibid., p. 93.
27 'Treaty on Friendship and Good Neighbourliness', CTK News Archive, February, 1992.
28 CTK News Agency, 'Profile', p. 2.
29 Nagengast, p. 93.
30 CTK News Agency, 'Profile', pp. 2–3.
31 V. Havel, 'Czechs and Germans on the way to a Good Neighbourship', Address by the president of the Czech Republic, Charles University, Prague 17 February 1995 (Prague: Office of the President, Press Department, 1995).
32 S. Kettle, 'Czechs and Germans still at odds', *Transition*, 9 February 1996, p. 24.
33 Ibid., p. 23.
34 *Der Spiegel*, 36/1996, p. 173.
35 CTK, 'Profile', p. 4.
36 *The Week in Germany*, 31 May 1996, p. 1.
37 *Der Spiegel*, 51/1996, p. 31.
38 See pp. 91–2: for full text of declaration: CTK News Archive, 20 January, 1997.
39 *Frankfurter Allgemeine Zeitung*, 31 January 1997.
40 *Taz*, 9, 3 (1998) p. 6.
41 Helms, p. 95.
42 *Der Spiegel*, 21/1996, p. 33.
43 *Die Welt online*, 14 February 2000.
44 H. Mommsen and J. Kořalka, *Ungleiche Nachbarn* (1993); J. K. Hoensch and D. Kováč, *Das Scheitern der Verständigung* (1994; D. Brandes and V. Kural, *Der Weg in die Katastrophe* (1994); H. Lemberg, J. Křen and D. Kováč, *Im geteilten Europa* (1998); Gemeinsame deutsch–tschechische Historikerkommission: *Konfliktgemeinschaft* (1998); D. Brandes, E. Ivaničkova and Jiří Pešek (eds), *Erzwungene Trennung* (1999). Originally inaugurated as 'German Czechoslovak'

Historians commission it consists since 1993 of three sections – a Czech, a German and a Slovak one.

45 F. P. Habel, 'Verteibungsverluste der Sudetendeutschen 1945/46: Neuester Forschungstand und politische Schätzungen', in Sudetendeutsches Archiv, *Odsun. Die Vertreibung der Sudetendeutschen* (Munich: Verlagshaus Sudetenland, 1995) pp. 175–92.

46 F. P. Habel, Eine Politische Legende. *Die Massenvertreibung der Tschechen aus dem Sudetengebiet 1938/39* (Munich: Langen Müller, 1996) p. 85. The author was not able to decipher the material presented in this book.

47 Strothmann, pp. 271–6.

48 H. Field, 'The Czech Republic: a Prime Contender for EU Membership' (unpublished paper, 2001) pp. 10–14.

49 Ibid., p. 3.

50 *Rheinischer Merkur*, **49** (2000) p. 5.

51 K. Pakla, 'Czech Privatization and Corporate Grievances', *Communist and Post-Communist Studies*, 30, 1 (1997) p. 93.

52 *Berichte zu Staat und Gesellschaft in der Tschechischen und in der Slowakischen Republik*, 1999 (4) p. 11.

53 Houvièka, p. 5.

54 *Electronic Telegraph*, 19 December 1999, pp. 1–3.

55 Note also V. Gomez and L. Allnut, 'Getting ready for the Big Bang', TOL, 27 December 2001, http://www.tol.cz.

Works Cited and Consulted

Abelshauser, W. 'Der Lastenausgleich und die Eingliederung der Vertriebenen und Flüchtlinge – eine Skizze' in R. Schulze, D. Von der Brelie-Lewien and H. Grebing, *Flüchtlinge und Vertriebene in der westdeutschen Nachkriegsgeschichte* (Hildesheim: August Lax, 1987) pp. 229–38.

Ahrens, W. *Verbrechen an Deutschen. Dokumente der Vertreibung* (Arget: Ahrens, 1984).

Alexander, M. *Der Deutsch–Tschechoslowakische Schiedsvertrag von 1925 im Rahmen der Locarno-Vertrage* (Munich: Oldenbourg, 1970).

Alexander, M. 'Die Diskussion über die Vertreibung der Deutschen aus der Tschechoslowakei', in R. Streibel, (ed.), *Flucht und Vertreibung. Zwischen Aufrechnung und Verdrängung* (Vienna: Picus 1994) pp. 158–73.

Anderson, B. R. *Imagined Communities: reflections on the origin and spread of nationalism* (London: Verso, 1983).

Anderson, M. S. *Europe in the Eighteenth Century 1713–1783* (London: Longmans, 1963).

Arndt, W. *Ostpreußen, Westpreußen, Pommern, Schlesien, Sudetenland 1945/6. Eine Bild-Dokumentation der Flucht und Vertreibung aus den deutschen Ostgebieten* (Friedberg: Podzun-Pallas Verlag, 1982).

Bade, K. J. (ed.), *Neue Heimat im Westen: Vertriebene-Flüchtlinge-Aussiedler* (Münster: Westfälischer Heimatbund, 1990).

Barraclough, G. *The Origins of Modern Germany* (Oxford: Basil Blackwell, 1966).

Bartov, O. *The Eastern Front, 1941–45, German Troops and the Barbarisation of Warfare* (Basingstoke: Macmillan – now Palgrave Macmillan, 1996).

Beneš, E. *Memoirs of Dr. Eduard Beneš* (London: George Allen & Unwin, 1954).

Beneš, E. *Tři roky druhé světové války, projevy a dokumenty 1938–1942* (London, n.d.).

Benrather Kreis, *Der Prager Vertrag vor dem Bundesverfassungsgericht* (Düsseldorf: Arbeitsgemeinschaft für Deutschland, 1977).

Benz, W. 'Fremde in der Heimat: Flucht-Vertreibung-Integration', in K. J. Bade, *Deutsche im Ausland – Fremde in der Heimat* (Munich: C. H. Beck, 1992) pp. 374–507.

Benz, W. 'Vierzig Jahre nach der Vertreibung. Einleitende Bemerkungen', in W. Benz, *Die Vertreibung der Deutschen aus dem Osten. Ursachen, Ereignisse, Folgen* (Frankfurt: Fischer, 1995) pp. 8–15.

Benz, W., ten Cate, Houwink and Otto, J. G. *Die Bürokratie der Okkupation. Strukuren der Herrschaft und Verwaltung im besetzten Europa* (Berlin: Metropol, 1998).

Bessel, R. 'Why did the Weimar Republic collapse?' in I. Kershaw, *Weimar: Why Did German Democracy Fail?* (New York: St. Martins Press – now Palgrave Macmillan, 1990).

Bittel, K. *Der Revanchismus als Kriegsvorbereitung in der Bonner Bundesrepublik* (Berlin: Kongress Verlag, 1961).

Blackbourne, D. and Eley, G. *The Peculiarities of German History. Bourgeois Society and Politics in Nineteenth Century Germany* (Oxford: Oxford University Press, 1984).

Böddeker, G. *Die Flüchtlinge. Die Vertreibung der Deutschen aus dem Osten* (Munich: Herbig, 1980).

Bohmann, A. *Das Sudetendeutschtum in Zahlen* (Munich: Sudetendeutscher Rat, 1959).

Bohmann, A. *Bevölkerung und Nationalität in der Tschechoslowakei* (Cologne: Verlag Wissenschaft und Politik, 1975).

Bosl, K. *Handbuch der Geschichte der Böhmischen Länder, vol. iv, Der Tschechoslowakische Staat im Zeitalter der Modernen Massendemokratie und Diktatur* (Stuttgart: Anton Hiersheim, 1970).

Boyer, C. 'Die Vergabe von Staatsaufträgen in der ČSR ein Vehikel zur Ruinierung der sudetendeutschen Wirtschaft?' in J. K. Hoensch and D. Kováč, *Das Scheitern der Verständigung: Tschechen, Deutsche und Slowaken in der Ersten Republik 1918–1938* (Essen: Klartext, 1994) pp. 81–118.

Boyer, C. *Nationale Kontrahenten oder Partner. Studien zu den Beziehungen zwischen Deutschen und Tschechen in der Wirtschaft der ČSR* (Munich: Oldenbourg, 1999).

Břach, R. 'Die Bedeutung des Prager Vertrags von 1973 für die deutsche Ostpolitik', in H. Lemberg, J. Křen and D. Kováč, *Im geteilten Europa. Tschechen, Slowaken und Deutsche und ihre Staaten 1945–1989* (Essen: Klartext, 1998) pp. 169–91.

Brandes, D. *Die Tschechen unter deutschem Protektorat.* Part One, *Besatzungspolitik, Kollaboration und Widerstand im Protektorat Böhmen und Mähren bis Heydrichs Tod* (Munich/Vienna: Oldenbourg, 1968).

Brandes, D. *Die Tschechen unter deutschem Protektorat.* Part Two, *Besatzungspolitik, Kollaboration und Widerstand im Protektorat Böhmen und Mähren von Heydrichs Tod bis zum Prager Ausfstand* (Munich/Vienna: Oldenbourg, 1975).

Brandes, D. 'Die Politik des Dritten Reiches gegenüber der Tschechoslowakei', in M. Funke, *Hitler, Deutschland und die Mächte. Materialien zur Außenpolitik des Dritten Reiches* (Düsseldorf: Droste, 1978) pp. 508–23.

Brandes, D. *Großbritanien und seine Osteuropäischen Allierten 1939–1943* (Munich: R. Oldenbourg, 1988).

Brandes, D. 'Nationalsozialistische Tschechenpolitik im Protektorat Böhmen und Mähren', in D. Brandes and V. Kural, *Der Weg in die Katastrophe: deutsch–tschechoslowakische Beziehungen 1938–1947* (Essen: Klartext, 1994) pp. 39–56.

Brandes, D. *Der Weg zur Vertreibung 1938–1945. Pläne und Entscheidungen zum 'Transfer' der Deutschen aus der Tschechoslowakei und aus Polen* (Munich: Oldenbourg, 2001).

Brandes, D. and Kural, V. (eds), *Der Weg in die Katastrophe: deutsch–tschechoslowakische Beziehungen 1938–1947* (Essen: Klartext, 1994).

Brandes, D., Ivaničkova E. and Pešek, Jiří (eds.) *Erzwungene Trennung. Vertreibung und Aussiedlung in und aus der Tschechoslowakei 1938–1947 im Vergleich mit Polen, Ungarn und Jugoslawien* (Essen: Klartext, 1999).

Brenner, C. 'Die Geschichte der böhmischen Länder und die Geschichte des tschechischen Volkes: eine Geschichte oder zwei?', in ' "Unsere Geschichte": Die tschechisch–deutsche Vergangenheit als Interpretationsproblem', *Bohemia*, **35** (1994) 377–83.

Brügel, J. W. 'The Germans in Pre-War Czechoslovakia, in Czechoslovakia', in V. S. Mamatey and R. Luža, *A History of the Czechoslovak Republic 1918–1948* (Princeton: Princeton University Press, 1973) pp. 167–87.

Brügel, J. W. *Tschechen und Deutsche* (Munich: Nymphenburger Verlagshandlung, 1974).

Buben, V. *Šest let okupace Prahy* (Prague: 1946).

Burian, P. Der 'Transfer und seine Konsequenzen', in K. Bosl, *Das Jahr 1945 in der Tschechoslowakei* (Munich: Oldenbourg, 1971) pp. 201–15.

Burian, P. 'Der Staat und seine neue Verfassung', in H. Lemberg and P. Heumoos, *Das Jahr 1919 in der Tschechoslowakei und in Ostmitteleuropa* (Munich: Oldenbourg, 1989) pp. 203–14.

Burian, P. 'Die nationalen Minderheiten in Parliament und Regierung', in H. Lemberg, *Ostmitteleuropa zwischen den Weltkriegen 1918–1938* (Marburg: Verlag Herder, 1997) pp. 225–38.

Calvocoressi, P. Wint, G. and Pritchet, J. *Total War. Causes and Consequences of the Second World War* (Harmondsworth: Penguin, 1989).

Celovský, B. 'The transferred Sudeten-Germans and their political activity', in *Journal of Central European Affairs*, **17**, 2 (1957) 127–49.

Celovsky, B. *Das Münchener Abkommen 1938* (Stuttgart: Deutsche Verlagsanstalt, 1970).

Cohan, G. B. *The Politics of Ethnic Survival: Germans in Pragues 1861–1914* (Princeton: Princeton University Press, 1981).

Cornejová, I. 'Wie finster war die "Finsternis" ', in ' "Unsere Geschichte": Die tschechisch–deutsche Vergangenheit als Interpretationsproblem', *Bohemia*, **35** (1994) 384–7.

Cornwall, M. 'Edvard Beneš and Czechoslovakia's German Minority, 1918–1943', in J. Morison, *The Czech and Slovak Experience*, (New York: St. Martin's Press – now Palgrave Macmillan, 1992) pp. 167–202.

DeZayas, Alfred M., *Nemesis at Potsdam: the Anglo-Americans and the expulsion of the Germans; background, execution, consequences* (London: Routledge & Kegan Paul, 1979).

Doyle, W. *The Old European Order 1660–1800* (Oxford: Oxford University Press, 1978).

Eubank, K. 'Munich', in V. S. Mamatey and R. Luža, *A History of the Czechoslovak Republic 1918–1948* (Princeton: Princeton University Press, 1973) pp. 239–52.

Evans, R. J. *Rethinking German History. Nineteenth Century Germany and the Origins of the Third Reich* (London: Allen and Unwin, 1987).

Felak, J. 'Slovak Considerations of the Slovak Question: The Ludak, Agrarian, Socialist and Communist Views on Interwar Czechoslovakia', in J. Morison, *The Czech and Slovak Experience* (New York: St. Martin's Press – now Palgrave Macmillan, 1991) pp. 136–62.

Field, H. 'The Czech Republic: a Prime Contender for EU Membership' (unpublished paper, 2001).

Foschepoth, J. 'Potsdam und danach – die Westmächte, Adenauer und die Vertriebenen' in *Die Vertreibung der Deutschen aus dem Osten. Ursachen, Ereignisse, Folgen* (Frankfurt: Fischer, 1995) pp. 86–113.

Frantzioch, M. *Die Vertriebenen: Hemnisse, Antriebskräfte und Wege Ihrer Integration in der Bundesrepublik Deutschland* (Berlin: Reimer, 1987).

Franzen, K. E. *Der Prager Vertrag vom 11. Dezember 1973 im Sudetendeutschen Urteil* (Cologne: self-published MA thesis, 1995).

Franzen, K. E. *Die Vertriebenen. Hitlers letzte Opfer* (Berlin/Munich: Propylaen, 2001).

Franzl, E. *Sudetendeutsche Geschichte. Eine volkstümliche Darstellung* (Munich: Kraft, 1958).

Franzl, E. *Die Vertreibung. Sudetenland. 1945/46* (Landshut: Aufstieg Verlag, 1967).

Gaida, H. J. *Die offiziellen Organe der ostdeutschen Landsmannschaften* (Berlin: Duncker & Humblot, 1973).

Galandauer, J. 'Tschechische Sozialdemokraten zwischen Internationalismus und Nationalismus (1889–1914)' in H. Mommsen and J. Koralka (eds) *Ungleiche Nachbarn. Demokratische und Emanzipation bei Deutschen, Tschechen und Slowaken (1815–1914)* (Essen: Klartext, 1993) pp. 91–106.

Gatz, K. 'East-German and Sudeten Germans Expellees in West Germany 1945–1960', unpublished PhD thesis, Indiana University, 1989.

Gebhart, J. 'Migrationsbewegung der tschechischen Bevölkerung in den Jahren 1938–1939. Forschungsstand und offene Fragen' in D. Brandes, E. Ivaničkova and Jiří Pešek (eds), *Erzwungene Trennung. Vertreibung und Aussiedlung in und aus der Tschechoslowakei 1938–1947 im Vergleich mit Polen, Ungarn und Jugoslawien* (Essen: Klartext, 1999) pp. 11–22.

Gedye, G. E. R. *Fallen Bastions. The Central European Tragedy* (London: Gollancz, 1939).

Gemeinsame deutsch–tschechische Historikerkommission: *Konfliktgemeinschaft, Katastrophe, Entspannung. Skizze einer Darstellung der deutsch–tschechischen Geschichte seit dem 19. Jahrhundert* (Bonn: Bundeszentrale für politische Bildung, 1998).

Gisevius, H. B. *Bis zum bitteren Ende, Bd. II: Vom Münchener Abkommen biz zum 20. Juli 1944* (Zürich: Fretz und Wasmuth Verlag, 1946).

Goldstein, E. 'Neville Chamberlain, The British Official Mind and the Munich Crisis', in I. Lukes and E. Goldstein, *The Munich Crisis. Prelude to World War Two* (London: Frank Cass, 1999) pp. 276–92.

Goscurth, H. *Tagebücher eines Abwehroffiziers 1938–1940*, ed. H. Krausnick and H. C. Deutsch (Stuttgart: Deutsche Verlagsanstalt, 1970).

Grosser, T. 'Die Integration der Vertriebenen in der Bundesrepublik Deutschland'. Annäherungen an die Situation der Sudetendeutschen in der westdeutschen Nachkriegsgesellschaft am Beispiel Baiers', in H. Lemberg, J. Křen and D. Kováč, *Im geteilten Europa. Tschechen, Slowaken und Deutsche und ihre Staaten 1945–1989* (Essen: Klartext, 1998) pp. 41–94.

Grube F. and Richter G. *Flucht und Vertreibung: Deutschland zwischen 1944 und 1947* (Hamburg: Hoffmann und Campe, 1980).

Habel, F. P. *The Sudeten Question. Brief Exposition and Documentation* (Munich: Sudeten German Council, 1984).

Habel, F. P. *Die Sudetendeutschen* (Munich: Herbig, 1992).

Habel, F. P. 'Verteibungsverluste der Sudetendeutschen 1945/46: Neuester Forschungstand und politische Schätzungen', in Sudetendeutsches Archiv, *Odsun. Die Vertreibung der Sudetendeutschen* (Munich: Verlagshaus Sudetenland, 1995) pp. 175–92.

Habel, F. P. *Eine Politische Legende. Die Massenvertreibung der Tschechen aus dem Sudetengebiet 1938/39* (Munich: Langen Müller, 1996).

E. Hahn, 'Die Sudetendeutschen in der deutschen Gesellschaft: ein halbes Jahrhundert politischer Geschichte zwischen "Heimat" und "Zuhause" ', H. Lemberg, J. Křen and D. Kováč, *Im geteilten Europa. Tschechen, Slowaken und Deutsche und ihre Staaten 1945–1989* (Essen: Klartext, 1998) pp. 111–31.

Hamann, B. *Hitlers Wien. Lehrjahre eines Diktators* (Munich: Piper, 1996).

Hans, E. and Brand, W. *Der Witikobund. Weg-Wesen-Wirken* (Munich: Eigenverlag des Witikobundes, 1969).

Haun, H. 'Die Patenschaften als Stützenpfeiler der Schirmherrschaft', U. Reichert-Flügel (ed.), *Unter dem weißblauen Schild. 30 Jahre Schirmherrschaft Bayerns über die Sudetendeutschen* (Munich: Verlagshaus Sudetenland) pp. 88–9.

Hauner, M. 'Září 1938: kapitulovat či bojovat?', *Svědectví* **13** (1975) 151–68.

Hauner, M. 'Zrada, sovítizace, nebo historicky lapsus? Ke kritike dvou dokumentú k éeskoslovensko-sovítskym vztahum z roku 1938', *Soudobé díjiny*, **6**, 4 (1999) 545–71.

Heumoos, P. 'Interessensolidarität gegen Nationalgemeinschaft. Deutsche und tschechische Bauern in Böhmen 1848–1918', in F. Seibt, (ed.) *Die Chancen der Verständigung. Absichten und Ansätze zu übernationaler Zusammenarbeit in den böhmischen Ländern 1848–1918* (Munich: R. Oldenbourg, 1987) pp. 87–100.

Heumoos, P. *Die Emigration aus der Tschechoslowakei nach Westeuropa und dem Nahen Osten 1938–1945* (Munich: Oldenbourg, 1989).

Heumoos, P. 'Mythos, Aufklärung, Identität' in "Unsere Geschichte": Die tschechisch-deutsche Vergangenheit als Interpretationsproblem', *Bohemia*, 35 (1994) pp.415–21.

Hilf, R. *Deutsche und Tschechen* (Opladen: Leske & Budrich, 1986).

Hirschfeld, G. 'Zwischen Kollaboration und Widerstand – Europa unter deutscher Besatzung', in *Brockhaus Bibliothek Weltgeschichte*, Vol. 5, X, 2, 1999, 634–43.

Hirschfeld G. and Mann, P. *Collaboration in France. Politics and Culture during Nazi Occupation, 1940–1944* (Oxford: Berg, 1989).

Höbelt, L. 'Deutschösterreich und die Sudetendeutschen', in H. Lemberg and P. Heumoos, *Das Jahr 1919 in der Tschechoslowakei und in Ostmitteleuropa* (Munich: Oldenbourg, 1989) pp. 159–66.

Hobsbawm, E. *Das Zeitalter der Extreme. Weltgeschichte des 20. Jahrhunderts* (Munich: Deutscher Taschenbuch Verlag, 1998).

Hochfelder, H. 'Über die Ziele sudetendeutscher Politik', in R. Eibicht (ed.) *Die Sudetendeutsche und ihre Heimat. Erbe-Auftag-Ziel* (Wesseding: Gesamtdeutscher Verlag) pp. 50–9.

Hoensch, J. K. 'Zum sudetendeutsch–tschechischen Verhältnis in der Ersten Republik', in E. Lemberg and G. Rhode (eds), *Das deutsch–tschechische Verhältnis seit 1918* (Stuttgart: Kohlhammer, 1969) pp. 199–231.

Hoensch, J. K. 'Tschechoslowakismus oder Autonomie. Die Auseinandersetzung um die Eingliederung der Slowakei in die Tschechoslowakische Republik', H. Lemberg and P. Heumoos, *Das Jahr 1919 in der Tschechoslowakei und in Ostmitteleuropa* (Munich: Oldenbourg, 1989) pp. 129–58.

Hoensch, J. K. 'Grundzüge und Phasen der deutschen Slowakei-Politik im Zweiten Weltkrieg', in D. Brandes and V. Kural, *Der Weg in die Katastrophe: deutsch–tschechoslowakische Beziehungen 1938–1947* (Essen: Klartext, 1994) pp. 93–118.

Hoffmann, D. Kraus, M. and Schwartz, M. *Vertriebene in Deutschland. Interdisziplinäre Ergebnisse und Forschungsperspektiven* (Munich: Oldenbourg, 2000).

Hoffmann, S. 'Collaborationism in France during world War II', in *Journal of Modern History*, **40** (1968) 375–95.

Houvièka, V. *Betrachtungen zurr Sudetendeutschen Frage* (Prague: Foreign Ministry of the Czech Republic, 1999).

Hrabovec, E. *Vertreibung und Abschub. Deutsche in Böhmen und Mähren* (Frankfurt: Peter Lang, 1995).

Imhof, M. 'Die Vertriebenenverbände in der Bundesrepublik Deutschland. Geschichte, Organisation und Gesellschaftliche Bedeutung', Inaugural-Dissertation, Philipps-Universität Marburg, 1975.

International Military Tribunal, *Trials of the Major War Criminals before the Nuremberg International Military Tribunal. Nuremberg 1945–46* (Nuremberg: 1947–9) Vol. XXXVI.

Isupov, V. A. *Demografcheskie katastrofy i krisizy v Rossii v pervoi polovine XX veka*, (Novosibirsk: Academician Polyakov, 2000).

Jaworski, R. *Vorposten oder Minderheit. Der sudetendeutsche Volkstumskampf in den Beziehungen zwischen der Weimarer Republik und der ČSR* (Stuttgart: Deutsche Verlagsanstalt, 1977).

Kaiser, V. 'Das Ende des Krieges und die Vertreibung der Deutechen aus dem Aussiger Gebiet' in D. Brandes, E. Ivaničkova and Jiří Pešek, *Erzwungene Trennung. Vertreibung und Aussiedlung in und aus der Tschechoslowakei 1938–1947 im Vergleich mit Polen, Ungarn und Jugoslawien* (Essen: Klartext, 1999) pp. 197–213.

Kann, R. A. *A History of the Habsburg Empire 1526–1918* (Berkeley, CA: London: University of California Press, 1975).

Kather, L. *Die Entmachtung der Vertriebenen. Die entscheidenden Jahre* (Munich/Vienna: Günter Olzog, 1964).

Kather, L. *Die Entmachtung der Vertriebenen. Die Jahre des Verfalls* (Munich/Vienna: Günter Olzog, 1965).

Kershaw, I. *Hitler 1889–1936. Hubris* (Harmondsworth: Penguin, 1998).

Kershaw, I. *Hitler 1936–1945. Nemesis* (London: Allan Lane, 2000).

Kettle, S. 'Czechs and Germans still at odds', *Transition*, 9 February 1996, pp. 22–5.

Konopka, V. *Živé tradice* (Prague: Nase Vojsko, 1959).

Kořalka, J. 'Nationsbildung und nationale Identität der Deutschen, Oesterreicher, Tschechen und Slowaken um die Mitte des 19. Jahrhunderts', in H. Mommsen and J. Kořalka (eds), *Ungleiche Nachbarn. Demokratische und nationale Emanzipation bei Deutschen, Tschechen und Slowaken (1815–1914)* (Essen: Klartext, 1993) pp. 33–48.

Kornrumpf, M. *In Baiern angekommen. Die Eingliederung der Vertiebenen. Zahlen-Daten-Namen* (Munich: Günter Olzog, 1979).

Kovaccs, E. 'Die katholische Kirche im Spannungsfeld von Nationalismus und Patriotismus zwischen 1848 und 1918', in F. Seibt, (ed.) *Die Chancen der Verständigung. Absichten und Ansätze zu übernationaler Zusammenarbeit in den böhmischen Ländern 1848–1918* (Munich: R. Oldenbourg, 1987) pp. 49–62.

Krallert-Sattler, G. *Kommentierte Bibliographie zum Flüchtlings- und Vertriebenenproblem in der Bundesrepublik Deutschland, in Oesterreich und in der Schweiz* (Vienna: Braunmueller, 1989).

Křen, J. 'Nationale Selbstbehauptung im Vielvölkerstaat: Politische Konzeption des tschechischen Nationalismus 1890–1938', in J. Křen, V. Kural and D. Brandes, *Integration oder Ausgrenzung. Tschen und Deutsche 1890–1945* (Bremen: Donat & Temmen, 1986) pp. 15–65.

Krüger, P. 'Die Friedensordnung von 1919 und die Entstehung neuer Staaten in Ostmitteleuropa', in H. Lemberg and P. Heumoos, *Das Jahr 1919 in der Tschechoslowakei und in Ostmitteleuropa* (Munich: Oldenbourg, 1993) pp. 93–116.

Kubů, E. 'Die brüchigen Beziehungen, Die Weimarer Republik und die Tschechoslowakei' in J. K. Hoensch and D. Kováč, *Das Scheitern der*

Verständigung: Tschechen, Deutsche und Slowaken (1918–1938) (Essen: Klartext, 1993), pp. 15–28.

Kučera, J. 'Statistische Berechnungen der Vertreibungsverluste – Schlußwort oder Sackgasse', in D. Brandes and V. Kural, *Der Weg in die Katastrophe: deutsch–tschechoslowakische Beziehungen 1938–1947* (Essen: Klartext, 1994) pp. 187–200.

Kučera, J. 'Statistik auf dem Holzweg. Einige Bemerkungen zur Berechnung der Sudetendeutschen Vertriebenenverlust', in R. G. Plaschka, H. Haelsteiner, A. Suppan and A. A. Drabek (eds) *Nationale Frage und Vertreibung in der Tschechoslowakei und Ungarn 1938–1945* (Vienna: Oesterreichische Akademie der Wissenschaften, 1997) pp. 145–54.

Kučera, J. *Minderheit im Nationalstaat. Die Sprachenfrage in den tschechisch–deutschen Beziehungen 1918–1938* (Munich: Oldenbourg, 1999).

Kural, V. 'Die Tschechoslowakei als Nationalstaat? Das sudetendeutsche Problem', in J. K. Hoensch and D. Kováč, *Das Scheitern der Verständigung: Tschechen, Deutsche und Slowaken (1918–1938)* (Essen: Klartext, 1993), pp. 63–70.

Kural, V. 'Tschechen, Deutsche und die sudetendeutsche Frage während des Zweiten Weltkriegs' in D. Brandes, E. Ivaničkova and Jiří Pešek (eds), *Erzwungene Trennung. Vertreibung und Aussiedlung in und aus der Tschechoslowakei 1938–1947 im Vergleich mit Polen, Ungarn und Jugoslawien* (Essen: Klartext, 1999) pp. 91–4.

Kurz, K. 'Der Wandel des Dorfes Gersdorf, Kreis Herzfeld, durch das Einströmen der Heimatvertriebenen', in E. Lemberg and L. Krecker, *Die Entstehung eines neuen Volkes aus Binnendeutschen und Ostvertirebenen* (Marburg: N. G. Elwert Verlag, 1950) pp. 32–43.

Lehmann, A. *Im Fremden ungewollt zuhaus: Flüchtlinge und Vertriebene in Westdeutschland 1945–1990* (Munich: Beck, 1991).

Lemberg, E. *'Die Sudetendeutschen im Exil,' Sudetendeutsche rufen Europa* (Munich: Volksbote, 1950).

Lemberg, E. 'Bemerkungen zu einem Geschichtsbild', *Der neue Ackermann*, 2, 4 (1954) 28–37.

Lemberg, H. (ed.) *Ostmitteleuropa zwischen den Weltkriegen 1918–1938* (Marburg: Verlag Herder, 1997).

Lemberg, H. and Heumoos, P. (eds) *Das Jahr 1919 in der Tschechoslowakei und in Ostmitteleuropa* (Munich: Oldenbourg, 1989).

Loeber, D. 'Die Minderheitenschutzverträge – Entstehung, Inhalt und Wirkung', in H. Lemberg, (ed.) *Ostmitteleuropa zwischen den Weltkriegen 1918–1938* (Marburg: Verlag Herder, 1997) pp. 189–200.

Luft, R. 'Die Mittelpartei des mährischen Großgrundbesitzes 1879–1918. Zur Problematik des Ausgleichs in Mähre und Böhmen' in F. Seibt (ed.), *Die Chancen der Verständigung. Absichten und Ansätze zu übernationaler Zusammenarbeit in den böhmischen Ländern 1848–1918* (Munich: R. Oldenbourg, 1987) pp. 187–244.

P. Lüttinger, *Integration der Vertriebenen. Eine empirische Analyse* (Frankfurt/Main: 1989).

Luža, R. *The Transfer of the Sudeten Germans. A Study of Czech–German relations 1933–1962* (London: Routledge and Kegan Paul, 1964).

Luža, R. 'The Czech Resistance Movement', in V. S. Mamatey and R. Luža, *A History of the Czechoslovak Republic 1918–1948* (Princeton: Princeton University Press, 1973) pp. 343–61.

Macartney, C. A. *The Habsburg Empire 1790–1918* (London: Weidenfeld and Nicholson, 1968).

Macek, J. 'Zur Problematik der Geschichte der abgetrennten Gebiete besonders des sogenannten Sudetenlandes in den Jahren 1938–1945', in D. Brandes and V. Kural, *Der Weg in die Katastrophe: deutsch–tschechoslowakische Beziehungen 1938–1947* (Essen: Klartext, 1994) pp. 57–75.

Magraw, R. 'Socialism, Syndicalism and French Labour before 1914' in D. Geary (ed.) *Labour and Socialist Movements in Europe before 1914* (Oxford: Berg, 1989) pp. 49–100.

Mamatey, V. S. 'The Establishment of the Republic', in V. S. Mamatey and R. Luža, *A History of the Czechoslovak Republic 1918–1948* (Princeton: Princeton University Press, 1973) pp. 3–38.

Mastny, V. *The Czechs under Nazi Rule. The Failure of National Resistance* (New York: Columbia University Press, 1971).

Menzel, W. *Die nationale Entwicklung in Böhmen, Mähren und Schlesien. Von der Aufklärung bis zur Revolution von 1848* (Nurenberg: Helmut Preußler Verlag, 1985).

Miltová, J. 'Die NS-Pläne zur Lösung der tschechischen Frage', in D. Brandes, E. Ivaničkova and Jiří Pešek (eds), *Erzwungene Trennung. Vertreibung und Aussiedlung in und aus der Tschechoslowakei 1938–1947 im Vergleich mit Polen, Ungarn und Jugoslawien* (Essen: Klartext, 1999) pp. 23–35.

Mommsen, H. 'Die mitteleuropäische Sozialdemokratie im Konflikt zwischen Internationalismus and nationaler Loyalität', in H. Mommsen and J. Koralka (eds) *Ungleiche Nachbarn. Demokratische und Emanzipation bei Deutschen, Tschechen und Slowaken (1815–1914)* (Essen: Klartext, 1993) pp. 91–106.

Moraw, P. 'Das Mittelalter' in F. Prinz, *Deutsche Geschichte im Osten Europas. Böhmen und Mähren* (Berlin: Siedler Verlag, 1993).

Mühlfenzl, R. *Geflohen und Vertrieben. Augenzeugen berichten* (Königstein/Taunus: Athenäum, 1981).

Nagengast, E. 'Coming to terms with a European Identity': the Sudeten Germans between Bonn and Prague', *German Politics*, 5, 1 (1996) 81–100.

Naumann, F. *Mitteleuropa*, published February 1915, and reproduced in T. Nipperdey (ed.), *Friedrich Naumanns Werke*, Vol. 4, *Schriften zum Parteiwesen und zum Mitteleuropaproblem* (Cologne: Westdeutscher Verlag, 1964) pp. 485–767.

Nawratil, H. *Vertreibungsverbrechen an Deutschen. Tatbestand, Motive, Bewältigung* (Munich: Universitätsverlag, 1982).

Němec, L. 'Solution of the Minorities Problem', in V. S. Mamatey and R. Luža, *A History of the Czechoslovak Republic 1918–1948* (Princeton: Princeton University Press, 1973) pp. 416–27.

Neuhoff, H. 'Der Lastenausgleich aus der Sicht der Vertriebenen', in H. J. von Merkatz, *Aus Trümmern wurden Fundamente. Vertriebene/Flüchtlinge/Aussiedler. Drei Jahrzehnte Integration* (Düsseldorf: Walter Rau, 1979) pp. 129–49.

Neumann, F. *Der Block der Heimatvertriebenen und Entrechteten 1950–1960. Ein Beitrag zur Geschichte und Struktur einer politischen Interessenpartei* (Marburg: Anton Hain: Meisenheim am Glain, 1966).

Newton, D. *British Policy and the Weimar Republic, 1918–1919,* (Oxford: Clarendon Press, 1997).

Nittner, E. *Dokumente zur Sudetendeutschen Frage, 1916–1967* (Munich: Ackermann Gemeinde, 1967).

Nittner, E. *Die Ackermann Gemeinde. Bilanz und Auftrag* (Munich: Kultur-und Bidungswerk der Ackermanngemeinde, 1978).

Nittner, E. 'Traditionen der Sudetendeutschen', in R. Schulze, D. Von der Brelie-Lewien and H. Grebing, *Flüchtlinge und Vertriebene in der westdeutschen Nachkriegsgeschichte* (Hildesheim: August Lax, 1987) pp. 89–97.

Ohlbaum, R. *Baierns vierter Stamm, die Sudetendeutschen: Herkunft, Neubeginn, Persönlichkeiten* (Munich: Aufstieg-Verlag, 1980).

Otruba, G. 'Das Kapital. Zusammenarbeit aus Sachzwang anstelle sachfremder Integration?', in F. Seibt, (ed.), *Die Chancen der Verständigung. Absichten und Ansätze zu übernationaler Zusammenarbeit in den böhmischen Ländern 1848–1918* (Munich: R. Oldenbourg, 1987) pp. 63–86.

Overmanns, R. ' "Amtlich und wissenschaftlich erarbeitet." Zur Diskussion über die Verluste während der Flucht und Vertreibung der Deutschen aus der ČSR', in D. Brandes, E. Ivaničkova and Jiří Pešek (eds), *Erzwungene Trennung. Vertreibung und Aussiedlung in und aus der Tschechoslowakei 1938–1947 im Vergleich mit Polen, Ungarn und Jugoslawien* (Essen: Klartext, 1999) pp. 149–77.

Pakla, K. 'Czech Privatization and Corporate Grievances', *Communist and Post-Communist Studies*, **30** 1 (1997), 83–94.

Prinz, F. *Deutsche Geschichte im Osten Europas. Böhmen und Mähren* (Berlin: Siedler Verlag, 1993).

Prinz, F. 'Heimatvertriebene als Industriepioniere. Der Beitrag der Sudetendeutschen zu Bayerns Wirtschaft', in U. Reichert-Flügel (ed.), *Unter dem weißblauen Schild. 30 Jahre Schirmherrschaft Bayerns über die Sudetendeutschen* (Munich: Verlagshaus Sudetenland, 1985) pp. 63–5.

Rable, K. 'Zur Frage der Deutschenvertreibung aus der Tschechoslowakei', *Bohemia*, **2** (1960) 414–92.

Ragsdale, H. 'Soviet Military Preparation and Policy in the Munich Crisis: New Evidence', *Jahrbücher für Geschichte Osteuropas*, **47**, 2 (1999) 210–26.

Reichling, G. *Die deutschen Vertriebenen in Zahlen* (Bonn: Kulturstiftung der deutschen Vertriebenen, 1986).

Remak, J. 'The healthy invalid: how doomed was the Habsburg Empire?', *Journal of Modern History*, **41** (1969) 127–43.

Rhode, G. 'Das Protectorat Böhmen und Mähren', in E. Lemberg and G. Rhode (eds), *Das deutsch–tschechische Verhältnis seit 1918* (Stuttgart: Kohlhammer, 1969) pp. 59–91.

Roberts, F. 'The Berlin Crisis', *Politics and Society in Germany, Austria and Switzerland*, Vol. 1, 2, (1989), pp. 3–12.

Roth, G. D. 'Ein Wirtschaftpotential in Bayern. Sudetendeutsche Siedlungen', *Bayerland Impressum*, **4** (1978) 37–42.

Ryder, A. J. *Twentieth Century Germany* (New York: Columbia University Press, 1973).

Scharrer, M. *Die Spaltung der deutschen Arbeiterbewegung* (Stuttgart: Cordeliers, 1983).

Schieder, T. *Die Vertreibung der Deutschen Bevölkerung aus der Tschechoslowakei*, Part IV/1 of the series *Dokumentation der Vertreibung der Deutschen aus Ost/Mitteleuropa* (Berlin: Heyne's Erben, 1957).

Schillinger, R. 'Der Lastenausgleich' in W. Benz, *Die Vertreibung der Deutschen aus dem Osten. Ursachen, Ereignisse, Folgen* (Frankfurt: Fischer, 1995) pp. 231–43.

Schnürch, R. 'Konsequenzen sudetendeutscher Heimatpolitik', R. Eibicht (ed.), *Die Sudetendeutsche und ihre Heimat. Erbe-Auftag-Ziel* (Wesseding: Gesamtdeutscher Verlag) pp. 83–94.

Schoenberg, H. W. *Germans from the East. A study of their migration, resettlement, and subsequent history* (The Hague: Martinus Nijhoff, 1970).

Schorske, C. E. *Fin-de-siècle Vienna. Politics and Culture* (New York: Knopff, 1979).

Schwartz, M. ' "Vom Umsiedler zum Staatsbürger". Totalitäres und Subversives in der Sprachpolitik der SBZ/DDR', D. Hoffmann, M. Kraus, and M. Schwartz, *Vertriebene in Deutschland. Interdisziplinäre Ergebnisse und Forschungsperspektiven* (Munich: Oldenbourg, 2000) pp. 135–66.

Seibt, F. (ed.), *Die Chancen der Verständigung. Absichten und Ansätze zu übernationaler Zusammenarbeit in den böhmischen Ländern 1848–1918* (Munich: R. Oldenbourg, 1987).

Seibt, F. *Deutschland und die Tschechen. Geschichte einer Nachbarschaft in der Mitte Europas* (Munich: Piper, 1993).

Seton-Watson, H. *Eastern Europe between the Wars 1918–1941* (New York: Harper and Row, 1967).

Seton-Watson, R. W. *A History of the Czechs and Slovaks* (London: Hutchinson, 1943).

Skorpil, P. 'Probleme bei der Berechnung der Zahl der tschechoslowakischen Todesopfer des nationalsozialistischen Deutschlands', in D. Brandes and V. Kural, *Der Weg in die Katastrophe: deutsch–tschechoslowakische Beziehungen 1938–1947* (Essen: Klartext, 1994) pp. 161–4.

Slapnicka, H. 'Die böhmischen Länder und die Slowakei', in K. Bosl, *Handbuch der Geschichte der Böhmischen Länder, Vol. iv, Der Tschechoslowakische Staat im Zeitalter der Modernen Massendemokratie und Diktatur* (Stuttgart: Anton Hiersheim, 1970) pp. 2–150.

Slapnicka, H. 'Die Ohnmacht des Parlamentarismus gegüber der nationalistischen Übermacht', in F. Seibt (ed.), *Die Chancen der Verständigung. Absichten und Ansätze zu übernationaler Zusammenarbeit in den böhmischen Ländern 1848–1918* (Munich: R. Oldenbourg, 1987) pp. 147–74.

Slapnicka, H. 'Die rechtlichen Grundlagen für die Behandlung der Deutschen und Magyaren in der Tschechoslowakei 1945–1948', in R. G. Plaschka, H. Haselsteiner, A. Suppan and A. A. Drabek (eds) *Nationale Frage und Vertreibung in der Tschechoslowakei und Ungarn 1938–1945* (Vienna: Oesterreichische Akademie der Wissenschaften, 1997) pp. 155–92.

Smelser, R. M. *The Sudetenproblem 1933–1938. Volkstumspolitik and the Formulation of Nazi Foreign Policy* (Middletown: Wesleyan University Press, 1975).

Snejdárek, A. 'Über die Anfänge des sudetendeutschen Revanchismus in Westdeutschland', *Wissenschaftliche Zeitschrift der Karl-Marx Universität Leipzig*, Sonderband IV (1964) pp. 140–52.

Staněk, T. 'Vertreibung und Aussiedlung der Deutschen 1945–8' in D. Brandes and V. Kural, *Der Weg in die Katastrophe: deutsch–tschechoslowakische Beziehungen 1938–1947* (Essen: Klartext, 1994) pp. 165–86.

Staněk, T. '1945 – Das Jahr der Verfolgung. Zur Problematik der außergerichtlichen Nachkriegsverfolgung in den böhmischen Ländern' in D. Brandes, E. Ivaničkova and Jiří Pešek, *Erzwungene Trennung. Vertreibung und Aussiedlung in und aus der Tschechoslowakei 1938–1947 im Vergleich mit Polen, Ungarn und Jugoslawien* (Essen: Klartext, 1999) pp. 117–47.

Statistisches Bundesamt, *Die deutschen Vertreibungsverluste* (Wiesbaden: Kohlhammer, 1958).

Steele, J. *Why Switzerland?* (Cambridge: Cambridge University Press, 1978).

Stiftung Ostdeutscher Kulturrat (ed.), *Bestandsverzeichniss der deutschen Heimatvertriebenenpresse* (Munich: Saur, 1982).

Strakosch, H. E. *Austria. An Imperial Destiny* (Adelaide: Rigby, 1973).

Streibel, R. (ed.), *Flucht und Vertreibung. Zwischen Aufrechnung und Verdrängung* (Vienna: Picus, 1994).

Strothmann, D. ' "Schlesien bleibt unser": Vertiebenenpolitiker und das Rad der geschichte', in W. Benz, *Die Vertreibung der Deutschen aus dem Osten. Ursachen, Ereignisse, Folgen* (Frankfurt: Fischer, 1995) pp. 265–76.

Sudetendeutsches Archiv, *Odseun. Die Vertreibung der Sudetendeutschen* (Munich: Verlagshaus Sudetenland, 1995).

Suppan, A. 'Soziale und wirtschaftliche Lage im Protektorat Böhmen und Mähren', in R. G. Plaschka, H. Haselsteiner, A. Suppan and A. A. Drabek (eds) *Nationale Frage und Vertreibung in der Tschechoslowakei und Ungarn 1938–1945* (Vienna: Oesterreichische Akademie der Wissenschaften, 1997) pp. 9–32.

Taborsky, E. 'Politics in Exile, 1939–1945' in V. S. Mamatey and R. Luža, *A History of the Czechoslovak Republic 1918–1948* (Princeton: Princeton University Press, 1973) pp. 322–42.

Tampke, J. 'Causes, Course and consequences of the Division of Germany. An Essay on Cold War and Post Cold War Policies', in A. Bonnell, G. Munro and M. Travers Power, *Conscience and Opposition. Essays in German History in Honour of John A. Moses* (New York: Peter Lang, 1996) pp. 387–404.

Taylor, A. J. P. *The Origins of the Second World War* (London: Hamish Hamilton, 1961).

Taylor, A. J. P. *The Habsburg Monarchy 1809–1918* (London: Hamish Hamilton, 1972).

Ther, P. *Deutsche und polnische Vertriebene. Gesellschaft und Vertriebenenpolitk in der SBZ/DDR und in Polen 1945–1956* (Göttingen: Vandenhoek & Ruprecht, 1998).

Trachtenberg, M. 'Versailles after Sixty Years', *Journal of Contemporary History*, **17** (1982) 487–506.

Turnwald, W. *Dokumente zur Austreibung der Sudetendeutschen* (Munich: Arbeitsgemeinschaft zur Wahrung sudetendeutscher Interessen, 1951).

Ueberschär, G. R. *Generaloberst Franz Halder, Generalstabsched, Gegner und Gefangener Hitlers* (Göttingen: Muster-Schmidt, 1991).

Urban, V. *Hitler's Spearhead* (London: Trinity Press, 1945).

USA, Department of State, *Foreign Relations of the United States. Diplomatic Papers.* Vol. 3, 1941 (Washington: United States Government Printing Office, 1959).

Walker, M. *The Cold War* (London: Vintage, 1993).

Wambach, M. *Verbändestaat und Parteienoligopol. Macht und Ohnmacht der Vertriebenenverbände* (Stuttgart: Ferdinand Enke, 1971).

Wandycz, P. S. 'Foreign Policy of Edvard Beneš, 1919–1938' in V. S. Mamatey and R. Luža (eds), *A History of the Czechoslovak Republic 1918–1948* (Princeton: Princeton University Press, 1973) pp. 216–38.

Weick, E. 'Gibt es einen Rechtsradikalismus in der Vertriebenenpresse?' in I. Fetcher (ed.) *Rechtsradikalismus* (Frankfurt/Main: Europäische Verlagsanstalt, 1967) pp. 95–124.

Weinberg, G. L. *Germany, Hitler and World War Two* (Cambridge: Cambridge University Press, 1995).

Weinberg, G. L. 'Reflections on Munich after 60 years' in I. Lukes and E. Goldstein, *The Munich Crisis 1938. Prelude to World War Two* (London: Frank Cass, 1999) pp. 1–12.

Weiß, H. 'Die Organisation der Vertriebenen und ihre Presse' in W. Benz, *Die Vertreibung der Deutschen aus dem Osten. Ursachen, Ereignisse, Folgen* (Frankfurt: Fischer, 1995) pp. 244–64.

Wheatcroft, S. G. 'Ausmaß und Wesen der deutschen und sowjetischen Repressionen und Massentötungen 1930 bis 1945' in D. Dahlmann and G. Hirschfeld, *Lager, Zwangsarbeit, Verteibung und Deportation. Dimension der Massenverbrechen in der Sowjetunion und in Deutschland 1933–1945* (Essen: Klartext. 1999) pp. 67–109.

Whetten, L. L. *Germany's Ostpolitik. Relations between the Federal Republic and the Warsaw Pact Countries* (London: Oxford University Press, 1971).

Wille, M. 'Die Vertriebenen und das politisch-staatliche System der SBZ/DDR', in D. Hoffman, M. Kraus and M. Schwartz, *Vertriebene in Deutschland. Interdisziplinäre Ergebnisse und Forschung sperspektiven* (Munich: Oldenbourg, 2000), pp. 203–18.

Wingfield, N. M. *Minority Politics in a Multinational State. The German Social Democratic Party, 1918–1938*, (New York: Columbia University Press, 1989).

Winter, E. *Barock, Absolutismus und Aufklärung in der Donau-Monarchie* (Vienna: Europa Verlag, 1971).

Wiskemann, E. *Czechs and Germans* (Oxford: Oxford University Press, 1938).

Wiskemann, E. *Germany's Eastern Neighbours* (London: Oxford University Press, 1956).

Wolkogonow, D. *Stalin. Triumph and Tragedy* (London: Weidenfeld and Nicholson, 1991).

Zeman, Z. A. B. *The Break-Up of the Habsburg Empire 1914–1918* (London: Oxford University Press, 1961).

Zeman, Z. A. B. *The Masaryks. The Making of Czechoslovakia* (London: I. B. Tauris & Co, 1990).

Zeman, Z. A. B. *The Making and Breaking of Communist Europe* (Oxford: Basil Blackwell, 1991).

Zeman, Z. A. B. *The Life of Edvard Beneš, 1884–1948* (Oxford: Clarendon Press, 1997).

Ziemer, G. *Deutscher Exodus. Verteibung und Eingliederung von 15 Millionen Ostdeutschen* (Stuttgart: Seewald, 1973).

Zimmermann, V. *Die Sudetendeutschen im NS-Staat. Politik und Stimmung der Bevölkerung im Reichsgau Sudetenland* (Essen: Klartext, 1999).

Index